OXFORD CHINESE THOUGHT

Series Editors
Eric L. Hutton and Justin Tiwald

Zhu Xi: Selected Writings
Edited by Philip J. Ivanhoe

Treatise on Awakening Mahāyāna Faith
Translated by John Jorgensen, Dan Lusthaus, John Makeham, Mark Strange

Zhu Xi

Selected Writings

———◄◆►———

Edited by

PHILIP J. IVANHOE

OXFORD
UNIVERSITY PRESS

Oxford University Press is a department of the University of Oxford. It furthers
the University's objective of excellence in research, scholarship, and education
by publishing worldwide. Oxford is a registered trade mark of Oxford University
Press in the UK and certain other countries.

Published in the United States of America by Oxford University Press
198 Madison Avenue, New York, NY 10016, United States of America.

CIP data is on file at the Library of Congress
ISBN 978–0–19–086126–1 (pbk.)
ISBN 978–0–19–086125–4 (hbk.)

1 3 5 7 9 8 6 4 2

Paperback printed by Webcom, Inc., Canada
Hardback printed by Bridgeport National Bindery, Inc., United States of America

Contents

Series Editors' Preface

CHINESE WRITINGS FROM pre-modern times constitute a vast body of texts stretching back over 2,500 years, and while Western studies of China have been growing, many riches from the Chinese tradition have remained untranslated or have been given only partial translations, sometimes scattered across multiple publication venues. This situation obviously poses a problem for those who want to learn about Chinese thought but lack the ability to read Chinese. However, it also poses a problem even for scholars who specialize in Chinese thought and can read Chinese, because it is not easy to read across all the time periods and genres in the Chinese corpus. Not only did the Chinese language change over time, but in some genres particular vocabularies are developed and familiarity with certain earlier texts—sometimes quite a large number of texts—is presumed. For this reason, scholars who focus on one tradition of Chinese thought from a given era cannot simply pick up and immediately understand texts from a different tradition of thought in another era. The lack of translations is thus an impediment even to specialists who can read Chinese but wish to learn about aspects of Chinese thought outside their normal purview. Furthermore, scholars are often hampered in their teaching by the lack of translations that they can assign to students, which then becomes a barrier to promoting greater understanding of Chinese history and culture among the general public.

By offering English translations of Chinese texts with philosophical and religious significance, *Oxford Chinese Thought* aims to remedy these problems and make available to the general public, university students, and scholars a treasure trove of materials that has previously been largely inaccessible. The series focuses on works that are historically important or stand to make significant contributions to contemporary discussions, and the translations seek to strike a reasonable balance between the interests of specialists and the needs of general readers and students with no skills in Chinese. Translators for the series are leading scholars and experts in the traditions and texts that they render, and the volumes are meant to be suitable for classroom use while meeting the highest standards of scholarship.

This first volume in the series, on Zhu Xi (1130–1200), well exemplifies our aim to give readers greater access to Chinese texts that have not been represented or have been inadequately represented among existing translations to date. Zhu Xi is without a doubt one of the most important and influential thinkers in history, having established what became Confucian orthodoxy and the educational requirements for nearly all government officials for several centuries, not just in China but throughout much of East Asia. He left behind a massive body of writings and recorded conversations that, as of a recent printing from 2002, comprises twenty-seven volumes, each of which is several hundred pages long. While a small portion of this material has been translated, the vast majority of it has not. Furthermore, previous translations of Zhu Xi's work, though undeniably valuable, have tended to adopt a very specific focus, such as his views on learning or his commentarial work. As a result, it has been difficult for readers lacking knowledge of Chinese to gain an understanding of Zhu's thought that encompasses the incredibly broad variety of topics covered in his writings. The present volume constitutes an important step toward filling this gap left by previous translations. We hope that it will serve to spur greater interest in Zhu Xi and may eventually lead to a complete translation of all his works.

Eric L. Hutton and Justin Tiwald

Preface

THIS VOLUME, *ZHU XI: SELECTED WRITINGS*, is the first in a new series of translations of Chinese philosophical texts, *Oxford Chinese Thought*, edited by Eric L. Hutton and Justin Tiwald, aimed at providing English-speaking readers access to a range of China's most interesting and influential traditional philosophical writings. While parts of Zhu Xi's works are available in English, this volume offers the first selection of Zhu's writings across a broad spectrum of his core concerns that is designed to be attractive to students and scholars from a wide range of disciplines. It contains lightly annotated, accurate, and readable translations that represent much more of his work than is currently available and includes thoughtful introductions to the full range of his concerns. Our primary audience is scholars and students of East Asian Confucianism, broadly construed, to whom we offer an essential resource for gaining a comprehensive understanding of Zhu Xi's thought. The complete Chinese text for the translated passages, compiled and meticulously edited by Eric L. Hutton, is available on the Oxford University Press website: http://global.oup.com/us/companion.websites/9780190861261/

A Note on the Cover Illustration

THE COVER PRESENTS the final three characters of a monumental piece of calligraphy by Zhu Xi, one hundred and seven characters in length with each character being over five inches tall. The composition quotes and paraphrases three sections of the "Great Appendix" to the *Book of Changes*. The red seal below the final character belongs to Zhu himself. The large seal in the upper left belongs to the Qianlong Emperor and is one of four seals attesting to the fact that the piece was part of Qing Palace Collection. Appearing at the end of the scroll, the three characters 朱熹書 mean [the characters were] "written by Zhu Xi," but on the cover of our work they can also be read as "Zhu Xi's Writings."

Acknowledgments

THE SERIES EDITORS and I would like to thank Peter Ohlin of Oxford University Press for his initial interest in developing this series and for helping us to craft the form and style of this volume. We thank the University of Utah and in particular its College of Humanities, Philosophy Department—and especially their Charles H. Monson Award—and Confucius Institute, along with their administrative staff, for supporting and hosting a workshop held 20–21 October 2017, which enabled the contributors to this volume to meet and discuss drafts of their individual contributions and larger issues concerning the format and content of this volume, and Nalei Chen for his participation in the workshop and offering a number of helpful suggestions that have enhanced this work. We also thank the *Sungkyun Institute for Confucian Studies and East Asian Philosophy* for its generous support in the production of this volume.

Conventions

WE HAVE ESTABLISHED and followed a number of policies in an effort to make the translations provided in this volume accessible and consistent; the most important are described below.

1. We include Chinese characters whenever we believe these might help readers understand or make connections among the translated passages. We employ the format: translation, italicized Romanization, and Chinese character, e.g., humaneness (*ren* 仁).

2. We employ standard translations for expressions such as "it was asked" (*huo wen* 或問 or *wen* 問) and "Zhu Xi (or whoever) said (or replied)" (*yue* 曰).

3. We do not footnote every interlocutor's name. In most cases, when the name of the person posing the question is not important for the sense, it is omitted, but individual translators have discretion in this regard.

4. We mostly employ gender neutral language, e.g., using "human beings" for *ren* 人 instead of "man," "noble person" for *junzi* 君子 instead of "gentleman," and the plural forms of words such as "sages" (*sheng ren* 聖人). We do so, on the one hand, because Zhu believed all human beings possess a full complement of moral pattern-principle and he was interested in everyone's moral cultivation[1] and, on the other, in order to be more inclusive. However, we do not do so in cases where such a policy would introduce strong anachronism or misleading implications, for example, in passages about ministers where it would imply that women had the opportunity to attain such offices as well as men.

---

1. There are impressive arguments in the tradition defending claims such as that women can become sages, which seem to be implied by a number of core neo-Confucian beliefs, e.g., that all people possess a full endowment of pattern-principle.

5. When referencing the original Chinese text of *The Classified Sayings of Master Zhu* (*Zhuzi yulei* 朱子語類), we provide the chapter (*juan* 卷) and page numbers of the version edited by Li Jingde 黎靖德 and collated by Wang Xingxian 王星賢 (Beijing: Zhonghua shu ju, 1986), e.g., (*ZZYL*, Chapter 12, p. 199). For other texts, we provide the information needed to locate the passage and the edition used for the translation. When citing or referring to standard works that are widely available in English translation, e.g., the *Analects, Doctrine of the Mean*, etc., we do not provide a specific edition but only the chapter and section numbers needed to locate the passage.

6. We take "neo-Confucian" to be an English proper name denoting various movements in the late Tang and through the Qing aimed at reviving and reinvigorating the Confucian tradition.[2] We employ the lower-case to highlight that it is not a "school" of philosophy in the sense either of a group of people who embrace the same set of beliefs and practices or the sense of having a single lineage or institutional organization. We treat Chinese terms that refer to particular parts of neo-Confucianism differently, for example, Learning of the Way (*Daoxue* 道學).

7. We use standard translations for titles of classic works but individual translators have discretion in this regard. Whenever translators depart from the standard translation they add a note at the first occurrence explaining their motivations and aims.

8. We use standard translations for key terms of art, for example "feelings" (*qing* 情), but individual translators have discretion in this regard. Whenever translators depart from the standard translation they add a note at the first occurrence explaining their motivations and aims.

9. For several terms of art we employ a hyphenated translation, e.g., "heart-mind" (*xin* 心), "pattern-principle" (*li* 理), "master-governor" (*zhuzai* 主宰). Our intent is to give a range of meanings that are representative of such terms; readers should not take these as exhaustive of the sense of these terms. Individual translators have discretion in this regard and whenever they depart from the standard translation they add a note at the first occurrence explaining their motivations and aims.

---

2. For a discussion of this term, see Tillman 1992 and de Bary 1993.

Bibliography

de Bary, William Theodore. 1993. "The Uses of Neo-Confucianism: A Response to Professor Tillman." *Philosophy East & West* 43(3): 541–555.

Tillman, Hoyt Cleveland. 1992. "A New Direction in Confucian Scholarship: Approaches to Examining the Differences between Neo-Confucianism and *Tao-hsüeh*." *Philosophy East & West* 42 (3): 455–474.

About the Translators

Ari Borrell is a bibliographer for Chinese literature at the Modern Languages Association. His research interests focus on the interactions of Buddhist and neo-Confucian elites in the Song dynasty.

Beverly Bossler is a professor of history at University of California, Davis. Her work focuses on gender and social relations in the Tang, Song, and Yuan dynasties. Her publications include *Courtesans, Concubines, and the Cult of Female Fidelity* (2013) and *Gender and Chinese History: Transformative Encounters* (2015, editor).

Daniel K. Gardner is the Dwight W. Morrow Professor of History at Smith College. He has written extensively on the Confucian and neo-Confucian traditions in China. His books include *Learning to Be a Sage: Selections from the* Conversations of Master Chu, *Arranged Topically* (1990), *Zhu Xi's Reading of the* Analects (2003), and *Confucianism: A Very Short Introduction* (2014).

Philip J. Ivanhoe is distinguished chair professor in the College of Confucian Studies and Eastern Philosophy at Sungkyunkwan University, Seoul, Korea where he is Director of the *Sungkyun Institute for Confucian Studies and East Asian Philosophy* and Editor-in-Chief of the *Journal of Confucian Philosophy and Culture*. He specializes in the history of East Asian philosophy and religion and its potential for contemporary ethics.

Yung Sik Kim is a professor emeritus of Seoul National University, where he was professor in the Department of Asian History and the Program in History and Philosophy of Science until he retired in 2013. He received his PhD from Princeton University in 1980, and works on various aspects of Confucian scholars' thought and knowledge, in particular their attitudes toward scientific, technical, and occult knowledge. He is the author of *The Natural*

Philosophy of Chu Hsi (2000) and *Questioning Science in East Asia: Essays on Science, Confucianism, and the Comparative History of Science* (2014).

Ellen Neskar is the Merle Rosenblatt Goldman Chair of Asian Studies at Sarah Lawrence College, where she teaches pre-modern Chinese philosophy and history. She specializes in the intellectual and religious history of the Song dynasty.

On-cho Ng is a professor of history, Asian studies, and philosophy at the Pennsylvania State University, where he also serves as head of the Department of Asian Studies. He is an intellectual historian of Late Imperial China, and has written extensively on Confucian historiography, hermeneutics, and religiosity.

Hoyt Cleveland Tillman is a professor of Chinese history in the School of International Letters and Cultures at Arizona State University, and specializes in the history of Chinese thought, especially Confucianism during the Song to Yuan periods. His academic honors include being the first Sinologist to receive the senior research prize from the Alexander von Humboldt Foundation in 2000 and serving as an affiliated researcher at Peking University's Center for Studies of Ancient Chinese History since 2004. In contrast to others who focus on orthodoxy, his English, Chinese, and Korean publications emphasize diversity and alternatives within Confucianism.

Justin Tiwald is a professor of philosophy at San Francisco State University. He has published on classical Confucian, Daoist, and neo-Confucian accounts of moral psychology, well-being, and political authority, as well as the implications of Confucian views for virtue ethics, individual rights, and moral epistemology. His books include *Neo-Confucianism*, with Stephen C. Angle (2017); *Ritual and Religion in the* Xunzi, with T. C. Kline III (2014); and *Readings in Later Chinese Philosophy*, with Bryan W. Van Norden (2014).

Curie Virág is Senior Research Fellow and Co-Project Director in the School of History, Classics, and Archaeology at the University of Edinburgh, and Visiting Professor in the Departments of Philosophy and Medieval Studies at Central European University. Her primary interests concern pre-modern Chinese philosophy and intellectual history (Warring States to twelfth century), focusing on the emotions, cognition, and subjectivity. She is actively engaged in cross-cultural and comparative research, and currently co-directs the research project "Classicising Learning in Medieval Imperial Systems: Cross-cultural Approaches to Byzantine Paideia and Tang/Song Xue," funded by the European Research Council. Her published work includes *The Emotions in Early Chinese Philosophy*.

Chronology of Important Events in Zhu Xi's Life

1130	Born 18 October in the Youqi District of Fujian Province.
1140	Zhu's father resigns over policy disagreements and begins tutoring Zhu Xi at home.
1143	Zhu's father dies; Zhu Xi begins studying with Liu Zihui, Liu Mianzhi, and Hu Xian.
1148	Passes highest level of Imperial Examinations and obtains Presented Scholar degree.
1149	Marries daughter of Liu Mianzhi; her posthumous name was "Person of Great Virtue" (Shiren 碩人). (date approximate)
1151	Appointed Registrar of the District of Tong'an, takes up position in 1153.
1153	Birth of first child, a son named Shu 塾 (courtesy name Shouzhi 受之).
1160	Formally becomes Li Tong's student.
1172	Writes "Explanation of the Meaning of the Western Inscription" (*Ximing jieyi* 西銘解義).
1173	Writes "Elucidation of the Diagram of the Supreme Ultimate" (*Taiji tushuo* 太極圖說).
1175	Compiles, with Lü Zuqian, *A Record for Reflection* and debates Lu Jiuyuan 陸九淵 (1139–1193) at Goose Lake Monastery.
1177	Composes his *Collected Commentaries on the Analects* and *Collected Commentaries on the Mengzi*.
1179	Accepts position as Prefect of the Nankang Military District and revives the White Deer Grotto Academy.
1182	Indicts Tang Zhongyou 唐仲友 (1136–1188), Prefect of Taizhou 台州 and relative of the Prime Minister, for official misconduct.

1189   Writes commentaries on the *Great Learning* and *Doctrine of the Mean*.

1190   Accepts position as Prefect of Zhangzhou 漳州 in Fujian 福建 Province.

1196   Zhu's Learning of the Way (*Daoxue* 道學) is proscribed by the Emperor as "false learning." In the same year, Zhu is accused by Shen Jizu 沈繼祖 (Presented Scholar degree 1169) of six "great crimes" and five "evil deeds."

1200   Zhu passes away from natural causes on 23 April.

Introduction

ZHU XI 朱熹 (18 October 1130, d. 23 April 1200)—courtesy names (*zi* 字): Yuanhui 元晦 and Zhonghui 仲晦; pen name (*hao* 號): Huian 晦庵— was born in the Youqi District (Youqi xian 尤溪縣) of Fujian Province (Fujian sheng 福建省).[1] His *Chronological Biography* (*Nianpu* 年譜)[2] claims that from a very early age he showed remarkable ability and inquisitiveness. He is described as a "clever and serious" youth (Wang 1998, 2). At age four (*sui* 歲) when his father pointed skyward and declared, "That is Heaven," we are told Zhu Xi asked, "What lies above Heaven?" (Wang 1998, 2). At age eight, it is reported that he read through the *Classic of Filial Piety* (*Xiaojing* 孝經) in a single sitting and wrote above its title, "Those who fail to follow this are not fully human" (Wang 1998, 2). Around the same time, in the company of other children, he once sat apart from them, playing in the sand. Sitting upright, he drew patterns in the sand and when people went and looked at them, they discovered he had inscribed the eight hexagrams of the *Classic of Changes* (*Yijing* 易經)(Wang 1998, 2). At the age of ten, upon reading the *Mengzi* 孟子 (*Mencius*), when he came to the line, "The sages and I are the same in kind" (*Mengzi* 6A7), he was overcome by a feeling of indescribable joy; earlier he had thought that becoming a sage was easy, but now, he felt

---

1. Excellent accounts of Zhu Xi's life can be found in Brian McKnight, "Chu Hsi and His World," in Chan 1986, 408–436; Chan 1987; and several chapters in Chan 1989. A short but highly insightful introduction to his life, thought, and contributions to neo-Confucianism is Thompson 2017.

2. I have relied on what most scholars regard as the standard version of this text, *Zhu Xi's Chronological Biography* (*Zhu Xi nianpu* 朱熹年譜) by Wang Maohong 王懋竑 (1668–1741) 1998. For a thorough account of Zhu's different biographies, see "The Hsing-chuang" in Chan 1989, 1–11.

how difficult it was (Wang 1998, 3). Such precocious beginnings presaged—almost certainly retrospectively—his remarkable career.

Zhu Xi received his early education at home from his father Zhu Song 朱松 (1097–1143), who began instructing his son soon after having been forced from office because of his opposition to the appeasement policy the Song court had adopted toward the Jurchen in 1140. Following Zhu Song's death in 1143, Zhu Xi studied with three of his father's friends, Liu Zihui 劉子翬 (1101–1147), Liu Mianzhi 劉勉之 (1091–1149), and Hu Xian 胡憲 (1086–1162). All three of these scholars were deeply interested in Daoism and Buddhism as well as Confucianism and as a consequence Zhu Xi was exposed to and developed a sophisticated knowledge and appreciation of all three traditions.

Zhu passed the official Presented Scholar (*jinshi* 進士) exam in 1148, at just nineteen years of age, and continued his studies, waiting for his first governmental appointment. In 1153, he was offered and took up a position as Registrar of the District of Tong'an (*Tong'an xian zhubu* 同安縣主簿), a post he retained until 1156. He began serious study of Confucian philosophy under the neo-Confucian master Li Tong 李侗 (1093–1163) the same year he accepted his first official position, and formally became Li's student in 1160 at the age of thirty. From this point on, he focused all his energies on Confucianism and in particular the interpretation that came down from the Cheng brothers: Cheng Hao 程顥 (1032–1085) and Cheng Yi 程頤 (1033–1107).

Zhu Xi held views that were opposed to the court on a number of important issues and so he chose to avoid government service after his time as Registrar of the District of Tong'an. This arrangement afforded him much more time for study, reflection, and writing. In 1179, however, he returned to government service, accepting a position as Prefect of the Nankang Military District (*Nankang jun* 南康軍), and revived the White Deer Grotto Academy (*bailudong shuyuan* 白鹿洞書院), a famous former school at the foot of Wulau Peak (*Wulao feng* 五老峰) on Mount Lu (*Lushan* 廬山). Three years later, he was demoted for attacking the performance and integrity of some influential officials. From this point onward, his official career took a convoluted and unstable course.[3] He was appointed to and demoted from a succession of positions and was dismissed from his last official post, accused of several serious crimes. A petition was drafted, calling for his

---

3. For an account of Zhu Xi's official career, see Schirokauer 1962.

execution. Despite his checkered official career and its ignominious conclusion, his interpretation of neo-Confucianism soon became dominant at the Song court, and eight years after his death, in 1208, Emperor Ningzong of the Song 宋寧宗 honored him with the posthumous name "Duke of Culture" (*Wen Gong* 文公); ever since, he has often been referred to as "Zhu, Duke of Culture" (*Zhu Wen Gong* 朱文公). Twenty years later, Emperor Lizong of the Song 宋理宗 granted him the additional posthumous title "Duke of the State of Hui" (*Huiguo Gong* 徽國公), and in 1241, he was awarded the highest honor a Confucian can receive, when his spirit tablet was placed in the Hall of the Complete Symphony (*Dacheng Dian* 大成殿), the main Confucian temple in Kongzi's hometown, Qufu 曲阜. Since that time and down to the present day, Zhu Xi has been revered as one of the "Twelve Wise Ones" (*Shi'er zhe* 十二哲), the most accomplished, influential, and admired scholars in the Confucian tradition.

As noted earlier, Zhu Xi's interpretation of neo-Confucianism, which self-consciously sought to continue and develop the philosophy of the Cheng brothers (and especially the thought of Cheng Yi), became the orthodox school in China and beyond, commonly known as the Learning of Pattern-Principle (*lixue* 理學) or the Cheng-Zhu Learning of Pattern-Principle (*Cheng-Zhu lixue* 程朱理學).[4] During the Yuan dynasty 元代 (1271–1368), Zhu Xi's edition and interpretation of the Four Books[5] was adopted as the basis for the Imperial Examination System, which was the pathway to officialdom and success in traditional Chinese society.[6] It remained the orthodox tradition until the collapse of the Qing dynasty 清代 (1644–1911) and had a profound and enduring influence on how the tradition was understood in Korea, Japan, and Vietnam.[7]

There are a number of interrelated reasons why Zhu Xi's interpretation of the Confucian tradition proved to be so influential and enduring; chief among these is the sheer brilliance and power that it displays. Another important

---

4. For introductions to the philosophy of the Cheng-Zhu School, see Graham 1987; Chan 1989; Tillman 1992; and chapters 4, 5, 8, and 9 in Makeham 2010.

5. The Four Books (*Sishu* 四書) are the *Great Learning* (*Daxue* 大學), *Analects* (*Lunyu* 論語), *Book of Mencius* (*Mengzi* 孟子), and the *Doctrine of the Mean* (*Zhongyong* 中庸). Zhu Xi's commentary on the Four Books is called the *Collected Commentaries on the* Four Books *Arranged in Sections and Sentences* (*Sishu zhangju jizhu* 四書章句集注).

6. For Zhu Xi's ascendancy in the Yuan, see Liu Ts'un-yan, "Chu Hsi's Influence in Yuan Times," in Chan 1986, 521–550.

7. For a study of the Confucian tradition in China, Korea, and Japan, see Huang 2010 and Ivanhoe 2016. See also the contributions by Youn Sa-soon and Yamazaki Michio in Chan 1986.

virtue of his reading of the tradition is its comprehensiveness: he commented on all the Confucian classics in a way that related and synthesized their various concerns into an orderly system of thought that presented the tradition as neatly organized and coherent, drew a clear and bright contrast between Confucianism and the competing schools of Buddhism and Daoism, and offered followers both a powerful theoretical account of the tradition's core teachings as well as a concrete course of practice they could take up and pursue on a daily basis. Zhu Xi carried out extensive philological and philosophical research on the Five Classics,[8] bringing them within the ambit of his grand synthesis. In addition, as noted earlier, he provided what became the definitive edition and commentary on the Four Books. Zhu Xi highlighted these four texts and elevated them to central importance within the Confucian canon; in so doing he shifted the attention of the tradition, focusing it squarely on issues concerning the ethical and spiritual cultivation of the self, that offered Confucians an attractive alternative to the regimens of cultivation found in Daoism and Buddhism. Zhu's neo-Confucian synthesis had all the metaphysical sophistication and appeal of these popular competitors, as well as corresponding spiritual exercises for the cultivation of the heart-mind, but in addition it linked these to a political and social program of renewal and strengthening that people of his and subsequent ages found profoundly attractive and appealing and that claimed for Confucianism a distinctive this-worldly, practical set of concerns.[9]

Like many Confucians before and after him, Zhu Xi was not only a scholar and theoretician but also a renowned teacher, who had a core of devoted disciples and who likely instructed several thousand students. The *Classified Sayings of Master Zhu* (*Zhuzi yulei* 朱子語類) purports to record his oral presentations and conversations, while the *Collected Writings of Master Zhu* (*Zhuzi wenji* 朱子文集) contains his poetry, essays, letters, and other prose works. In addition to the extensive comments on all the classical texts of Confucianism that can be found scattered throughout those two massive works and his *Collected Commentaries on the Four Books*, Zhu published annotated editions of other classical works, including the *Classic of Changes* and the *Odes*, collections of the essential works of selected neo-Confucian masters such as the Cheng brothers, i.e., the *Extant Works of the Cheng*

---

8. The Five Classics include the *Classic of Changes, Odes* (*Shijing* 詩經), *Book of Documents* (*Shangshu* 尚書), *Book of Rites* (*Liji* 禮記), and the *Spring and Autumn Annals* (*Chunqiu* 春秋).

9. Peter K. Bol does a splendid job showing how neo-Confucian philosophy entailed and guided its followers to engage in a range of practical social and political endeavors. See Bol 2010.

[Brothers] from Henan (*Henan Chengshi yishu* 河南程氏遺書), and, together with Lü Zuqian 呂祖謙 (1137–1181), the highly influential anthology
of neo-Confucian teachings, *A Record for Reflection* (*Jinsilu* 近思祿).[10] He
also published an edited and annotated edition of the Huang-Lao Master Wei
Boyang's 魏伯陽 (*c.* 100–170) *Classic of Changes' Unity of the Three* (*Zhouyi
cantong qi* 周易參同契), a Daoist work on inner alchemy, based upon the
cosmology found in the *Classic of Changes*.

This collection of selected translations of Zhu Xi's works, by leading
scholars from around the world, presents a representative range of his and
our interests and concerns. Each chapter begins with a short description by
the translator aimed at introducing the topic and relating it to some of Zhu
Xi's larger concerns. Taken together, the aim of the volume is to present an
accurate and comprehensive introduction to Zhu Xi's philosophy that can
be used not only to understand its historical expression and place within
the Confucian tradition but also some of its potential value as a resource for
contemporary ethical, political, and social thought. The volume includes a
brief chronology of important events in Zhu Xi's life, included in the front
matter, and a list of key terms of art, along with their standard translations[11]
and common alternatives. Each chapter includes a list of works cited as well
as suggestions for further readings on the topics that it features. Chapter 1
consists of selected passages concerning Zhu Xi's metaphysics, epistemology,
and ethics. Since these three topics provide much of the foundation and inform almost everything Zhu Xi wrote about, this introduction offers a concise
description of each of these central features of Zhu's philosophy and explores
some of the most important relationships among them.

Under the influence of Daoist and Buddhist metaphysical beliefs, neo-
Confucians developed a dramatically more robust sense of connection—a
belief in a kind of identity or oneness between self and world—that provided
the foundation for a more extensive and demanding imperative to care for the

---

10. Translated into English by Wing-tsit Chan as *Reflections on Things at Hand: The Neo-
Confucian Anthology*, Chan 1967. In subsequent centuries students of Confucianism used
this work as a kind of introduction to and primer on the founding figures of Song dynasty
neo-Confucianism.

11. The "standard translation" is the one recommended by the editors and followed by most
of the translators. Since these English correlates of the original Chinese are never perfect, our
contributors on occasion opt out of the standard translation and provide alternative English
renderings of some of these terms. Whenever this is done, it is noted and a brief explanation
provided.

world *as oneself* (1:20, 22).[12] Rather than seeing the world as an interconnected system or web, as earlier Chinese thinkers tended to do, they believed each and every thing in the world contained within itself all the pattern-principles (*li* 理)—a term we will discuss in more detail later in this Introduction—in the universe (1:1). This idea, which we might identify as "all in each," came most directly from certain teachings within Huayan 華嚴 Buddhism. One can see this idea illustrated in many Buddhist temples around the world by displays in which the figure of the Buddha—representing our original nature and containing all the pattern-principle in the universe—is placed within a circle of mutually reflecting mirrors. The effect is that the image of the Buddha is projected and appears everywhere, with the pattern recurring in infinitely expanding repetitions.

The translation "pattern-principle" is more a gesture toward the meaning of *li* 理 than a fully adequate translation. Like *qi* 氣[13] and certain other terms of art, there is no wholly adequate English word in the same semantic neighborhood that can be used to translate *li* 理; this should not come as a great surprise, for these are terms that serve as the core of the distinctive metaphysics of neo-Confucianism.[14] In a number of passages, Zhu Xi identifies two interrelated, characteristic aspects of *li* 理: pattern-principle is what makes a thing the kind of thing it is and, at the same time, provides a standard, norm, or paradigm for the thing in question.

As for the things under heaven, each has that which makes it what it is (*suoyi ran zhi gu* 所以然之故) and a standard to which it

---

12. These numbers refer to chapters and sections in this volume—in this case chapter 1, sections 20 and 22—that illustrate the point under discussion. For a study of such a conception of oneness, see Ivanhoe 2017. For an anthology that explores how such a sense of oneness might inspire new contemporary understandings of the self and its relationship to the world, see Ivanhoe, Flanagan, Harrison, Schwitzgebel, and Sarkissian 2018.

13. *Qi* is a term of great importance, varied meanings, and venerable history. In some of its earliest and most common occurrences, it referred to vapor, steam, and human breath. In general, it was thought to be a kind of vital energy that exists in different densities and various levels of purity or turbidity. Its alternative forms give phenomena different degrees of substantiality: the purest and most refined *qi* being most ethereal while the most impure and turbid *qi* leading to dense and material existence. Associated with such contrasting states were associated levels of movement and vitality: the former types of *qi* being most active and lively while the latter being most inert and dead. *Qi* also played important roles in cosmological speculation being the "stuff" out of which everything in the universe condensed and coalesced and into which it eventually would expand and dissipate. This Introduction further explains how *qi* relates to *li* in the Zhu Xi's metaphysics.

14. The most insightful and helpful discussion of *li* 理 in Zhu Xi's philosophy is Kim 2000, 19–30.

ought to accord (*suo dangran zhi ze* 所當然之則). This is called its pattern-principle.[15]

The pattern-principle of a thing conveys what a thing is in itself (*ti* 體) and for neo-Confucians what a thing is in itself is inextricably linked to how that thing naturally functions (*yong* 用) or operates in the world (1:9, 13, 18). When Zhu Xi is pressed to explain the meaning of pattern-principle, he tends to describe both the form and function of a thing or type of thing. For example, the pattern-principle of boats is that they "can only travel upon water" (1:7); the pattern-principle of carts is that they "can only travel upon land" (1:7); the pattern-principle of bricks is that they lend themselves to building things like steps (1:6); the pattern-principle of chairs is "having four legs and so being something one can sit upon" (1:53). If one removes one of the legs of a chair, "one can no longer sit in it; it has lost the pattern-principle of a chair" (1:53). Folding fans are what they are because they are "made in this particular way and should be used in this particular way" (1:53): this is their pattern-principle. Pattern-principles should not be thought of as fundamental building blocks out of which different things are constructed; they are closer to blueprints than atoms, but closer still to paradigmatic ideals or images that capture and convey not only the structure and form of a thing or type of thing but also its characteristic function or activity in the world.

Throughout his writings, Zhu uses the term *li* 理 in two distinct but related senses: individuated pattern-principle and unified pattern-principle. Individuated pattern-principle is explained earlier in this Introduction; this is the aspect of *li* 理 that makes an individual thing or type of thing the thing or type of thing it is. At the same time, though, each and every individuated pattern-principle is a manifestation of the single, unified pattern-principle. The dual aspects of pattern-principle are captured in a famous teaching of Cheng Yi's—"Pattern-principle is one but its manifestations are many" (*li yi fen shu* 理一分殊). At times Zhu speaks as if unified pattern-principle is the sum or aggregate of all individuated pattern-principle, but he more often speaks as though the former somehow contains within itself all the latter and the latter are in some sense reflections or manifestations of the former; there is a multifaceted and complex relationship between the unity of pattern-principle and its various manifestations that Zhu Xi himself admits is difficult

---

15. *Questions on the* Great Learning (*Daxue huowen* 大學或問) in Zhu, Yan, and Liu 2002.

to explain fully. He at times equates the single, unified pattern-principle with the "Supreme Ultimate" (*taiji* 太極) (1:1). Zhu suggests that the relationship between the supreme ultimate and its myriad manifestations is like that between the moon and its innumerable reflections in various bodies of water, large and small, and makes clear that the supreme ultimate fixes and regulates the form and function of the myriad things. All of this makes clear that the relationship between the supreme ultimate and its myriad manifestations is something much stronger and more mysterious than mere aggregation.

Another way in which Zhu Xi talked about this set of ideas concerning the unity underlying the vast diversity in the universe is by saying that each thing contains within it a shared "original nature" (*ben xing* 本性 or *benti zhi xing* 本體之性), which consists of all the pattern-principles of the world (1:3). This shared "original nature" is manifested in the phenomenal world of individual things as discrete expressions of "physical nature" (*qizhi zhi xing* 氣質之性). Individual things and types of things are what they are not because of a difference in their original natures or stock of pattern-principles but because their endowment of *qi*, which differs in quality and balance, only allows certain pattern-principles to manifest themselves. *Qi* naturally occurs in different mixtures and various grades and qualities; some things have more *yin* than *yang*; some *qi* is slow, dull, heavy, turbid, and dark; some is quick, bright, light, lively, and clear. The more imbalanced and impure one's *qi* the less pattern-principle is able to be manifested and it is only such manifested *li* that contributes to how a thing appears and functions and determines whether and what it can think or feel. Humans are unique among all things in being endowed with the most perfectly balanced or purest form of *qi* and hence they are the most intelligent and sensitive creatures on earth. Moreover, they alone have the capacity to refine their individual endowment of *qi*, their "talent" (*cai* 才) (1:18), and thereby increase their understanding and character even to the point where they attain a form of enlightenment and become sages. Non-human animals show more limited levels of and constricted capacities for intelligence and feeling, while plants and inanimate things complete a spectrum that passes into lower states of consciousness and eventually fades into unknowing and unfeeling things (1:2, 4). This prepares the way to discuss some of Zhu Xi's core epistemological views.

As noted earlier, not only are human beings endowed with the purest and most well-balanced *qi*; they are unique among creatures in having the ability to refine and balance the particular endowment they receive at birth. If they work to refine and balance the *qi* that blocks the *li* within to the point where the pattern-principle of their heart-minds can shine forth and illuminate the things they encounter or bring to mind, then at that point they achieve proper understanding and appreciation of these phenomena. Such a view allowed Zhu Xi and other neo-Confucians to provide an account of how it is that human beings, when properly cultivated through learning, ritual practice, meditation, and reflection, can understand the myriad phenomena of the world.[16] Roughly, the idea is that the pattern-principle in our heart-minds can join or meet the pattern-principle in things or events and attain "understanding" (*lihui* 理會, literally "pattern-principle meeting"). It is only because of the pernicious influence of imbalanced or unrefined *qi* that some of the pattern-principle endowed within us is obscured; we can't "see" our way to understanding, and we remain either wholly ignorant or lost in partial or distorted understanding. In order to improve and advance along the Way, one must cultivate oneself, eliminating the self-centered desires that generate and sustain imbalanced or unrefined *qi* and allowing the pattern-principle within the heart-mind to gradually come into play and guide understanding and action.

Zhu Xi described a complex and systematic process to facilitate the refining of *qi* and thereby gaining a full understanding and appreciation of pattern-principle. He distinguished two primary stages in this process of learning: Lesser Learning and Greater Learning (1:23–26). Lesser Learning was designed to shape young people to accord with pattern-principle in the course of carrying out actual affairs such as practicing rituals, music, archery, charioteering, calligraphy, and mathematics. The idea is to inculcate proper habits that would on the one hand refine the *qi* while on the other resonate with the pattern-principle of a child's heart-mind. Such learning often occurred at a preconscious level (1:25) but in every case helped prepare the young for the more explicitly theoretical lessons to come. Greater Learning "concerns explaining the pattern-principle underlying such affairs" (1:24). Broadly speaking, such learning concerned grasping the pattern-principle of things and affairs and seeing how they all fit together to form the grand scheme of the Way.

Greater Learning consisted in investigating the things (*gewu* 格物) one encountered in life with an aim to grasp their underlying pattern-principles, but it also consisted in and was tightly linked to a systematic study of the classics. Study of such works gave one access to the thoughts of the sages and worthies, who wrote in order to pass on their insights and experiences (1:39).

---

16. Plato solved a similar problem by arguing that human souls have prior contact with the forms before being born and are able to recollect this experience in acts of knowing.

This enables one to make rapid progress in the effort to extend one's knowledge (*zhizhi* 致知) (1:37–38). In order for such study to prove effective in refining *qi* and leading to enhanced understanding it had to be experienced directly by students and properly influence and help cultivate their feelings as well as their thoughts. A distinctive feature of Zhu Xi's approach to learning is that he rejected the idea of relying on untutored emotional intuitions as one's guide. Even though his highest virtue was humaneness and his goal was to care for all the world, he insisted that emotions themselves are originally and inextricably connected to *qi* and tend to mislead; we should instead, as we have discussed, shape ourselves early in life through correct practice and then study and master a set of lessons that explain the pattern-principles underlying proper conduct.[17] As we make progress along the Way, though, we must work in the corresponding and appropriate feelings to inform and motivate our practice of the Way. We must see and feel the significance of the Way by studying for "our own sake" (1:32), i.e., with an aim to improve ourselves morally.

Zhu Xi insisted that learning must bring together and combine proper emotional and theoretical understanding; appealing to an idea first seen in the *Mengzi*, he taught that students must "get it for themselves" (*zide* 自得). They must "taste" the lessons they work at and learn to savor their "flavor" for themselves (1:29, 35). Only such embodied understanding can effectively shape the moral self in the required ways. In order to achieve this goal, students must assiduously maintain an attitude of reverential attention (*jing* 敬) throughout their studies. For Zhu, reverential attention described a serious, focused, and steadfast attitude and state of attentiveness—a Confucian version of Buddhist mindfulness—that functioned to both guard and guide the self in the process of moral cultivation. It guards one from losing one's focus and letting one's attention drift onto ideas, issues, or interests that hinder or distract from moral improvement; it guides one by keeping one's attention focused on those things that advance moral understanding. Reverential attention is the psychological state that keeps us focused on the pattern-principle that leads us to a full and proper understanding and appreciation of the Way. As we progress in learning and advance along the path of moral cultivation, we come to see and appreciate not only how to act but also

---

17. This distinguished another major lineage within the neo-Confucian tradition, the Lu-Wang School, which taught that from the start one must seek and cultivate the feeling of connection and care with other people, creatures, and things. For a study that explores this difference, see Ivanhoe 2016.

the larger and grander patterns and processes of the Way. We gain a clearer and more vivid understanding and sense of our relationship, proper function, and fundamental oneness with other people, creatures, and things. We now begin to see how intimately Zhu's metaphysics and epistemology are related to his ethical views and the imperative to care for the world as one's self.

Given the general picture we have described, Zhu Xi and neo-Confucians in general developed and embraced a new and powerful justification for universal care: our shared pattern-principle supplies a deep and intricate connection between ourselves and other people, creatures, and things. Such a view provided an explanation for *why* people are emotionally affected not only by the suffering of other people, but also by the suffering of non-human animals, the harming of plants, and even the wanton destruction of inanimate objects. For example, Zhou Dunyi 周敦頤 (1017–1073) famously refused to cut the grass growing in front of his window saying, "I regard it in the same way as I regard myself." Zhang Zai 張載 (1020–1077) expressed the same sentiment when he heard the braying of a donkey and declined to eat young bamboo shoots because he could not bear to violate the shared pattern-principle of incipient growth he felt they manifested.[18] Like other neo-Confucians, these men experienced a profound feeling of oneness not only with other human beings but with the entire universe. The self was in some deep sense not only connected or intermingled with other people, creatures, and things but coextensive with the universe, and this provided a clear and powerful justification to care for all the world. If, fundamentally, we are one body (*yiti* 一體) with all the world, we naturally should care for it in the same way that we care for ourselves (1:22).

Daoists, in general, rely upon a distinctive style of reasoning, which, roughly, proceeds from claims about how all phenomena, including the self, arise from and at the most basic level remain nothing (*wu* 無) to claims about the radical equality of things and an imperative to feel and show parental care (*ci* 慈) for all; Buddhists employ a similar style, arguing that all things arise from emptiness (*kong* 空) and fundamentally remain empty, and those who understand this fact about the world and the self will therefore embrace a stance and attitude of great compassion (*mahākaruṇā*) and loving kindness (*maitrī*).[19] While Zhu and other neo-Confucians were moved by their

---

18. The first two stories are recorded in the same passage in chapter three of Cheng and Cheng 2004. For the anecdote about bamboo shoots, see Chan 1967, 248, n. 42.

19. There are important differences between the views sketched here, but the point is that Daoist arguments that move from metaphysical claims about "nothing" to normative claims

long association with Daoism and Buddhism, they insisted that neither the world nor the self is fundamentally nothing or empty; instead all things are abundantly full of pattern-principle, which itself has proclivities toward life or a ceaseless system of life-production (*sheng sheng* 生生). As we have seen, each and every person shares with all other people, creatures, and things a complete and perfect endowment of pattern-principle; it is shared pattern-principle—not "nothing" or "emptiness"—that serves as the foundation for the deep interpenetration and identity among things, which gives rise to and supports their core virtue of humaneness (*ren* 仁), expressed in terms of an imperative to care for other people, creatures, and things as oneself. For neo-Confucians, to be inhumane or unfeeling (*buren* 不仁) was to be in the grip of a delusion about the true nature of the world and the self. Those who do not feel the suffering of the world or fail to seek its flourishing simply do not understand and fully appreciate that they and the world are "one body" (*yiti* 一體); they are like a person with a paralyzed (*buren* 不仁) arm who is insensitive to and ignores someone injuring his afflicted limb.[20] Their moral failing is the result of ignorance, a failure to see the true nature of themselves and the world of which they are a part.

Philip J. Ivanhoe
Seoul, Korea

Works Cited

Bol, Peter K. 2010. *Neo-Confucianism in History.* Harvard East Asian Monographs. Reprint. Cambridge: Harvard University Asia Center.

Chan, Wing-tsit, trans. 1967. Tr. *Reflections on Things at Hand: The Neo-Confucian Anthology.* New York: Columbia University Press.

_____, ed. 1986. *Chu Hsi and Neo-Confucianism.* Honolulu: University of Hawaii Press.

_____. 1987. *Chu Hsi: Life and Thought.* Hong Kong: Chinese University Press.

_____. 1989. *Chu Hsi: New Studies.* Honolulu: University of Hawaii Press.

Cheng Hao 程顥, and Cheng Yi 程頤. 2004. *Collected Works of the Two Chengs (Er Cheng ji* 二程集). Beijing: Zhonghua Shuju.

Graham, Angus C. 1989. *Two Chinese Philosophers: The Metaphysics of the Brothers Cheng.* Reprint. La Salle, IL: Open Court Press.

---

about "parental care" are like Buddhist arguments that move from "emptiness" to "great compassion" and "loving kindness."

20. This analogy, which was invoked by numerous neo-Confucians, has considerable intuitive appeal since, like the English word "unfeeling," to be *buren* 不仁 could mean either to be insensitive to *other people's suffering* or to have a paralyzed limb.

Huang Chun-chieh. 2010. *Humanism in East Asian Confucian Contexts*. Bielefeld, Germany: Transcript Verlag.

Ivanhoe, Philip J. 2016. *Three Streams: Confucian Reflections on Learning and the Moral Heart-Mind in China, Korea, and Japan*. New York: Oxford University Press.

_____. 2017. *Oneness: East Asian Conceptions Virtue, Happiness, and How We Are All Connected*. New York: Oxford University Press.

Ivanhoe, Philip J., Owen Flanagan, Victoria Harrison, Eric Schwitzgebel, and Hagop Sarkissian, eds. 2018. *The Oneness Hypothesis: Beyond the Boundary of the Self*. New York: Columbia University Press.

Kim, Yung Sik. 2000. *The Natural Philosophy of Chu Hsi 1130–1200*. Philadelphia, PA: American Philosophical Society.

Makeham, John, ed. 2010. *Dao Companion to Neo-Confucian Philosophy*. Dordrecht; London: Springer.

Schirokauer, Conrad. 1962. "Chu Hsi's Political Career: A Study in Ambivalence." In *Confucian Personalities*. Edited by A. Wright and D. Twichett. Stanford, CA: Stanford University Press.

Thompson, Kirill. 2017. "Zhu Xi" *The Stanford Encyclopedia of Philosophy*. Edited by Edward N. Zalta. https://plato.stanford.edu/entries/zhu-xi/.

Tillman, Hoyt Cleveland. 1992. *Confucian Discourse and Chu Hsi's Ascendancy*. Honolulu: University of Hawaii Press.

Wang Maohong 王懋竑. 1998. *Zhu Xi's Chronological Biography* (*Zhu Xi nianpu* 朱熹年譜). Reprint. Beijing: Zhonghua shuju.

Zhu Jieren 朱傑人, Yan Zuozhi 嚴佐之, Liu Yongxiang 劉永翔, eds. 2002. *Questions on the* Great Learning (*Daxue huowen* 大學或問). In *The Complete Works of Master Zhu* (*Zhuzi quanshu* 朱子全書). Vol. 6. Shanghai: Shanghai guji chubanshe and Hefei: Anhui jiaoyu chubanshe.

Metaphysics, Epistemology, and Ethics

Philip J. Ivanhoe

Introduction

As described in greater detail in the Introduction to this volume, under the in-fluence of Daoism and Buddhism, neo-Confucians developed a set of robust metaphysical beliefs that describe a kind of identity or oneness between one-self and world. It is this underlying unity between the self and other people, creatures, and things rather than natural human feelings of attachment or empathy that provides the ultimate foundation for a comprehensive and de-manding imperative to care for the world *as oneself.* While similar in struc-ture to the Daoist and Buddhist precedents that in many ways inspired this vision—in arguing from metaphysical claims about how the self and the world really are to normative claims about how we should feel, perceive, act, and or-ganize society—neo-Confucians insist that their view differs fundamentally from either of these traditions. Most importantly, rather than holding that the world and the self are fundamentally "nothing" or "empty"—as Daoists and Buddhists respectively believe—they claim that all things are abundantly full of pattern-principle (*li* 理), which supports the nurturance and cease-less production of life. Neo-Confucians contend that each and every person shares with all other people, creatures, and things a complete and perfect en-dowment of pattern-principle. This shared "original nature" (*ben xing* 本性) serves as the foundation for the deep interpenetration and identity among things that is characteristic of their view and gives rise to and supports the core Confucian virtue of benevolence (*ren* 仁), which for neo-Confucians is a universally, though graded expression of care for all people, creatures, and things. Those who remain "unfeeling" to the suffering of the world or fail to seek its flourishing simply do not understand or fully appreciate the fact that they are "one body" (*yiti* 一體) with all things. Their moral failing is the result of ignorance, a failure to see the true nature of themselves and the world of which they are a part and to act in light of such understanding.

Given the metaphysical view sketched above and the related ethical imperative to care for all the world as in some sense oneself, the epistemological challenge for Zhu Xi and other neo-Confucians was how to attain an accurate and complete understanding of the true nature of the world and the self. Among neo-Confucians this challenge has given rise to distinctive approaches to learning as the means to attain true understanding of both self and world. Unlike other important neo-Confucian thinkers, Zhu rejected the idea that untutored emotional intuitions—a sense or feeling of our underlying unity with the world—could guide us to full moral virtue. Even though his highest virtue was benevolence and his goal was to care for all the world, Zhu insisted that emotions, being originally and inextricably connected to *qi*, tend to mislead. We should instead shape ourselves early in life through correct practice and then study and master a set of lessons that explain the pattern-principle underlying proper conduct. Nevertheless, as we make progress along the Way, we need to work in the corresponding and appropriate feelings to inform, guide, and motivate our practice of the Way. We must see and feel the significance of the Way by studying for "our own sake"—i.e., with an aim to improve ourselves morally—and "get it for ourselves" (*zide* 自得)—i.e., come to a personal understanding in which proper feelings inform, guide, and motivate correct knowledge.

In order to achieve true and proper understanding, we must assiduously maintain an attitude of reverential attention (*jing* 敬) throughout our studies and everyday lives. For Zhu, reverential attention describes a serious, focused, and steadfast attitude—a Confucian version of Buddhist mindfulness—that functions to both guard and guide the self in the process of moral cultivation. Reverential attention keeps us focused on the pattern-principle that leads us to a full and proper understanding and appreciation of the Way, and as we progress in learning and advance along the path of moral cultivation, we come to see and appreciate not only how to act and feel in this or that situation or type of circumstance but also the larger and grander patterns and processes of the Way. We gain a clearer and more vivid understanding and sense of our relationship, proper function, and fundamental oneness with other people, creatures, and things.

Translation

1. It was asked, "Human beings and other things all are endowed with the pattern-principle of Heaven and earth as their nature and receive the *qi* of Heaven and earth as their physical form. If the quality of people's character is not the same, surely this is because there are differences in the turbidity or clarity, density or thinness of their *qi*. As for other things, I am not sure whether such differences are because they do not possess a complete endowment of pattern-principle or because they are obscured by the turbidity of their endowment of *qi*."

   Zhu Xi replied, "It is solely because of the *qi* they receive that they only have certain [capabilities]. For example, dogs and horses have a certain physical constitution and so are only capable of doing certain things."

   A further question was asked, "Since each and every thing possesses the Supreme Ultimate (*taiji* 太極)[1] can we say that there is none which does not have a complete endowment of pattern-principle?"

   Zhu Xi replied, "One can say that they all have a complete endowment or one can say that some have partial endowments. If you talk about it in terms of pattern-principle, then none is without a complete endowment. If you talk about it in terms of *qi* then there cannot but be partial endowments.[2] This is why Lü Yushu[3] said, "There are respects in which the nature of other things is close to the nature of human beings. There are respects in which the nature of human beings is close to the nature of other things." (*ZZYL*, chapter 4, pp. 57–58)

2. It was asked, "Isn't it because the *qi*-material (*qizhi* 氣質) (nature of various things) is not the same, in terms of turbidity and murkiness, that there are partiality and completeness in the nature that Heaven endows?"

---

1. The Supreme Ultimate is the name for the complete and perfect collection of all principles. Often it is likened to a pure and perfect full moon, which is reflected fully in every body or drop of water.

2. Here, Zhu is invoking the two basic aspects or modes of nature: there is the nature of Heavenly pattern-principle (*tian li zhi xing* 天理之性) also known as the fundamental nature (*benxing* 本性) and there is the *qi*-material nature (*qizhi zhi xing* 氣質之性).

3. Yushu is the courtesy name of Lü Dalin 呂大臨 (ca. 1042–ca. 1090) who was a philosopher and a great scholar of Chinese antiquities. He studied under Zhang Zai 張載 and after Zhang's death with the brothers Cheng Hao 程顥 and Cheng Yi 程頤. His book *Illustrated Antiquities* (*Kaogutu* 考古圖) is the oldest Chinese description of various antiques.

Zhu Xi replied, "It is not a case of being partial or complete. It is like the light of the sun or the moon. If one is on open ground, one sees all of it. If one is inside a thatched hut some of the light is obstructed and blocked: some you see; some you don't see. When there is turbidity and murkiness, it is *qi* that makes things turbid and murky; as a result, there is obstruction and blockage, like being inside a thatched hut. Nevertheless, it is possible for human beings to penetrate through the obstruction and blockage. Birds and beasts have this same nature, but they are constrained by their physical form. They are profoundly obstructed and cut off from birth and have no way to penetrate through. As for the benevolence of tigers and wolves, the sacrifices made by badgers and otters, and the dutifulness of bees and ants, they are able to penetrate through (the obstruction and blockage) in these ways; like a slender shaft of light (penetrating the roof or walls of the thatched hut). As for monkeys and apes, their physical form is like that of human beings and so they are the most intelligent of all creatures. The only thing they lack is the ability to speak." (*ZZYL*, chapter 4, p. 58)

3. Someone said, "The natures of human beings and other things are the same."

Zhu Xi replied, "The natures of human beings and other things *fundamentally* are the same; they only differ because of their respective endowments of *qi*. It is like how there is no water that is not pure. If you pour water into a white bowl, it all will appear one color. If you pour it into a black bowl, it all will appear another color. If you pour it into a green bowl, it all will appear yet another color."

[He] went on to say, "It is most difficult to talk about the nature. If you want to say it is the same [in all things], this can be appropriate. If you want to say it is different [in different things], this too can be appropriate. It is like sunlight (penetrating through) small cracks (in the roof or walls of a thatched hut). Because of the different lengths and sizes of the cracks, the amount of sunlight is different; nevertheless, it all is the light of the sun." (*ZZYL*, chapter 4, p. 58)

4. Someone asked, "Human beings are able to extend [their feelings of concern] while other things are not able to extend."

Zhu Xi replied, "It would not be correct to say that other things lack this ability; it is only because of the obscuration of *qi* that they seem to lack it." (*ZZYL*, chapter 4, p. 58)

5. Zhu Xi said, "It is not human beings alone who are the most intelligent among all those between heaven and earth; one's heart-mind is the same as the heart-mind of birds, beasts, grass, and trees. It is only that human beings are born with what is most balanced between heaven and earth." (*ZZYL*, chapter 4, p. 59)

6. It was asked, "Withered and decayed things also have the nature. What are your thoughts about this?"

   Zhu Xi replied, "This is correct; right from the start, they possess this pattern-principle. And so, we say that there is nothing in heaven and earth that is beyond the nature."

   As he walked along the street, he said, "The bricks of these stairs have the pattern-principle of bricks." As he sat down, he said, "This bamboo chair has the pattern-principle of bamboo chairs."

   Zhu Xi continued, "One can say that withered and decayed things lack the impulse of life, but one cannot say they lack the pattern-principle of life. For example, rotten wood cannot be put to any use;[4] it can only be tossed in the stove to burn; it lacks the impulse of life. And yet, when one burns a particular kind of wood a particular kind of *qi* is released and, in each case, it is different. This is because the pattern-principle originally is like this." (*ZZYL*, chapter 4, p. 61)

7. It was asked, "Human beings and other things equally receive pattern-principle from Heaven, but do insentient things also have pattern-principle?"

   Zhu Xi replied, "They certainly have pattern-principle. For example, boats can only travel upon water; carts can only travel upon land." (*ZZYL*, chapter 4, p. 61)

8. Zhu Xi said, "The nature is simply pattern-principle. Nevertheless, if there were no heavenly *qi* and earthly material, this pattern-principle would have no place to settle. When only the clearest and brightest *qi* is received, there is no obstruction or impediment, and this pattern-principle flows forth freely; when there is some obstruction or impediment, it flows forth and Heavenly pattern-principle triumphs; when there is a great deal of obstruction or impediment, self-centered desires triumph. From this we can see that the original nature is in every respect

---

4. A reference to *Analects* 8.5, which says, "Rotten wood cannot be carved. . . ."

good. This is what Mengzi was referring to by saying 'human nature is good,'[5] what Zhou Dunyi was referring to by 'the perfectly pure absolute good,'[6] and what Cheng Yi was referring to by 'the root of the nature'[7] and 'the nature traced back to its root and source.'[8] It is only owing to the turbidity and murkiness of *qi*-material that [this nature] is cut off. And so, 'Within the material nature there is that which the cultivated person does not regard as his nature. . . . Through learning, he returns to it and the nature of Heaven and earth thereby is preserved.'[9] And so, when you talk about the nature, you must include a discussion of *qi*-material in order to present a complete account." (*ZZYL*, chapter 4, p. 66)

9. Zhu Xi said, "Pattern-principle is Heaven in and of itself;[10] the Mandate (*ming* 命) is the functioning of pattern-principle. The nature is what human beings receive; the emotions are the functioning of the nature." (*ZZYL*, chapter 5, p. 82)

10. It was asked, "The heart-mind is consciousness. The nature is pattern-principle. How is it that the heart-mind and pattern-principle are able to interpenetrate one another and form a unity?"

   Zhu Xi replied, "There is no need for them to interpenetrate one another; they interpenetrate from the very beginning."

   It was asked, "How is it that they interpenetrate from the very beginning?"

   Zhu Xi replied, "If pattern-principle lacked the heart-mind it would have nowhere to settle down." (*ZZYL*, chapter 5, p. 85)

11. Zhu Xi said, "The heart-mind must be understood as both vast and pervasive; it must also be understood as productive. For example, Master Cheng talked about 'Benevolence is the heart-mind of Heaven and earth

---

5. *Mencius* 6A1–6.

6. Zhou Dunyi 周敦頤, *Comprehending the Classic of Changes* (*Tongshu* 通書), chapter 1.

7. Cheng Yi 程頤 and Cheng Hao 程顥, *The Extant Works of the Cheng Brothers from Henan* (*Henan Chengshi yishu* 河南程氏遺書), chapters 18, 19, 22A, and 25.

8. *The Extant Works of the Cheng Brothers from Henan*, chapter 3, which has 極本窮源之性 (i.e., 極 in place of 反).

9. Zhang Zai 張載, *Correcting Youthful Ignorance* (*Zhengmeng* 正蒙), chapter 6.

10. The word translated "in and of itself" is *ti* 體, which traditionally has been translated as "substance." An alternative translation of this line is "Pattern-principles are the essence of Heaven."

producing [the myriad] things.'[11] Only Heaven and earth are vast, their production of things pervasive, and they continue to produce without end." (*ZZYL*, chapter 5, p. 85)

12. It was asked, "When the physical body moves, is it connected with the heart-mind or not?"

Zhu Xi replied, "How could it not be connected with the heart-mind; it is the heart-mind that causes it to move."

It was asked, "Before the feelings of happiness, anger, grief, and joy have been manifested the physical body can move and the ears and eyes can hear and see. In such cases, is the heart-mind already manifested or not yet manifested?"

Zhu Xi replied, "Cases in which happiness, anger, grief, and joy are yet to be manifested are quite common, but in seeing, hearing, and acting the heart-mind is directed toward these activities. If the physical body is moving but the heart-mind is not in any way aware, then the heart-mind is not present and the actions are devoid of understanding. How, though, can one say that the heart-mind is not yet manifested? To be not yet manifested is not to be wholly insentient. Even before it is manifested the heart-mind is ever awake; it is never asleep." (*ZZYL*, chapter 5, p. 86)

13. Zhu Xi said, "The heart-mind as it is in itself is the nature. The nature is like the meat stuffing inside a pastry bun that is the heart-mind. We can say that the heart-mind is replete with all pattern-principle and that the nature is the reason for this being so." (*ZZYL*, chapter 5, p. 89)

14. Zhu Xi said, "Cheng Yi's 'the nature is pattern-principle'[12] and Zhang Zai's 張載 (1020–1077) 'the heart-mind comprehends and unifies the nature and feelings'[13]—these two sentences are indestructible!" (*ZZYL*, chapter 5, p. 93)

15. It was asked, "What is the difference between the heart-mind, the nature, and feelings?"

---

11. There is no line exactly like this in the extant works of the Cheng brothers, though both say things close enough to this in meaning to serve as the basis of Zhu Xi's attribution.

12. *The Complete Works of the Two Chengs* (*Er Cheng quanshu* 二程全書), chapters 19 and 24; the line is also found in *A Record for Reflection*, chapter 1.

13. "Missed Issues Concerning the Nature and Pattern-Principle," in *The Complete Works of Master Zhang* (*Zhangzi quanshu* 張子全書), chapter 14; these lines are also found in *A Record for Reflection*, chapter 1.

Zhu Xi replied, "Cheng Yi said, 'the heart-mind can be compared to the seeds of a fruit; the life-generating pattern-principles within it are the nature; what comes forth with the warmth of spring are feelings.'[14] If you extend and follow out the implications of this teaching, it can explain all things." (*ZZYL*, chapter 5, p. 95)

16. It was asked, "Thoughts are the application of the heart-mind. Does this mean that the heart-mind is manifested?"

Zhu Xi replied, "To be applied is to be manifested."

It was asked, "Feelings are also manifestations [of the heart-mind]. What is the difference?"

Zhu Xi replied, "Feelings are manifestations of the nature. Feelings are what is manifested in regard to this or that; thoughts are what one decides one would like in regard to this or that. Caring for a living thing[15] is a case of feeling; what leads one to care for that living thing is thought. Feelings are like boats and carts; thoughts are like people making use of boats and carts." (*ZZYL*, chapter 5, p. 95)

17. Zhu Xi said, "An intention is to publicly declare what one would like. Thought is carried out privately and in secret. Intention is like launching an open attack; thought is like encroaching or infiltrating." (*ZZYL*, chapter 5, p. 96)

18. It was asked, "How do feelings differ from talent (*cai* 才)?"

Zhu Xi replied, "Feelings are simply the route along which [the nature] is manifested; talent is the capacity to proceed along the route. For example, consider the feelings of alarm and concern.[16] Some feel this in earnest while others do not; this difference is the result of differences in natural talent."

A further question was asked, "If this is how it is, then the functioning of talent and the heart-mind are similar in kind?"

---

14. *The Complete Works of the Two Chengs*, chapters 19 and 24; these lines are also found in *A Record for Reflection*, chapter 1.

15. *Mengzi* 7A46 says, "A noble person cares for living things but is not benevolent toward them and is benevolent toward the people but does not love them as family. The noble person loves his family as family, is benevolent toward the people, and takes care of living things." Zhu Xi comments, "*Living things* (*wu* 物) refers to birds, beasts, grasses, and trees. *Caring* (*ai* 愛) refers to taking them only in the proper season and managing one's use of them."

16. The natural reactive attitude upon seeing an innocent child in imminent danger (*Mengzi* 2A6).

Zhu Xi replied, "Talent is the strength of the heart-mind; it is the power of *qi* that enables one to act. The heart-mind is the master-governor that oversees and controls; this is what makes the heart-mind great. If we compare the heart-mind to water, then the nature is the pattern-principle of water. The nature is established when the water is calm; feelings come into play when the water moves. [Self-centered] desires arise when the flow of the water is excessive. Talent is the power of *qi* the water has that enables it to flow, and so, if the flow is swift or slow, this is because of differences in natural talent. Cheng Yi says, 'The nature is endowed by Heaven; talent is endowed by *qi*.'[17] This explains the matter. The only thing that is set and unchanging is the nature; feelings, the heart-mind, and talent all are intermixed with *qi*. The heart-mind originally is the same [in all human beings]; it is only at birth that it becomes differentiated. Feelings can be good or bad."

Zhu Xi added, "If one wants to understand this clearly, one only needs to consider Cheng Hao's saying, 'The thing as it is in itself is called the changes; its pattern-principle is called the Way; its functioning is called the spiritual.'[18] The changes is the heart-mind; the Way is the nature; the spiritual is the feelings. These are the heart-mind, the nature, and the feelings of Heaven and earth." (*ZZYL*, chapter 5, p. 97)

19. It was asked, "How does one distinguish the Way from pattern-principle?"

Zhu Xi replied, "The Way is a path or route; pattern-principle is its structure and articulation."

It was asked, "Is it like the patterns [of the grain] in wood?"

Zhu Xi replied, "Yes."

It was asked, "If this is so, then they [i.e., the Way and pattern-principle] are really the same?"

Zhu Xi replied, "The Way is comprehensive; pattern-principle is the innumerable patterning veins within the Way."

Zhu Xi added, "The Way is vast and great; pattern-principles are fine and detailed." (*ZZYL*, chapter 6, p. 99)

20. Zhu Xi said, "Sincerity (*cheng* 誠) is the actualization of pattern-principle; it is also the achievement of oneness. Since the Han dynasty,

---

17. *The Complete Works of the Two Chengs*, chapter 2; this line is also found in *A Record for Reflection*, chapter 1.

18. *The Complete Works of the Two Chengs*, chapter 1; this line is also found in *A Record for Reflection*, chapter 1.

people have explained sincerity exclusively in terms of the achievement of oneness; it was not until Cheng Yi that it was talked about in terms of the actualization of pattern-principle.[19] Later students have all abandoned talk of the achievement of oneness and pay no attention to this explanation. In some passages, the *Doctrine of the Mean* explains sincerity as the actualization of pattern-principle, while in other passages it describes it as the achievement of oneness.[20] It is not acceptable to take sincerity to be only the actualization [of pattern-principle] and to deny that the achievement of oneness is sincerity." (*ZZYL*, chapter 6, p. 102)

21. Zhu Xi said, "Sincerity fully describes the heart-mind as it is in itself; 'conscientiousness' (*zhong* 忠) describes reacting to affairs and responding to things; these are the basic terms concerning ethical pattern-principle. As for Zengzi's discussion of conscientiousness and 'sympathetic concern' (*shu* 恕), this refers to the affairs of sages. And so, conscientiousness and sincerity are discussed together and benevolence and sympathetic concern are discussed together." (*ZZYL*, chapter 6, p. 103–4)

22. Yu Zhengshu[21] said, "To be without self-centered desires is benevolence."

Zhu Xi replied, "It is acceptable to say that one is benevolent only after one is without self-centered desires, but it is not acceptable to say that being without self-centered desires is benevolence. When one is without self-centered desires, benevolence begins to appear just as when there are no obstructions blocking the way, water begins to flow."

Yu Fangshu[22] then said, "To be one body with heaven, earth, and the myriad things is benevolence."

Zhu Xi replied, "To be without self-centeredness is a prerequisite for being benevolent; to be one body with heaven, earth, and the myriad things is a consequence of being benevolent. Only after someone is

---

19. *The Complete Works of the Two Chengs*, chapter 40.

20. *The Doctrine of the Mean*, chapters 16 and 20, respectively.

21. Yu Daya 余大雅, whose pen name (*zi* 字) was Zhengshu 正叔, was one of Zhu Xi's disciples. A native of Jiangxi Province, he exchanged several letters with Zhu Xi, and their conversations as well as references to their discussions are found in impressive numbers throughout Zhu's written works.

22. Yu Dayou 余大猷, whose pen name (*zi* 字) was Fangshu 方叔, was Daya's younger brother and also one of Zhu's disciples. Conversations and references to discussions between him and Zhu Xi are found in many of Zhu's written works, including several letters: one between Dayou and Zhu and two between Zhu and others all discussing Dayou's views on human nature and *qi*.

without self-centeredness does that person become benevolent; only after someone is benevolent does that person become one body with heaven, earth, and the myriad things. The aim is to recognize, between these two (i.e., being without self-centered desires and forming one body with heaven, earth, and the myriad things), what benevolence really comes down to. If you want to understand what benevolence means you must look at it together with the three words: 'rightness,' 'ritual,' and 'wisdom.' If you want to really see what benevolence is like, you must begin with the purposeful practice (*gongfu* 功夫)[23] of 'overcoming the self and complying with ritual.'[24] People today talk about benevolence in the same way they all say candy is sweet; if one has never eaten a piece of candy, one does not know what the flavor of its sweetness tastes like. Sages never talk in excess; students should seek to embody [benevolence] and experience it for themselves." (*ZZYL*, chapter 6, p. 117)

23. Zhu Xi said, "Lesser Learning consists in studying affairs; Greater Learning consists in studying the principles underlying the affairs that one studies in Lesser Learning." (*ZZYL*, chapter 7, p. 124)

24. Zhu Xi said, "Lesser Learning concerns affairs, such as serving one's lord, serving one's father, serving one's elder brother, associating with friends, etc. At this point, students were only taught to carry out such affairs according to proper norms and models. Greater Learning concerns explaining the pattern-principle underlying such affairs." (*ZZYL*, chapter 7, p. 125)

25. Zhu Xi said, "In ancient times, Lesser Learning successfully nurtured people without their full awareness so that when they matured they already would possess the proper form of sages and worthies and then would simply embellish upon this. Today, since people have completely lost the purposeful practice of Lesser Learning, they just teach people to take reverential attention as their governing ideal and to control their bodies and heart-minds and under such conditions apply themselves to purposeful practice."

Zhu Xi added, "For the ancients, Lesser Learning consisted of teaching people how to carry out affairs; in this way, they nurtured their

---

23. The standard translation of 功夫 is "purposeful practice," though it often means something closer to what Pierre Hadot called "spiritual exercises." See Hadot 1995.

24. *Analects* 12.1.

heart-minds and without their full understanding or awareness, became good. As they gradually matured, they gradually gained in experience and mastered other affairs and things until there was nothing they could not do. People today lack a proper root or foundation; they simply work to understand numerous idle and distracting curiosities and apply themselves in further reflection upon and analysis of such things; in this way, inadvertently, they harm their heart-minds." (*ZZYL*, chapter 7, p. 125)

26. Zhu Xi said, "The other evening, Qiyuan 器遠[25] said, 'Reverential attention is not the equal of Lesser Learning.' My view, though, is that Lesser Learning can never equal reverential attention; reverential attention encompasses Lesser Learning. Reverential attention penetrates throughout the higher and lower[26] stages of purposeful practice. Though one has reached the level of a sage, reverential attention still is essential for success. As for Yao and Shun, from beginning to end, they maintained reverential attention. For example, Yao's virtue was praised as 'reverentially attentive, enlightened, cultured, and reflective'[27]—the first and foremost among these four [excellent traits] is reverential attention. When it was said of Shun that 'he simply attained a dignified expression and faced south'[28] or 'he simply maintained an earnest and dignified expression and the entire world became peaceful'[29]—such are examples of reverential attention." (*ZZYL*, chapter 7, p. 126)

27. Zhu Xi said, "The everyday purposeful practice of the School of the Sages (i.e., Confucianism) seems superficial and commonplace, but if one extends its underlying pattern-principle there is nothing it does not comprehend and integrate.[30] If one fills it

---

25. Cao Shuyuan 曹叔遠, who passed the Presented Scholar examination in 1190, was a disciple of Chen Fuliang 陳傅良 (1137–1203), a neo-Confucian philosopher sometimes at odds with Zhu Xi.

26. A reference to *Analects* 14.35, which says, "... I study the lower to comprehend the higher ..."

27. See the "Canon of Yao" chapter of the *Book of Documents*.

28. See *Analects* 15.5.

29. See Zhu Xi's *The* Doctrine of the Mean *in Chapters and Lines* (*Zhongyong zhangju* 中庸章句), chapter 33.

30. *Analects* 4.15 talks about how Kongzi's way has one thread running through and integrating (*guan* 貫) its many aspects.

out[31] in all its breadth it will match that of heaven and earth. And so, being a sage or worthy and 'setting in their proper places heaven and earth and nurturing the myriad things'[32] is simply following this one pattern-principle." (*ZZYL*, chapter 8, p. 130)

28. Zhu Xi said, "Recognizing the primacy of Heavenly pattern-principle establishes the basis. It is like someone who wishes to build a house. One must first ram the earth to make a strong and firm foundation; then one can build the house upon it. If one does not have a foundation of one's own it is pointless to go and buy the wood needed to build a house. Soon one will simply be building the house on someone else's land and one will have no place to call one's own." (*ZZYL*, chapter 8, p. 130)

29. Zhu Xi said, "If you do not see where to begin it doesn't matter whether you proceed quickly or slowly—you will not succeed. If you have some recognition of the opening parts of the path, the essential thing is to not give up. If you give up, you will not succeed. If you delay and have to restart your journey along the path how much effort have you wasted! It is like the case of a chicken caring for her eggs. Her care apparently provides them warmth, but it is only because she cares for them consistently that they hatch. If she were to put them in boiling water, they would die; if she were to stop caring for them, they would grow cold. However, she knows where to begin and naturally does not stop. She naturally wants to offer care and she naturally has a taste for doing so. It is like eating a piece of fruit. Prior to recognizing the taste, you don't care whether you eat it or not, but once you have tasted it, even if you want to stop, you naturally cannot." (*ZZYL*, chapter 8, p. 132)

30. Zhu Xi said, "Students must establish a firm intention. The reason people today are so anxious and unsettled is because they do not take learning to be something they need to work at. When they encounter some affair or situation, they handle it in a confused and unsystematic manner. This is only because they have not established a firm intention." (*ZZYL*, chapter 8, p. 134)

---

31. *Mengzi* 2A6 etc. talks about the need to extend and fill out (*chong* 充) one's incipient moral feelings to embrace all the world.

32. This line is quoted from the *Doctrine of the Mean*, chapter 1.

31. Zhu Xi said, "Zonggao[33] once remarked, 'It is like having a cartload of weapons and trying each of them out one by one—first you try this one and then another—this is not the way to kill someone. If I have just a short dagger, I can kill someone.'"[34] (*ZZYL*, chapter 8, p. 137)

32. Zhu Xi said, "The problem is that students don't work for their own sake.[35] And so, they spend little time each day with their heart-minds contemplating moral pattern-principle and a great deal of time contemplating idle matters. As a result, they are not well-versed in moral pattern-principle but intimately familiar with idle matters." (*ZZYL*, chapter 8, p. 139)

33. Zhu Xi said, "The gate through which one enters upon the Way is to immerse oneself in the patterns and processes of the Way so one gradually becomes intimate with them and over time becomes one with them. People today believe one enters the pattern-principle of the Way over here while one's own person stands on the outside, so there is never any mutual interaction with them." (*ZZYL*, chapter 8, p. 140)

34. Zhu Xi said, "It is like climbing a mountain. Most people want to get to the highest places but do not understand that if they do not grasp the pattern-principle of the lowest places they will never understand the pattern-principle of the highest places." (*ZZYL*, chapter 8, p. 142)

35. Zhu Xi said, "If you just hold a whole fruit in your hand you will not know whether the flesh inside is sour, salty, bitter, or acidic. You must chew into it in order to know its taste." (*ZZYL*, chapter 8, p. 145)

36. Zhu Xi said, "After you have become intimately familiar with the pattern-principle of the Way, everything else will seem unreal; one will come to regard the myriad things of the world—confused, lost, lustful, and addicted—as no more than a play one truly cannot bear to watch."

---

33. The famous Song dynasty Chan (Zen) master Dahui Zonggao 大慧宗杲 (1089–1163), whose works Zhu Xi knew well.

34. A version of this story, employing the metaphor of weapons, appears in the *Jade Path in Crane Copse* (*Haolin yulu* 鶴林玉露) by Luo Dajing 羅大經 (1196–1242) of the Song dynasty. In that version, Zigong's broad learning (familiarity with various kinds of weapons) is compared unfavorably to Zengzi's grasp of the essential (use of a short dagger).

35. The reference is to *Analects* 14.24, "The Master said, 'In ancient times, scholars learned for their own sake; these days they learn for the sake of others'" (Slingerland 2003, 164). The idea is that learning should be aimed at improving—not advancing—the self.

In response to a letter Zhu Xi also said, "The myriad things of the world change and are annihilated in the blink of eye; none is worthy of being retained in one's heart. The ultimate Way consists only in fully understanding pattern-principle and cultivating the self." (*ZZYL*, chapter 8, p. 147)

37. Zhu Xi said, "One cannot be one-sided in one's effort in regard to extending knowledge and exerting strenuous effort.[36] If you are one-sided in regard to either, then that task will suffer. It is as Cheng Yi said, 'Use reverential attention to cultivate one's character; advancement in learning lies in extending knowledge.'[37] He provides these two distinct explanations but the distinction only concerns the proper order and importance. In terms of order, the extension of knowledge comes first; in terms of importance, exerting strenuous effort is most important." (*ZZYL*, chapter 9, p. 148)

38. Zhu Xi said, "Extending knowledge, reverential attention, and overcoming the self[38]—if we compare these three tasks to a home, then reverential attention is the person who guards the gates and doors; overcoming the self is the act of warding off thieves; extending knowledge is thoroughly investigating affairs in and outside one's home. Cheng Yi said, 'Use reverential attention to cultivate one's character; advancement in learning lies in extending knowledge.'[39] He did not talk about overcoming the self because reverential attention conquers the entire range of depravities and naturally results in overcoming (the self). If one has sincerity, then there is no reason to talk about defending against depravity. It is like someone who is good at guarding the gates and doors—this is the same as warding off thieves, and so there is no reason

---

36. "Extending knowledge" is the first of the "eight steps" that are described in the opening section of the *Great Learning*: "Extending knowledge lies in the investigation of things." "Exerting strenuous effort" is found in the *Doctrine of the Mean*, chapter 20: "To be fond of learning is to be near to wisdom. To exert strenuous effort is to be near to benevolence. To understand shame is to be near to [moral] courage."

37. *The Extant Works of the Cheng Brothers from Henan*, chapter 19.

38. Overcoming the self is offered as an important goal in *Analects* 12.1: "To overcome the self and return to ritual propriety is benevolence." The idea is not for a complete elimination of any sense of oneself but to reach a state of moral development where one no longer suffers from the vice of self-centeredness. Zhu Xi's *Collected Commentaries on the* Analects (*Lunyu jizhu* 論語集注) glosses this line by saying, "To overcome is to conquer; the self refers to one's self-centered desires."

39. *The Extant Works of the Cheng Brothers from Henan*, chapter 19.

to separately talk about warding off thieves. If one compares the cultivation of one's character and overcoming the self, then, of course, each of these can be understood as constituting a separate task. Cultivating one's character is like taking good care of one's health; overcoming the self is like taking medicine to eliminate an illness. In general, if one does not take good care of one's health then one must take medicine. If one takes good care of one's health, one naturally is free from illness; what then would be the point of taking medicine? If one is perfectly reverentially attentive, one naturally is free of depravity or perversion; what then would be the point of overcoming the self? The only reason there is depravity or perversion is because one does not have a perfectly reverentially attentive heart-mind; the only appropriate [response] in such cases is to urge [greater] reverential attention. And so, if one is reverentially attentive, there is no self to be overcome; this is the natural effect of being reverentially attentive. If one is just beginning to learn, the imperative is to achieve every aspect of purposeful practice and to exert oneself to the utmost in every regard." (*ZZYL*, chapter 9, pp. 151–152)

39. Zhu Xi said, "Reading books already is second best. This is because, when human beings are born, they are completely endowed with all the Heavenly pattern-principle. The reason we need to read books is because we are lacking in broad experience. Sages are people with broad experience, and so they wrote these down in books and gave them to people to read. When we read books, it is only because we need to become acquainted with many Heavenly pattern-principles; once we truly come to understand these, we find they all are things with which we were originally endowed and not things that later were added on to us from outside." (*ZZYL*, chapter 10, p. 161)

40. Zhu Xi said, "In reading books limit the amount but apply great effort. If you are able to read two hundred characters [at a sitting] only read one hundred, but apply yourself fiercely to those one hundred characters as a form of purposeful practice. Gain a fine and detailed understanding, be able to recite and master [what you have read]. If you proceed in this manner, even those who are not good at memorization will remember; even those not good at understanding will understand. If you just read indiscriminately and broadly, it will not benefit you at all. When reading a book, do not compare yourself to those who have never read it but rather to those who already have read it." (*ZZYL*, chapter 10, p. 165)

41. Zhu Xi said, "When people today read books, even before they have read to here [in the work], their heart-minds already are there, at a later point in the work. As soon as they reach here, they want to set it aside. If one proceeds in this manner, one is not seeking to attain a personal understanding. One must spread one's attention and concern backward and forward [over the work] as if one desires to never let it go; then one will attain true understanding."

He also said, "A reader can be compared to someone contemplating this house. If they are standing outside and can see there is this house, then we say they can see it, but they don't have any direct knowledge about it. They must enter the house and systematically look throughout it to see how large it is and how many windows it has. Once they have looked it over, repeatedly looked throughout it, and memorized it completely, then they know it." (*ZZYL*, chapter 10, p. 173)

42. Zhu Xi said, "People engaged in learning certainly want to get it with their own heart-minds and embody it within their own persons, but if they do not read books then they will not understand what it is that their heart-minds are to get." (*ZZYL*, chapter 11, p. 176)

43. Zhu Xi said, "When students read books, they must compose themselves and sit up straight, move their gaze slowly [across the page], recite softly, immerse themselves in an open and amorphous state of mind, and reflect and examine themselves carefully."

He also said, "When you read a single line in a book, you must experientially explore that one line and ask yourself *how will I apply this in the future?*"

He also said, "One should read about what is proper, but one should also read about what is not proper; one should read about what is pure and refined, but one should also read about what is impure and coarse." (*ZZYL*, chapter 11, p. 179)

44. Zhu Xi said, "There has never been anyone who was able to advance in learning with a heart-mind that was unsettled. The heart-mind of human beings is master of the myriad affairs; to go east or go west, how is this achieved?" (*ZZYL*, chapter 12, p. 199)

45. Zhu Xi said, "If the heart-mind of human beings always is clearly and lucidly present, there is no need to restrain or control the self; it naturally will fall into accord with proper standards and norms. It is only when the heart-mind of human beings is scattered and slow that one needs to

establish numerous proper standards and norms in order to guide and support it. Then, only if one always raises the alarm and instructs the self to stay within proper standards and norms will *this mind*[40] not become lax and indulgent and instead will be clearly and lucidly present. Once one's heart-mind is always awake and alert, one measures and compares it with proper standards and norms; this is the way for inside and outside to mutually nourish one another." (*ZZYL*, chapter 12, p. 200)

46. Zhu Xi said, "If people do not understand their own maladies it is because they never thoroughly investigated and awakened themselves." (*ZZYL*, chapter 12, p. 201)

47. Zhu Xi said, "Reverential attention is not just how one should be while seated, when one rises up and sets to walking one should always want to maintain this state of mind." (*ZZYL*, chapter 12, p. 210)

48. Zhu Xi said, "There is dead reverential attention and living reverential attention. If one just has the reverential attention of maintaining singleness of mind but one is not able to regulate the affairs that one encounters according to [the standard of] rightness and distinguish rightness from what is wrong—this is not living [reverential attention]. Once one has gained complete mastery, reverential attention will yield rightness and rightness will yield reverential attention. When still, one will investigate whether one is reverentially attentive or not; when active, one will investigate whether one is according with rightness or not. For example, 'When abroad act as if you are receiving an honoured guest; employ the people as if you are taking part in a great sacrifice'[41]—when is it not the time to be reverentially attentive? 'Sit as if you are the impersonator of the deceased (i.e., with great solemnity); stand as if you are offering a sacrifice'[42]—when is it not the time to be reverentially attentive? It is imperative that reverential attention and rightness uphold and support one another, that they be an infinite and seamless ring; then inner and outer both will be thoroughly penetrated." (*ZZYL*, chapter 12, p. 216)

---

40. "This mind" (*cixin* 此心) is a term of art among neo-Confucians, designating the moral mind.

41. *Analects* 12.2.

42. These guidelines are offered in an opening section of the "Summary of the Rites" (*Quli* 曲禮) chapter of the *Book of Rites* (*Liji* 禮記).

49. Zhu Xi said, "Reverential attention and rightness are just one thing. Reverential attention is like standing steady on your two legs; walking is rightness. Reverential attention is like having two eyes; opening one's eyes and seeing things is rightness." (*ZZYL*, chapter 12, p. 216)

50. Zhu Xi said, "Here with me, less time is devoted to lectures and discussions and more time to implementation and practice. In your various affairs, apply your own understanding; thoroughly examine them on your own; cultivate your character on your own; read books on your own; search out and investigate the pattern-principle of the Way on your own. I am merely someone who can lead you along the path and certify your progress; someone who can join together with you to discuss and deliberate about doubtful and difficult points." (*ZZYL*, chapter 13, p. 223)

51. Zhu Xi said, "Inquiry and learning is like climbing up a tower; you ascend one level after another. Even if you don't ask others about the next higher level, you can see it on your own, but if you don't actually go there yourself and instead remain suspended in delusional phantasies about it you will not have understood even the lowest level." (*ZZYL*, chapter 13, p. 223)

52. Zhu Xi said, "The reason people are distressed about poverty and lowliness and eager for wealth and high station is only because they have yet to see the pattern-principle of the Way. If they see the pattern-principle of the Way, poverty and lowliness do not detract from them; wealth and high station do not add to them; their only desire is to understand the pattern-principle of the Way." (*ZZYL*, chapter 13, p. 241)

53 . . . Zhu Xi said, "Dressing, eating, working, and acting are *merely* things; the pattern-principles of things are the Way. It would not be correct to call things the Way. It is like this chair having four legs and so being something one can sit upon; this is the pattern-principle of a chair. If you remove one of the legs, one can no longer sit in it; it has lost the pattern-principle of a chair. The lines 'What is above form is called the Way. What is within form are called implements'[43] mean that inside the implements that are within form there is the Way, which is above form.

---

43. See the first part of the "Great Treatise" (*Xici* 繫辭) commentary of the *Classic of Changes*, chapter 12.

It is not correct to take the implements that are within form to be the Way, which is above form. It is like this fan; it is a thing which has a fan's pattern-principle of the Way. That a fan is made in this particular way and should be used in this particular way is the pattern-principle, which is above form. As for heaven, earth, and what is between: above there is heaven, below there is earth and in between are the sun, moon, stars, planets, mountains, streams, grasses, woods, humans, things, birds and beasts—all of these are implements that are within form. Nevertheless, each of the implements that are within form has inside of it its own pattern-principle of the Way. This is the Way, which is above form. (*ZZYL*, chapter 62, p. 1496)

Bibliography

Hadot, Pierre. 1995. *Philosophy as a Way of Life: Spiritual Exercises from Socrates to Foucault.* Oxford and New York: Blackwell.

Slingerland, Edward G. III, trans. 2003. *Confucius Analects with Selections from Traditional Commentaries.* Indianapolis, IN: Hackett Publishing Company.

Zhang Zai 張載. 1987. *Correcting Youthful Ignorance (Zhengmeng* 正蒙). In *The Complete Works of Master Zhang (Zhangzi quanshu* 張子全書). *Siku quanshu* 四庫全書, Vol. 697. Reprint. Shanghai: Shanghai guji chubanshe.

Zhou Dunyi 周敦頤. 1927–1936. *Comprehending the Classic of Changes (Tongshu* 通書), *Sibu beiyao*, Volume 1439. Reprint. Shanghai: Zhonghua shuju.

Zhu Xi, ed. 1927–1936. *The Complete Works of the Two Chengs (Er Cheng quanshu* 二程全書). *Sibu beiyao*, Volumes 1443–1456. Reprint. Shanghai: Zhonghua shuju.

_____, ed. 1978. *The Extant Works of the Cheng Brothers from Henan (Henan Chengshi yishu* 河南程氏遺書). Reprint. Taibei Shi: Taiwan shangwu yinshuguan.

_____. 1992. *Collected Commentaries on the* Analects *(Lunyu jizhu* 論語集注). Reprint. Chaoxing shuzi tushuguan.

_____. 2008. *The* Doctrine of the Mean *in Chapters and Lines (Zhongyong zhangju* 中庸章句). Electronic Resource. Chaoxing shuzi tushuguan.

Further Readings

Bol, Peter K. 1992. *Neo-Confucianism in History.* Cambridge, MA: Harvard University Press.

Chan, Wing-tsit. 1989. *Chu Hsi: New Studies.* Honolulu: University of Hawaii Press.

de Bary, William Theodore. 1981. *Neo-Confucian Orthodoxy and the Learning of the Mind-and-Heart.* New York: Columbia University Press.

Graham, Angus C. 1989. *Two Chinese Philosophers: The Metaphysics of the Brothers Cheng*. Reprint. La Salle, IL: Open Court Press.

Kim, Yung Sik. 2000. *The Natural Philosophy of Chu Hsi, 1130–1200*. Philadelphia, PA: American Philosophical Society.

Tillman, Hoyt Cleveland. 1992. *Confucian Discourse and Chu Hsi's Ascendancy*. Honolulu: University of Hawaii Press.

2

Moral Psychology and Cultivating the Self

Curie Virág

Introduction

The revival of the early Confucian ethical tradition by Zhu Xi and his neo-Confucian predecessors was a movement to reinstate moral self-realization as the proper goal of human life.[1] Zhu sought to restore what he regarded as the true Way of antiquity, in which the most important of human aspirations was to fulfill one's potential to grasp and embody the normative patterns of the cosmos, and to actualize them in one's conduct. Like the ancients before him, Zhu was conscious of living in an era of moral decline—an era whose downward trajectory was to be traced back to the very founding of empire, when scholars stopped concerning themselves with right understanding and right living, and instead devoted themselves to scholastic exegesis and to the mastery of textual content. Zhu's ethical project was to promote what he regarded as the true and proper way to live, which was to fulfill the potentiality that human beings shared with the creative forces of Heaven and earth. Such personal fulfillment necessarily involved engaging in activity that contributed to the betterment of society, and to the flourishing of all under Heaven.

1. This chapter was completed with generous support from the European Research Council under the European Union's Horizon 2020 research and innovation program (grant agreement no. 726371). For a fuller discussion of self-cultivation in the ethics of Zhu Xi and in neo-Confucianism more generally, see "Self-cultivation as *Praxis* in Song Neo-Confucianism," in Virág 2014.

Although Zhu Xi's ethical vision and program were, at some basic level, a continuation of the early Confucian concern with moral self-perfection, there was much that was new. For one thing, Zhu provided an account of cosmic and human phenomena that was far more elaborate than anything articulated by the early Confucians. It explained the diverse profusion of things in the world in terms of the dynamic engagement of pattern-principle (*li* 理) and *qi* 氣, and offered a coherent and systematic picture of the order and workings of the cosmos. It also contained a more nuanced account of the psychological workings of the human being that explained how the nature (*xing* 性), the heart-mind (*xin* 心), and the feelings (*qing* 情) were integrated with one another. Zhu also gave a more conceptually developed, naturalistic explanation of human moral capacity and self-cultivation. With these theoretical endeavors, Zhu achieved more than a "synthesis" of the various cosmological and ethical ideas forwarded by his Northern Song neo-Confucian predecessors: he was also enacting the very human potential to embody and experience the patterned workings of the cosmos itself. It was by conceptualizing being one with the all-pervading pattern-principle of things in the world that one achieved integrity and unity in one's own person, thereby fully realizing one's humanity.

Zhu's theoretical and practical projects were thus interdependent, and assumed significance and meaning in relation to each other. On the theoretical side, intellection was at the forefront of self-cultivation practice—a fact that was evident in how Zhu Xi explained the enterprise of learning and reading books. For Zhu, arriving at a coherent and meaningful understanding of the text was crucial to learning and to personal realization: it was through the process of apprehending the pattern-principle of the text that one could realize the normative condition of one's self. Not insignificantly, the heart-mind, as Zhu Xi repeatedly pointed out, was a faculty whose characteristic activity was to unite and organize the entire person. At the same time, the achievement of an integrated life through self-cultivation proceeded not only from the conceptual apprehension of intelligible wholes but also through the experiential dimensions of self-cultivation practice, and through an emphasis on sensory and affective engagement.[2]

In view of the complex engagement of the conceptual and practical dimensions of Zhu Xi's approach to self-cultivation, the passages presented in this chapter cover wide-ranging topics and genres, including essays,

---

2. On the conception and significance of emotions in Zhu Xi's ethical theory, see Virág 2007.

commentaries on the classics, and records of conversations with students. They include discussions of the basic categories of traditional moral psychology (such as the nature, the heart-mind, the feelings and desires), in which Zhu responded to his students' requests to clarify, develop, and justify his ideas. They also cover Zhu's approach to learning (*xue* 學). Conceived as a matter of exhaustively investigating pattern-principle (*qiong li* 窮理), learning was not a matter of apprehending what was external to one's person, but about achieving a resonance between oneself and the object of one's investigations. This entailed such practices as maintaining tranquility (*jing* 靜), being in a state of reverential attention (*jing* 敬), and sitting in meditation (*jing zuo* 靜坐). It also involved training oneself to keep one's heart-mind open (*xuxin* 虛心) and to preserve the heart-mind (*cunxin* 存心)—exercises that enabled one to achieve a proper state of heightened engagement with oneself, with one's surroundings, and with the objects of one's attention. Such efforts, Zhu emphasized, were not about physically escaping from the world and finding solace in the absence of affairs, but were meant to enable the individual to achieve mastery in the face of things and events, and to respond calmly and appropriately to them.

Zhu's approach to self-cultivation as an endeavor to achieve a coherent cognitive grasp of the true nature of things, as well as a deep, affective engagement with the objects of one's concern, is perhaps best exemplified in his method of reading (*dushufa* 讀書法).[3] Zhu's account of proper reading places primary emphasis on having the right attitude and commitment to the enterprise. It also stresses the importance of arousing and animating the senses and of bringing the body in alignment with the activity of reading. In order for the text to become fully "one's own," and not merely something external to oneself, one must engage with it physically, as it were—be it through recitation, which allowed one's body to perform the words, or through imaginatively "entering" the text. In such ways, one dissolved the boundary between oneself and the text, and awakened the normative pattern-principles that one shared with the rest of the cosmos.

Translation

1. It was asked, "Is it the case that first there was pattern-principle, and then afterwards there was *qi*?"

---

3. Editor's note: See chapter 4, "Poetry, Literature, Textual Study, and Hermeneutics," in this volume for more on Zhu Xi's views on reading and literature.

Zhu Xi replied, "Pattern-principle and *qi* cannot, fundamentally, be spoken of in terms of before and after. But when we proceed to make inferences [about things],[4] then it would seem that first there is pattern-principle and then afterwards there is *qi*. . . ."

He was asked about the Way itself and its operation (*yong* 用).[5]

Zhu Xi replied, "If we imagine the ears as the thing itself, then hearing is its operation; if we consider the eyes as the thing itself, then seeing is its operation." (*ZZYL*, chapter 1, p. 3)

2. It was asked, "The natures of humans and things have a single source, so why are there differences among them?"

Zhu Xi replied, "With respect to the nature of humans, we speak of brightness and dimness; with respect to the nature of things, there is just unevenness and blockage. What is dim can be made bright but what is already uneven and blocked cannot be made clear and penetrating. In the words of Hengqu 橫渠 (Zhang Zai 張載, 1020–1077),[6] 'Among things there is none that does not possess this nature, but it is on account of their penetrability and dimness, openness and blockage, that we can distinguish between humans and things.' And in the concluding lines [of this quotation], he says 'If the blockage is solid, it cannot be cleared; if it is thick, it can be cleared but clearing it is difficult; and if it is thin, it is easy to clear.'"[7]

It was also asked, "If one habitually does what is not good, and one becomes deeply steeped in [such habits], then in the end he will not be able to recover [his original condition]."

Zhu Xi replied, "If the force of this tendency is very severe, then one cannot reverse it; but it also depends on how shallow or deep one's understanding is, and how much effort one makes." (*ZZYL*, chapter 4, p. 57)

3. That by which human beings come into being is none other than the union of pattern-principle and *qi*. The pattern-principle of Heaven is

---

4. On the significance of inference in Zhu Xi's thought, see Meng 2016, 278–279.

5. I occasionally translate *yong* 用 as "operation" rather than as "function," the standard rendering followed in this volume, when Zhu seems to be referring to something like the broader practical unfolding of something, rather than its specific and predetermined function.

6. Zhang Zai 張載 was an eleventh-century neo-Confucian thinker whose ideas were of central importance for Zhu Xi. Among other things, Zhang Zai provided the conceptual foundation for understanding all phenomena, both cosmic and human, in terms of the shared, underlying reality of *qi*. Zhang thus argued that, beneath the diversity of all things in the world was a single, all-encompassing unity.

7. Zhu Xi 1936, chapter 1, p. 28.

indeed vast and inexhaustible, but if it weren't for *qi*, then even if there were pattern-principle, there would be nothing to collect around it. Thus, it is necessary that the two kinds of *qi* (*yin* and *yang*) mix and interact with one another so that they congeal and collect together; afterwards pattern-principle has something to attach itself to. That all human beings are able to speak, act, think, and engage in projects is all *qi*, but pattern-principle is present within. . . . [T]he substance of those of the highest intelligence and those who are born understanding is *qi* that is clear and unadulterated, without a trace of dimness or turbidity.[8] This is why being born understanding and conducting oneself with ease are not abilities that one acquires through learning. This was the case with Yao and Shun. Next is a level second to being born understanding, in which one can only achieve understanding through learning, and can only arrive at it by putting it into practice. Still the next level is when the material endowment is imbalanced, and is also obscured. In this case one must exert considerable effort: "What others do once, do a hundred times; what others do ten times, do a thousand times."[9] Only then can one reach the level that is second to being born understanding. If one proceeds without stopping, then one's achievements will be the same (as those who are born understanding). . . . (*ZZYL*, chapter 4, pp. 65–66)

4. The nature itself cannot be described. The reason why we can speak of the nature as being good is that, by looking at the goodness of alarm and concern, deference and yielding, and the other [virtues] among the four beginnings, you can see that the nature is good. This is like when you see the clarity of flowing water: you know that the source of the water must be clear. The four beginnings are the feelings, and the nature is pattern-principle. When they are manifest, they are feelings, but at their root they are the nature. This is like when you look at a shadow and see the form. (*ZZYL*, chapter 5, p. 89)

---

8. *Analects* 16.9: "Confucius said, 'Those who are born understanding it are the best; those who come to understand it through learning are second. Those who find it difficult to understand and yet persist in their learning comes next. People who find it difficult to understand but do not even try to learn are the worst of all.'" (Translation adapted from Slingerland 2003, 196.)

9. An abbreviated reference to a passage in chapter 22 of the *Doctrine of the Mean*, with some of the characters omitted.

5. The object of awareness is the heart-mind's pattern-principle. The capacity for awareness is the wondrous efficacy (*ling* 靈) of *qi*. (*ZZYL*, chapter 5, p. 85)

6. The heart-mind is master (*zhu* 主) of the nature and operates through the feelings. Therefore, it is said, "Before happiness and anger, sorrow and delight are manifest, it is called 'balanced' (*zhong* 中) and when they are all manifest and hit their proper measure, it is called 'harmonious' (*he* 和)."[10] The heart-mind is the realm in which this endeavor takes place. (*ZZYL*, chapter 5, p. 94)

7. Explicating the word "heart-mind," he said, "One word will cover it—'life-production.' [The *Great Treatise* commentary of the *Classic of Changes* says,] 'The great potency (*de* 德) of Heaven and earth is to produce.'[11] Human beings are born having received the *qi* of Heaven and earth. Therefore, the heart-mind must be humane, and if it is humane, then it produces." (*ZZYL*, chapter 5, p. 85)

8. The heart-mind is *qi* that is refined and luminous. (*ZZYL*, chapter 5, p. 85)

9. The heart-mind refers to a master.[12] In movement and in stillness there is always a master; it is not the case that it does not operate in a state of stillness, and that only in a state of movement is there is a master. When I speak of a master, I mean that there is a seamless order that is naturally present within. The heart-mind unites and joins together the nature and feelings. But this does not mean that it is a raw, undifferentiated mass together with the nature and the feelings, with there being no distinctions. (*ZZYL*, chapter 5, p. 94)

10 . . . As I have discussed before, the heart-mind's capacious luminousness and consciousness are one and the same. But if we may distinguish

---

10. *Doctrine of the Mean* 1.4; see chapter 9 of this volume.

11. *Classic of Changes,* "Great Treatise" (*Xici* 繫辭) commentary, Part 1, chapter 2.

12. I translate *zhuzai* 主宰 here and throughout this chapter simply as "master" rather than "master-governor," the standard rendering followed in this volume. In this and many other passages, Zhu Xi often seems to be specifically interested in the way that the heart-mind serves as an organizing, unifying force, rather than its ability to rule over or control the self. Elsewhere, Zhu suggests something stronger by referring to the controlling activity of heart-mind, and I consider "master" to be sufficient for covering both of these senses.

between the human heart-mind and the heart-mind of the Way,[13] the former arises from the self-centeredness of the *qi* of the physical body, while the latter originates from the correctness of the nature and mandate, and this is why, in terms of their awareness, they are not the same. For this reason, while the former is precarious and unstable, the latter is mysterious and difficult to perceive. Nevertheless, among human beings, none fail to possess a physical form, and therefore, even those of the highest wisdom cannot but possess a human heart-mind; moreover, none fail to possess a nature, and so, even those of the lowest intelligence cannot but possess the heart-mind of the Way. The two are mingled in the square inch [of the heart-mind], and if one does not know which is the one that rules it, then that which is precarious will be even more precarious, and that which is mysterious will be even more mysterious. Then, the public-orientedness of Heavenly pattern-principle will ultimately have no way to overcome the self-centeredness of human desire. If you are focused and refined, then you will carefully examine the two and not mix them up. If you are single-minded, then you will protect the correctness of your original heart-mind and not depart from it. If you pursue your affairs from this perspective, and do not desist for even a moment, then inevitably the heart-mind of the Way will become the master of your person, and your human heart-mind will in every instance obey the mandate. Then that which is precarious will be stable, and that which is mysterious will be manifest. And in activity and tranquility (*dong jing* 動靜), and in one's speech and conduct, one will naturally avoid erring on the side of either excess or deficiency. (Preface to the commentary on the *Doctrine of the Mean*. *ZZWJ*,[14] chapter 76, p. 3828)

11. Capacious luminousness is originally how the heart-mind is in itself; it is not that I am able to make it capacious. As for the seeing and hearing of the eyes and ears, that by which they see and hear is the heart-mind. How can there be forms and images [preexisting] within it? Nevertheless, when the eyes and ears see and hear them, then there are also forms and

---

13. See the "Counsels of the Great Yu" chapter of the *Book of Documents*: "The human heart-mind is precarious, the heart-mind of the Way is subtle; be refined, be single-minded; hold fast to the mean (*zhong* 中)."

14. *ZZWJ* refers to *The Collected Writings of Master Zhu* (*Zhuzi Wenji* 朱子文集). See Zhu Xi 2000 in the bibliography.

images in it. As for the capacious luminousness of the heart-mind, how can there be things preexisting within it? (*ZZYL*, chapter 5, p. 87)

12. He was asked about the statement [in the *Doctrine of the Mean*], "The state before the feelings of happiness, anger, sorrow and delight have become manifest is called 'balance' (*zhong* 中)."

    Zhu Xi replied, "Happiness, anger, sorrow and delight can be compared to east, west, south, and north: when they do not incline in a particular direction, they are in a state of balance."

    He was also asked about the meaning of "harmony."

    Zhu Xi replied, "This is just the happiness that is fitting, the anger that is fitting. If, in a given situation, it is appropriate to be five parts happy but one is seven or eight parts happy, then it exceeds the proper measure; if one is three or four parts happy, then it does not reach the proper measure. (*ZZYL*, chapter 62, p. 1516)

13. He was asked about the difference between the state before happiness, anger, sorrow, and delight are manifest and the state after they are manifest.

    Zhu Xi replied, "During the time before they are manifest, they have no form or appearance that is visible, but after they are manifest, they are visible. It is similar to when you see a child about to fall into a well, and you have feelings of alarm and concern.[15] In that case, it is apparent that you have humaneness inside yourself. If you see an act of trespassing, and you have the heart-mind of shame and disdain, in that case, it is apparent that you have rightness inside yourself.[16] Since the heart-mind of alarm and concern belongs to humaneness, it must be that humaneness lies within, and thus in becoming manifest it produces feelings of alarm and concern. Since the heart-mind of shame and disdain belongs to rightness, it must be that rightness lies within; and thus in becoming manifest it produces the heart-mind of shame and disdain. We can compare it to the eyes pertaining to the liver, or the ears pertaining to the kidneys. If your vision is not clear or if you are hard of hearing, then it must be the case that your liver or kidneys are diseased; if your vision is clear and your sense of hearing is acute, then it must be the case that the *qi* of your liver and kidneys is without defects before you can be like this. Nevertheless, if

---

15. *Mencius* 2A6.

16. *Mencius* 7B31.

humaneness does not have the heart-mind of alarm and concern, it is just love. If rightness does not have the heart-mind of shame and disdain, it is just judgment. Only if one first has these (i.e., a heart-mind of alarm and concern or of shame and disdain) within will one be moved to respond, and then they will naturally become manifest . . . ." (*ZZYL*, chapter 53, pp. 1288–1289)

14. The nature is the state before movement, and the feelings are the state after movement. The heart-mind encompasses both the states before and after movement. Now, the heart-mind, before it has been set into motion, is the nature, and after it has been set into motion, is the feelings. This is what is meant by "the heart-mind unites the nature and the feelings."[17] Desires are what issue forth from the feelings. The heart-mind is like water; the nature is like the stillness of water; the feelings are like the flowing of water; and desires are like waves. But there are good waves and bad waves. Good desires are as in cases like "I desire to be humane."[18] Bad ones are those that come forth and rush headlong towards something, like great, tumultuous waves. For the most part, bad desires destroy and reject Heavenly pattern-principle. Like a river overflowing, there is nothing they do not harm. When Mencius said that the feelings could be considered good,[19] he meant proper feelings. Those that flowed out from the nature originally possessed nothing that was not good. (*ZZYL*, chapter 5, pp. 93–94)

15. It was asked, "Were the sages anxious to not show their anger?

Zhu Xi replied, "How could they go through life without showing their anger? When it was proper for them to be angry, it always showed on their faces. If one must punish someone for his crimes and deliberately smiles, this is wrong."

It was asked, "If that is so, were they anxious about becoming enraged?"

Zhu Xi replied, "When Heaven is angry, there is the rumbling of thunder. When Shun punished the 'four villains,'[20] he must have been

---

17. This statement is from Zhang Zai and is quoted on many occasions by Zhu Xi. See Zhang 2001, Coda, Part 1, pp. 1a–3b.

18. *Analects* 7.30.

19. *Mencius* 6A6.

20. The "four villains" (*si xiong* 四凶) refer to ancient mythological figures representing harmful, malevolent forces that were banished by the legendary sage-ruler Shun 舜 to restore peace and order to the realm. There are different versions of this tale in Warring States and Han

angry at the time. If one is angry when one should be angry, he is behaving in a balanced and appropriate manner. When the incident has passed, this anger dissipates, and what is more it does not accumulate inside." (*ZZYL*, chapter 95, p. 2445)

16. If one has this nature, it will be expressed in these feelings. By way of these feelings, one sees this nature. Based on one having these feelings today, one can see that originally there was this nature. (*ZZYL*, chapter 5, p. 89)

17. Renfu 仁父[21] asked about the statement, "Humaneness is the pattern-principle of love."

　　Zhu Xi replied, "This statement can only be clarified if you consider it from the point of view of the heart-mind, nature, and feelings. There is a master that is naturally mingled within the self. This is the heart-mind. There being humaneness, rightness, ritual propriety, and wisdom—this is the nature. Its issuing forth as alarm and concern, shame and disdain, deference and yielding, and approbation and disapproval—these are the feelings. Alarm and concern is love, and it is the beginning of humaneness. Humaneness is the thing itself, love is its operation." He also said, "In the phrase, 'the pattern-principle of love,' love emanates from humaneness. But you cannot discuss humaneness separately from love." (*ZZYL*, chapter 20, p. 464).

18. He was asked about the nature, the feelings, the heart-mind, and humaneness.

　　Zhu Xi replied, "Master Hengqu [Zhang Zai] spoke of it most excellently, saying, 'The heart-mind unites the nature and feelings.' Mencius said, 'The heart-mind of alarm and concern is the beginning of humaneness, and the heart-mind of shame and disdain is the beginning of rightness.' This ultimately states that the heart-mind, feelings and the nature are all good. The heart-mind has nothing that is not good. What the heart-mind issues forth are the feelings, and sometimes there is that which is not good. Thus, to say that what is not good is not the heart-mind is to miss the point.

---

texts, many of which appear in the context of early flood myths. One of the earliest accounts is that found in the *Commentary of Zuo* (*Zuo Zhuan* 左傳), where the four villains are wicked sons whose expulsion to the four cardinal directions marks the ruler's endeavor to establish the foundations of his authority by constructing orderly space around the center (Wen year 18). On the motif of the punishment of the four villains, see Lewis 2006, 72–76.

21. Courtesy name of Xu Rong 徐容, Zhu Xi's disciple.

Although the heart-mind in itself is originally completely good, the fact that when it is in operation there are things that are not good is due to the fact that the feelings are swayed by things. 'Nature' is the all-encompassing name for pattern-principle, and humaneness, rightness, ritual propriety, and wisdom are terms for individual pattern-principles that lie within the nature. Alarm and concern, shame and disdain, deference and yielding, and approbation and disapproval are terms for what feelings issue forth. These feelings are what emanate from the nature and are thus good. The issuing forth of these beginnings is most subtle, and they all emanate from the heart-mind, and therefore [Zhang Zai] said: 'The heart-mind unites the feelings and the nature.'" (*ZZYL*, chapter 5, p. 92)

19. "The heart-mind unites the nature and feelings." It is "still and un-moving"[22] and the pattern-principles of humaneness, rightness, ritual propriety, and wisdom are all contained within it. When it is in a state of movement, it is the feelings. It has been said that the condition of still-ness is the nature and the condition of movement is the heart-mind. But this takes one thing and splits it into two. The heart-mind and the na-ture cannot be explained in terms of the distinction between movement and stillness. Everything possesses a heart-mind and the space within this heart-mind must be empty [*xu* 虛]. This is like when you take a dish containing chicken hearts or pig hearts: you can see [that they are empty] if you cut into them. The human heart-mind is also like this. But this empty place still encompasses and stores the many pattern-principles of the Way (*dao li* 道理), fills Heaven and earth, and embraces past and present. Extending this even further, it covers Heaven and earth, and there is nothing that does not come from this. This is the reason why the human heart-mind is such a marvelous thing! The pattern-principles that reside in the heart-mind are called "the nature." The nature is like the heart-mind's field: it fills the space within, and there is nothing but these pattern-principles within it. The heart-mind is the dwelling place of the spirit-like intelligence, and constitutes the master of the entire person.[23] The nature is then the many pattern-principles of the Way; these are

---

22. *Classic of Changes*, "Great Treatise" commentary Part 1, chapter 7.

23. Cf. *Xunzi* chapter 21: "The heart-mind is the ruler of the body (*xing zhi jun* 形之君) and the master of the spirit-like intelligence [*shen ming* 神明]." Adapted from Hutton 2014, 227. The account of the heart-mind in this chapter also makes recurring reference to its "emptiness [*xu* 虛]," which is a quality that Zhu Xi emphasizes in this passage.

received from Heaven and fully contained in the heart-mind. When they issue forth as wisdom, knowledge, recollection, and contemplation, they are all feelings. Therefore, [Zhang Zai] said, "The heart-mind unites the nature and feelings." (*ZZYL*, chapter 98, p. 2514)

20. It was asked, "What Yanzi learned[24] is that when human beings are born, a nature endowed with the Five Constants[25] is mixed within their heart-minds. Before they have been stirred by things, they are simply still and unmoving. But they cannot avoid being stirred by things, and therefore happiness, anger, sorrow, delight, and the rest of the seven feelings emerge. Having already become manifest, it is easy for them to get carried away, and the nature begins to get damaged. And so, what Yanzi learned was to make this pattern-principle clear and bright, and he took it as his imperative to restrain his feelings so that they accord with what is within, and to resolutely overcome his self-centeredness. Once self-centered desires are done away with, Heavenly pattern-principles will naturally reveal themselves. Therefore, when the heart-mind is receptive and still, when stirred it will respond accordingly. Sometimes it will be angry at something; it will be angry at what is appropriate to be angry about, but the self is not involved in this. As soon as the anger has passed, the heart-mind will return to a state of stillness; how could there be any transferring [of one's anger]?[26] When we talk about making mistakes, it is merely that something is slightly off. Zhang Zai called it 'dissatisfaction within oneself;' that is, roughly, some small things that one is dissatisfied about in one's heart-mind—if as soon as one is aware of them, one immediately sets about removing them, and moreover, ensures that they will not sprout

---

24. *Analects* 6.3. "What Yanzi learned" refers to the kind of learning represented by Yan Hui, the favored disciple of Confucius. Zhou Dunyi singled out Yan Hui as living in accordance with the idea that moral self-perfection was the true and proper aim of learning. Cheng Yi continued to promote this learning in his essay, "Discussion of What Yanzi Loved to Learn" (*Yanzi suo hao he xue lun* 顏子所好何學論). On the cult of Yan Hui, see Hon 2005, 85.

25. The five constant virtues of humaneness (*ren* 仁), rightness (*yi* 義), ritual propriety (*li* 禮), wisdom (*zhi* 智), and trustworthiness (*xin* 信).

26. *Analects* 6.3 reads:

Duke Ai asked, "Who among your disciples might be said to love learning?"
Kongzi answered, "There was one named Yan Hui who loved learning. He never transferred his anger, and never made the same mistake twice. Unfortunately, his allotted lifespan was short, and he has passed away. Now that he is gone, there are none who really love learning—at least, I have yet to hear of one." (Slingerland, Op. cit. with slight modification.)

again—if the effort one makes to learn is like this—then we can say that one truly loves learning."

Zhu Xi replied, "What is called 'learning' is learning this, and nothing more. What Cheng Yi called 'aligning the feelings with the nature,' what the *Great Learning* referred to as 'illuminating bright virtue,' and what the *Doctrine of the Mean* called 'Heaven's mandate is called the nature' is all about this pattern-principle." (*ZZYL*, chapter 30, p. 776)

21. As for the efforts made by students, I only worry that they fail to grasp what is essential. But if they strive to investigate the pattern-principles of the Way, things will naturally settle into their place, and become integrated into an all-encompassing unity so that each thing will have its own differentiated order (*tiaoli* 條理). But if they don't do this, then in all matters they will face obstructions and obstacles. Students are constantly engaged in discussion, speaking frequently about "holding on to it (*cao shou* 操守)"[27] without having grasped what is essential, so they do not know what they should be holding onto. They talk about "extending and filling it out," of "experiencing it personally," and of "nurturing it," but this is all just about finding nice words for making conversation. It will work only if they apply effort in actual affairs. The idea that one must understand at the fundamental level is motivated by the same point. (*ZZYL*, chapter 8, p. 130)

22. In antiquity, children entered the school of Lesser Learning at a young age, and were only instructed in practical matters, ranging from ritual, music, archery, charioteering, calligraphy, and mathematics, to the cultivation of filiality and fraternal respect, devotedness and trustworthiness. At the age of sixteen or seventeen, they entered the school of Greater Learning, and from then on were instructed in matters pertaining to pattern-principle, from "the extension of knowledge" and "the investigation of things" to what constitutes devotedness, trustworthiness, filiality, and fraternal respect. (*ZZYL*, chapter 7, p. 124)

23. Lesser Learning concerns the realm of affairs, such as serving one's ruler, serving one's father, serving one's elder brother, and comportment towards one's friends. It only provides instruction about acting in accordance with models of conduct. Greater Learning elucidates the pattern-principles underlying such affairs. (*ZZYL*, chapter 7, p. 125)

---

27. Following Daniel Gardner's rendering of *cao shou* 操守 in Gardner 1990.

24. A single heart-mind is fully endowed with the myriad pattern-principles. Only if you are able to preserve the heart-mind can you exhaustively investigate pattern-principle. (*ZZYL*, chapter 9, p. 154)

25. For exhaustively investigating pattern-principle, what is fundamental is to open one's heart-mind and quiet one's thoughts. (*ZZYL*, chapter 9, p. 155)

26. Pattern-principle is not a separate thing in front of us; instead, it resides in our heart-minds. Only if people directly experience how it truly resides within them will the situation be acceptable. It is like what the practitioners of inner alchemy refer to as "lead and mercury, dragon and tiger." These are all things that reside in one's body, not outside of it.[28] (*ZZYL*, chapter 9, p. 155)

27. Replying to Hengqu (Zhang Zai)'s question regarding the idea that "in calming the nature one cannot but be engaged in activity (*dong* 動),"[29] Mingdao (Cheng Hao)'s idea was that one should neither loathe things and affairs, nor should one pursue them. Now, if people loathe things, they would completely cut themselves off from them, and if they pursue them, they would be enticed and driven by them. Only if one neither resists them nor drifts along with them, but responds freely and completely appropriately can one achieve goodness. Now, in Hengqu's conception, one has to cut oneself off from the realm of external things and achieve calmness within, while Mingdao thought it was necessary to harmonize and join together inner and outer, saying that "there is calmness in motion and there is calmness in stillness,"[30] and that, when responding to things, one will naturally not be bound by things. If one can be calm only when one is still, then when one is engaged in activity, I'm afraid

---

28. The inner alchemists invoked the traditional ingredients used in outer alchemy (*waidan* 外丹)—a practice devoted to the production of elixirs that promised longevity or immortality. Lead and mercury were the most important of these ingredients, and were identified with the forces of *yang* and *yin* (denoted by the dragon and tiger), respectively. The inner alchemists eschewed the use of external substances in favor of methods of physical and mental cultivation that were understood as mirroring the workings of the cosmos.

29. Cheng Mingdao (Cheng Hao), "Letter in Reply to Master Hengqu Regarding Calming the Nature (*Da Hengqu xiansheng ding xing shu* 答恆渠先生定性書)," in Cheng Yi and Cheng Hao 1999, chapter 2, p. 1a. This passage also appears in *A Record for Reflection*; see Zhu Xi 1936, chapter 2, p. 34.

30. Ibid.

that they will be tempted and carried away by things. (*ZZYL*, chapter 95, p. 2442)

28. It was asked, "It seems that maintaining tranquility (*jing* 靜) is something we must apply ourselves to."

    Zhu Xi replied, "Although it is said that one should maintain tranquility, this doesn't mean that we should abandon affairs and things in order to pursue tranquility. Since we are human beings, we must demonstrate service to our ruler and kin, interact with our friends, comfort our wives and children, and attend to our servants. We cannot completely abandon these obligations, close our doors and engage in quiet sitting, and when things and affairs arrive, fail to respond and manage them, saying, 'Wait until I go and do some quiet sitting. I don't need to respond.' Nor can we simply go off in blind pursuit of things and affairs. Between these two extremes, only if there is thoughtful resoluteness can it work . . . When things and affairs arrive, if one does not respond to them in accordance with pattern-principle, then although one may sit like a lump and not interact with things, the heart-mind will not achieve tranquility. Only if, in a state of activity, one is able to accord with pattern-principle, then can one achieve tranquility in times when there are no affairs. If one can preserve and nurture this stillness, then in this state of responding to and managing things, one begins to achieve efficacy. In times of activity one must exert oneself; in times of tranquility one must exert oneself. . . ." (*ZZYL*, chapter 45, p. 1161)

29. Reverential attention is none other than the heart-mind serving as the master. (*ZZYL*, chapter 12, p. 210)

30. Reverential attention isn't just sitting around. Whenever you pick up your feet and set about going somewhere, this heart-mind should always be in such a state of mind. (*ZZYL*, chapter 12, p. 211)

31. Reverential attention isn't just sitting there like a lump of earth, with the ears not hearing, the eyes not seeing, and the heart-mind not thinking, and then calling that reverential attention. It is just being in a state of awe and respect toward something, and not daring to be without restraint or discipline. If one is like this, then one will be restrained in one's body and heart-mind, as though one were in awe of something. If one is constantly like this, then the state of one's *qi* will naturally become differentiated [from other states]. If you preserve this heart-mind, then you can engage in learning. (*ZZYL*, chapter 12, p. 211)

32. In undertaking the task of learning, one must practice quiet sitting (*jing zuo* 靜坐). If you practice quiet sitting, then your inner foundation will be settled. Even if you cannot avoid pursuing things, you will have a place where you can be tranquil when you come around. You can compare it to a person being comfortable living at home; if he goes out and then returns, he feels at ease. If things outside are hectic but one has never put in the effort [of practicing quiet sitting] and then wants to collect oneself in the inside, one will not have a place to settle down. (*ZZYL*, chapter 12, p. 217)

33. He was asked about [Confucius's statement], "Hold fast to it, and then it will be preserved."[31]

    Zhu Xi replied, "The heart-mind isn't a dead thing; one should look at it as a living thing. Otherwise, it will be like the Buddhists entering the realm of stillness and practicing Chan meditation. Holding fast to it and preserving it is just when you respond to affairs and manage things; if everything is in accordance with pattern-principle, then it is preserved. If the way you deal with things isn't proper, then in that case the heart-mind isn't present. If you only pay attention to maintaining a state of calm here, and then suddenly some matter comes before you, your holding fast will be dispersed; this is [what Confucius spoke of as] 'Let it go and you will lose it.'"[32]

    Zhongsi[33] asked, "What about the time before you respond to affairs or manage things?"

    Zhu Xi replied, "Before you respond to affairs or manage things, you should maintain a state of vigilance and caution, and that is all."

    He was further asked, "If one is in a state of vigilance and caution, in that case is this to hold on to it?"

    Zhu Xi replied, "It is also necessary to hold on to it, but you do not need to stubbornly hold it there. Only teach it to wake up, and then you will hold fast to it. You don't need to restrain yourself like a lump of clay." (*ZZYL*, chapter 59, p. 1400)

34. If your heart-mind is not preserved, your entire person will not have a master. (*ZZYL*, chapter 12, p. 199)

---

31. Statement by Confucius quoted in *Mencius* 6A8.

32. Ibid.

33. Courtesy name of Chen Jingzhou 陳景周 (d. 1229), who passed the Presented Scholar examination in 1220.

35. For one who is bright, the [heart-mind] is simply bright. As for the others, they have to nurture it. Nurturing isn't like toiling away with hammer and chisel. If you just keep the heart-mind open and tranquil, eventually it will become bright on its own. (*ZZYL*, chapter 12, p. 204).

36. About these two lines, "The extension of knowledge resides in nurturing it; for nurturing knowledge nothing surpasses lessening desire"[34]: the extension of knowledge means pushing your knowing to its fullest extent and perfecting it. One who wishes to extend one's knowledge must first be able to nurture his knowledge. If you are able to nurture it, then your perceptions will be increasingly clear, and what you grasp will be increasingly solid. If you wish to nurture your knowledge, all you have to do is lessen your desires, and that is all. If your desires are lessened, then you will not be disturbed by mixed-up things, and your knowing will become ever more clear; if you are not afflicted by vicissitudes, what you grasp will become ever more solid. (*ZZYL*, chapter 18, p. 405)

37. Jingzhi[35] asked, " 'For nurturing the heart-mind, nothing is better than lessening desires.'[36] In this phrase, 'nurturing the heart-mind' is none other than keeping [one's heart-mind] in a state of balance and openness."

Zhu Xi replied, "This is certainly right. When you want the many things that are in front of you, your heart-mind rushes headlong towards all these things. [Lessening desires] is not about a total absence [of desire], it is just about reducing them so that one can gradually preserve one's heart-mind. If you covet many things, you want this and you also want that. One need not be talking about things that are corrupt or bad; if there are things in front of you that you desire greatly, then your original heart-mind (*ben xin* 本心) will be thrown into confusion. . . . Human beings only have one heart-mind, so how can we divide it up into many parts? If we keep applying our heart-minds to useless things, when we encounter situations where we ought to apply it, we will not have the strength to deal with them. . . ." (*ZZYL*, chapter 61, p. 1475)

---

34. This passage appears in *Questions on the Great Learning* (*Daxue huowen* 大學或問), in Zhu Xi 1999, chapter 1, p. 15a.

35. Courtesy name of Zhu Zai 朱在 (1169–1239), the third son of Zhu Xi.

36. *Mencius* 7B35.

38. It is necessary for students to establish their will (*zhi* 志).[37,38] That people these days are going about it so casually is because they have never regarded learning as an enterprise. When they encounter situations, they deal with them in a haphazard and ad hoc way. This is simply because their wills aren't established. (*ZZYL*, chapter 8, p. 134)

39. You mustn't wait. (*ZZYL*, chapter 8, p. 135)

40. Students today are completely uneager [to learn].[39] (*ZZYL*, chapter 8, p. 135)

41. In making an effort, people nowadays are never willing to start. Everyone wants to wait. So, for instance, if they have something to do this morning, but not in the afternoon, they say they could start in the afternoon; if they have something to do in the afternoon, then they say they could start in the evening. But they will be sure to wait until tomorrow. If there still remain a few days left in the month, it is certain they will wait until the next month; if there still remain a few months left in the year, they will not make an effort, invariably saying, "There is hardly any time left in the year, so we have to wait until next year." When they are like this, how will they make any progress? (*ZZYL*, chapter 8, p. 135)

42. In learning, we should first establish the main structure, and then come back to the interior to build the walls and take care of the fine details. People nowadays often set about building individual rooms before they understand the bigger project, so they rarely complete their work. (*ZZYL*, chapter 8, p. 130)

43. You mustn't be dependent on teachers or friends. (*ZZYL*, chapter 8, p. 135)

44. In learning, do not complain that there is no one to analyze things for you. You must go inside it yourself and carefully make an effort. You have to see things for yourself. (*ZZYL*, chapter 8, p. 136)

---

37. Editor's note: The standard translation for the word here translated "will" is "commitment"; other translations are "intention" and "volition."

38. *Analects* 2.4.

39. *Analects* 7.19.

45. You must polish and refine your mental energy so as to pursue understanding. The matters of the world cannot be understood in a state of relaxed leisure. (*ZZYL*, chapter 8, p. 138)

46. The gate for entering the Way is for you to put yourself personally into the realm of the pattern-principle of the Way, becoming gradually intimate with it, and eventually becoming one with it. But nowadays, the path for entering the pattern-principle of the Way lies here, while people stand out there, with the two having nothing to do with each other at all. (*ZZYL*, chapter 8, p. 140)

47. Broad learning refers to the pattern-principle of Heaven and earth and the myriad things, and to the method of cultivating oneself and governing others. These are all things that one should learn. Still, there is a proper sequence and order, and you have to prioritize that which is important and urgent. [Learning] can't be confused and disunified. (*ZZYL*, chapter 8, p. 142)

48. It is like climbing a mountain. Most people want to get to the highest point, but don't know the pattern-principle whereby if you do not proceed from understanding the lower points, you will never reach the higher points. (*ZZYL*, chapter 8, p. 142)

49. As for the words of the sages and worthies, we must constantly pass them before our eyes, roll them around in our mouths, and ruminate over them in our heart-minds. (*ZZYL*, chapter 10, p. 162)

50. There is value in a book only in its recitation.[40] If you recite it often, you will naturally achieve understanding. Now, even if we ponder it deeply and write it down on paper, this doesn't help matters, since in the end it is not really ours. There is value only in its recitation. I don't know how it is that the heart-mind naturally harmonizes with the *qi*, becomes so buoyant and vitalized, and naturally comes to remember things so securely. Even if you read the text to the point of familiarity, and contemplate it in your

---

40. In this passage, I translate *du* 讀 as "recitation" rather than as "reading," which is the other common rendering of this term. In Zhu Xi's time, and in late imperial China more generally, the most frequently used terms for reading, *du* 讀 and *song* 誦, referred specifically to the act of reading aloud. Here, and in other passages addressing the method of reading, Zhu Xi emphasizes the physical activity of reading texts out loud so as to engage one's entire body and senses. This reflects Zhu Xi's conviction that being one with the text meant physically embodying and enacting it, not just in internalizing its content. It also suggests Zhu Xi's resistance to a growing tendency in his own time towards the practice of silent reading.

heart-mind, it is still not as good as recitation. If you recite it over and over again, then before long what you didn't understand you come to understand, and what you understand becomes even more meaningful. If you do not recite the text to the point of familiarity, then it really does not become so meaningful. But I have not yet spoken about the recitation of commentaries, but only about reciting with intimate familiarity the original classics. Whether you are moving or at rest, sitting or lying down, if your heart-mind always dwells [on the recitation of the classics], then naturally you will achieve understanding. Having thought about it, I believe that recitation *is* what it means to learn. (*ZZYL*, chapter 10, p. 170)

51. If the heart-mind isn't settled, it cannot grasp pattern-principle. Now if you wish to read books, you must first settle your heart-mind, and make it like still water, or like a bright mirror. How can a dirty mirror reflect things? (*ZZYL*, chapter 11, p. 177)

52. When reading books, you cannot simply seek the moral significance of the text from what's on the page. You must turn around and consider it from your own self as the reference point. Since the time of the Qin and Han periods, there was nobody who discussed this; all they did was to go and look for it in the text, and did not try to understand it for themselves. You have not yet understood that the previous words of the sages reside there [within yourself]. Only if you avail yourself of these words and come to investigate it in yourself can you begin to grasp it. (*ZZYL*, chapter 11, p. 181)

Bibliography

Cheng Yi and Cheng Hao. 1999. *The Collected Writings of the Cheng Brothers* (*Er Cheng wenji* 二程文集). Siku quanshu edition. Electronic resource.

Gardner, Daniel. 1990. *Learning to Be a Sage: Selections from the Conversations of Master Chu, Arranged Topically*. Berkeley: University of California Press.

Harvard University, Academia Sinica, and Peking University. 2018. *China Biographical Database* (January 1, 2018). https://projects.iq.harvard.edu/cbdb.

Hon, Tze-ki. 2005. *The Yijing and Chinese Politics: Classical Commentary and Literati Activism*. Albany: SUNY Press.

Hutton, Eric L., trans. 2014. *Xunzi: The Complete Text*. Princeton, NJ, and Oxford: Princeton University Press.

Legge, James, trans. 1963. *The Sacred Books of China: The I Ching*. New York: Dover.

Lewis, Mark E. 2006. *The Flood Myths of Early China*. Albany: SUNY Press.

Kong Yingda 孔穎達. 1999. *The Correct Meaning of the Book of Rites* (*Li ji zhengyi* 禮記正義). Edited by Li Xueqin 李學勤. Beijing: Beijing daxue chubanshe.

Meng, Peiyuan. 2016. "How to Unite Is and Ought: An Explanation Regarding the Work of Master Zhu." In *Returning to Zhu Xi: Emerging Patterns within the Supreme Polarity*. Edited by David Jones and Jinli He. Albany: SUNY Press.

Slingerland, Edward G., trans. 2003. *Confucius. Analects with Selections from Traditional Commentaries*. Indianapolis, IN, and Cambridge, MA: Hackett.

Virág, Curie. 2014. "Self-cultivation as *Praxis* in Song Neo-Confucianism." In *Modern Chinese Religion. Value Systems in Transformation*. Edited by John Lagerwey. Leiden and Boston: Brill.

Virág, Curie. 2007. "Emotions and Human Agency in the Thought of Zhu Xi." *Journal of Song-Yuan Studies* 37: 55–64.

Zhang Zai. 2001. *The Recorded Sayings of Master Zhang* (*Zhangzi yulu* 張子語錄). *Sibu congkan* 四部叢刊. Electronic resource.

Zhu Xi. 1985. *The Classified Sayings of Master Zhu* (*Zhuzi yulei* 朱子語類). Edited by Li Jingde 黎靖德. Beijing: Zhonghua shuju.

Zhu Xi. 2000. *The Collected Writings of Master Zhu* (*Zhuzi wenji* 朱子文集). Edited by Chen Junmin 陳俊民. Taibei: Defu wenjiao jijinhui.

Zhu Xi. 1936. *A Record for Reflection* (*Jinsilu* 近思錄). Edited by Zhang Boxing 張伯行. Shanghai: Shangwu yinshuguan.

Zhu Xi. 1999. *Questions on the Four Books* (*Sishu huowen* 四書或問). *Siku quanshu* edition. Electronic resource.

Further Readings

Bol, Peter K. 2008. *Neo-Confucianism in History*. Cambridge, MA: Harvard University Press.

Bol, Peter K. 1989. "Chu Hsi's Redefinition of Literati Learning." In *Neo-Confucian Education: The Formative Stage*. Edited by William Theodore de Bary and John W. Chaffee. Berkeley: University of California Press.

Gardner, Daniel K. 1990. *Learning to Be a Sage: Selections from the Conversations of Master Chu, Arranged Topically*. Berkeley: University of California Press.

Ivanhoe, Philip J. 2000. *Confucian Moral Self Cultivation*, rev. 2nd ed. Indianapolis, IN: Hackett.

Shun, Kwong-loi. 2010. "Zhu Xi's Moral Psychology." In *Dao Companion to Neo-Confucian Philosophy*. Edited by John Makeham. Dordrecht; London: Springer.

Virág, Curie. 2014. "Self-cultivation as *Praxis* in Song Neo-Confucianism." In *Modern Chinese Religion. Value Systems in Transformation*. Edited by John Lagerwey. Leiden and Boston: Brill.

3

Politics and Government

Justin Tiwald

Introduction

Zhu Xi's views on governance and administration tend to receive less attention from contemporary scholars than his contributions to ethics and metaphysics, but there is little question that his ideas about such matters form an indispensable piece of the whole that is his system of thought. Questions about good and effective governance were major objects of reflection and debate for the educated elite of his day, especially for those who, like Zhu, served as state officials. Zhu wrote and spoke extensively about issues such as the management of the state bureaucracy, public education, rules and regulations, foreign affairs, and the selection and appointment of officials. At pivotal moments in his life he risked his career to take positions against the corruption of officials and the Southern Song's policy of appeasement toward the Jurchens and other neighboring states. And Zhu's vision of good governance serves as a kind of regulative ideal for his ethics. The very character traits that Zhu most esteems and wants for educated men are those that position them to be righteous, discerning, and caring advisors and administrators, and the fact that they make for capable advisors and officers of state is part of what justifies the Confucian virtues as Zhu understands them.

Broadly speaking, Zhu adopted and defended an approach to governance that we might call character-based rather than institution-based. That is, Zhu thought that among the many things that should be done to remedy the social and political ills through the apparatus of the state, the most important or primary task was to improve the moral character of the people who run the state. This can be contrasted with the idea that the primary task should instead be to reform the laws, rules, and regulations of which state and quasi-state institutions are constituted. Zhu did not deny that institutional reform and other forms of statecraft were important work, and indispensable for a harmonious social and political order, but in various ways he thought that improving the character of those who hold office should come first. Viable institutions must be established and run by virtuous and talented people if they are to be successful. Furthermore, in many cases where it might seem that different policies and procedures would make a difference in outcome, the real difference can be credited to the people that enact them. "In general," Zhu says, "established regulations invariably have defects and no regulations are without them. What's really important in this matter is getting the right person for the job. If the person is right then even if the regulations aren't good he will still amply make up the difference in score."[1]

Zhu Xi could be said to have several foes in political thought. He believed that Buddhist and Daoist quietism and escapism were largely responsible for the deterioration of the strong social bonds—including political bonds—on which a stable and harmonious society depends. Like many Confucians who were ascendant in political circles in the Southern Song, Zhu looked back with disapprobation on the policies of the famous reformer Wang Anshi 王安石 (1021–1086), a minister and Confucian thinker whose institutional vision was adopted (but eventually abandoned) in the Northern Song. Zhu's criticisms of Wang's reforms were varied and often nuanced, but what loomed largest were suspicion of the strong centralization of power that Wang advocated and Wang's failure to recognize how much successful governance depends on the rigors of Confucian moral cultivation. Zhu also opposed some more institution-based political thinkers described collectively as the "Yongjia School" of Confucianism, leading representatives of which included his contemporaries Chen Liang 陳亮 (1143–1194) and Ye Shi 葉適 (1150–1223). In his eyes, thinkers like Chen and Ye tended to downplay the importance of virtue and virtuous motives in the interest of maximizing benefit or profit (*li* 利).[2]

A somewhat more concrete area of dispute had to do with two competing ways of distributing regional authority. By Zhu's time, governance of areas outside the capital had long followed basic principles of what is translated

---

1. See passage 10 in this chapter.

2. Tillman 1982.

here as the "commandery" (*junxian* 郡縣) system.³ What was most perti-
nent and controversial about this system is that the regional governors were
appointed by the imperial court and the rules of appointment were devised
to limit the power of regional officials and the likelihood of developing particular attachments between the appointees and the people in their charge.
Governors were rotated on a regular basis and it was usually forbidden for an
appointee to be given authority over territory that included his home town.
This system was also meant to be meritocratic. Governors were usually drawn
from the ranks of degree-bearing scholars who earned their degree through the
civil service examination system. While many saw the advantages in this way
of handling regional governance, there remained throughout the Northern
and Southern Song a strong contingent of Confucian scholars who wanted to
revive a system translated here as an "enfeoffment" (*fengjian* 封建), according
to which regional governorships are given not to individuals for short periods
of time but to lineages, and most enfeoffed lords receive their position by
birthright. Proponents of the enfeoffment system included several major figures in the fellowship of philosophical Confucianism with which Zhu Xi
identified, probably the most prolific of whom was Hu Hong 胡宏 (1106–
1161). In defending the system, Hu and likeminded political thinkers often
invoked the widely shared view that it prevailed during China's golden ages,
but all found it attractive for many independent reasons as well, the most notable being the great stability they thought it afforded, the decentralization of
power which allowed regional centers to thrive even when the supreme mon-
arch was corrupt or incompetent, and especially the appealing notion that
there would be more genuine and natural affinities and intimacy between regional rulers and their subjects. As we will see, Zhu admits to being enamored
of this ancient governmental structure in his early years as a scholar, but says
that he came over time to see the commandery system as no less viable so long
as it is led and staffed by people of good character.⁴

Translation

1. On the way of governance there is nothing more to say so long as the
   ruler is respectful, moderate, and fond of goodness. [And to paraphrase

---

3. More literally, a system of "prefectures and counties."

4. For more on the debate about these two systems as captured by Hu Hong, Zhu Xi, and
others, see Angle and Tiwald 2017, 201–206.

the *Book of Documents*,] "When others say something that goes against the grain of your heart-mind you should seek to find out whether it is in accord with the Way; and when others say something that concurs with your volitions you should seek to find out whether it goes against the Way."[5] [When there is a ruler with these qualities and tendencies], how could the state not be well-governed? There is nothing more to say than this, for the model has been evident from ancient times and it is truly like this. (*ZZYL*, chapter 108, p. 2678)

2. The affairs of the empire have both a great foundation and lesser foundations. Rectifying the heart-mind of the ruler is the great foundation. Each of the myriad remaining affairs has a foundation of its own—for example, providing for the nourishment of the people is the foundation for managing the state's finances and selecting generals is the foundation for governing the military. (*ZZYL*, chapter 108, p. 2678)

3. Naturally there is a great foundation for the affairs of the empire, and each affair also has its own critical point. (*ZZYL*, chapter 108, p. 2678)

4. The affairs of the empire should be understood by their foundations, not by what shows on the surface. (*ZZYL*, chapter 108, p. 2678)

5. In learning, one starts from the broad and returns to the essential. In governing, one starts from the essential and makes it broad. (*ZZYL*, chapter 108, p. 2678)

6. It was asked: "Some say that those who advise rulers these days are all able to utter the two words 'cultivate virtue [*xiu de* 修德].' What I don't understand is this: where do they advise rulers to start the work of cultivation? There must be some particularly important places [at which to begin their work]."

   Zhu Xi replied: "Why put it that way? One simply needs to see to it that the present state of the ruler's heart-mind is without self-centeredness and it will turn to a state of great public-orientation [*gong* 公] for all the empire. If he completely rids himself of all self-centered intentions then when any person in his employ lacks worthiness he will seek an upright person to replace him."

   It was asked: "But how can he be fully aware of the worthies in his empire with just one set of eyes and ears?"

---

5. *Book of Documents* 3.5C.8, "The Shang Documents."

Zhu Xi said: "He just needs a good person to serve as prime minister, who will naturally put forward people for consideration or dismissal, and a good Censorate, which will know when they are not good so that naturally such officials will not remain in their positions."[6] (*ZZYL*, chapter 108, p. 2679)

7. The enfeoffment system isn't in fact feasible [in present times]. In the context of the Three Dynasties [the ancient Xia, Shang, and Zhou] enfeoffment had an advantage, which was to keep the feelings of ruler and subject closely attached and thereby preserve a long peace without worries. This was not like the commanderies of later generations, whose governors rotate out after one or two years. Even with a worthy person in charge, good governance cannot be achieved. (*ZZYL*, chapter 108, p. 2679)

8. Zhu Xi then went on to say: "The enfeoffment system just passed down from one dynasty to the next, but circumstances no longer allow it, as Liu Zongyuan correctly explained.[7] Jia Yi was also quite correct in remarking that 'establishing vassal states inevitably leads to circumstances of mutual suspicion.'[8] The fiefdoms naturally came to concentrate power below, so those who would rule from above were unable to control them.[9] How long could the heyday of the Zhou dynasty last! By the time they reached the Spring and Autumn period the various vassal states were strong and wealthy and the power of the Zhou kings gradually diminished. Later in the Warring States period Zhou authority was divided up between enfeoffed lords in the East and West, leaving King Nan with no other option but to live as a lodger in the lands of the Duke of the West. Despite the fact that the regulations [embodied in the enfeoffment system that the Zhou King inherited] had been established by sages, how could it be without defects!" The general meaning of the Master's remarks was

---

6. For much of the Song dynasty, the "Censorate" (*Taijian* 臺諫) refers to that office in imperial government that is responsible for identifying and censuring bad officials and also for remonstrating with the emperor.

7. Liu Zongyuan 柳宗元 (773–819) is the author of what was, for many centuries, the most widely read and influential polemic against the enfeoffment system. See Song 2011.

8. Jia Yi 賈誼 (200–169 BCE) was a poet and scholar in the Western Han.

9. More literally, "have a distribution of power such that the tail was too heavy to be wagged" (*you wei da bu diao zhi shi* 有尾大不掉之勢).

that defects are easily acquired in the enfeoffment and wellfield systems. (*ZZYL*, chapter 108, p. 2679)

9. It was asked: "What is proper for later generations: the enfeoffment or the commandery system?"

    Zhu Xi replied: "In the final analysis, whether we have order or disorder does not rest on this issue. Looking at the matter from the perspective of moral pattern-principles [*dao li* 道理], the enfeoffment system was set up because the sages did not want to treat the empire as their private possession, and thus parceled it out to relatives and worthies for them to manage together. But this could be achieved because their institutions weren't overly large. In the Han dynasty, Jia Yi recommended 'multiplying the number of enfeoffed lords and diminishing their power.' Later, Zhufu Yan took this proposal and used it under the rule of Emperor Wu."[10] (*ZZYL*, chapter 108, p. 2680)

10. The students were discussing the defects of the commandery and enfeoffment systems. Zhu Xi said, "In general established regulations invariably have defects and no regulations are without them. What's really important in this matter is getting the right person for the job [of implementing and administering those regulations]. If the person is right then even if the regulations aren't good he will still amply make up the difference in score. If the person isn't right and yet the regulations are good, how could this have any benefits for the actual affairs? Now suppose we were to say that the commandery system isn't as good as enfeoffment. But if the enfeoffed governors aren't the right people then generation after generation could succeed one another without ever being able to replace them. If the commandery system doesn't have the right person then after only two or three years when his term is finished he could be replaced with a good person, but this is not assured. The Grand Historian Fan's *Mirror of the Tang* discusses how in general [for the Tang administrations] everything turned on getting the right person for the job.[11] At first I scorned him for saying this but later, upon reflection, I understood why he said it."

---

10. Zhufu Yan 主父偃 (d. ca. 126 BCE) was a minister to Emperor Wu of the Han dynasty (156–87 BCE). The latter reigned from 141 to 87 BCE. For more on Jia Yi, see passage 8 in this chapter.

11. The Grand Historian Fan is Fan Zuyu 范祖禹 (1041–1098).

Zhu Xi also said, "If you want to remove any defects then you must do so in light of an understanding of their originating sources." (*ZZYL*, chapter 108, p. 2680)

11. Living in the present age, I don't see the benefit in completely throwing out the present regulations and implementing the government of the ancients; this would only have the disadvantage of upsetting things. Moreover, large and important matters are involved and there would be many obstacles, making it absolutely difficult to implement. The most essential thing is to accord with the regulations of the forefathers and expertly select the right people for government service; this will be sufficient to effect order. The important thing is just to select the right people for service. In Fan Zuyu's *Mirror of the Tang* he reasons in the above manner to conclude that according with the current commandery system is sufficient to effect order. When I was young I would regularly scorn this view, regarding it as simply an argument for passive acceptance of the status quo. But when I examine it now I think it's true.

Deming's record of this conversation adds the following: "Someone asked: 'As for governing in the present day, which system should be put first?' Zhu Xi answered: 'One simply needs to get the right people.'" (*ZZYL*, chapter 108, p. 2682)

12. When the ancients established regulations they were just general guidelines which subordinates were able to pursue on their own. The regulations of later generations are detailed and meticulous such that subordinates are only able to abide by them [strictly and without individual discretion]. Where such regulations are in place superiors aren't able to promote or dismiss subordinates [as they see fit]. (*ZZYL*, chapter 108, p. 2688)

13. This age suffers from two defects: defects in its regulations and defects in the current political situation. The defects in the regulations can all be altered at once quite easily, but the defects in the current political situation all reside in people. How can they be changed when people go about their business with a selfish heart-mind! The regulations of the last eight years of Emperor Renzong's reign can be considered defective. Duke Wang of Jing changed them all soon after [assuming his position], but this only gave rise to numerous new defects.[12] This is because people are hard to change. (*ZZYL*, chapter 108, p. 2688)

---

12. "Duke Wang of Jing" refers to Wang Anshi 王安石 (1021–1086), a famous minister who,

14. Yang proceeded to discuss the regulations governing the civil examination system, contending that they were fair even if they could not guarantee that the right people are selected for civil service positions. Zhu Xi responded: "The regulations governing the selection and appointment of officials are indeed fair. But even if a regulation is perfectly fair it won't be a good one if it doesn't take account of people. Only a regulation that produces fair results even in the face of private interests can be considered a good one." (*ZZYL*, chapter 108, p. 2688)

15. It was asked: "The Master said, 'One shouldn't investigate all of the elaborate details of the ancient rituals. One should select some of the rituals and ceremonies that are practiced today and use the ancient rituals to make adjustments to them so that they accord with human feelings. Only then will the ancient rituals have some benefit.' How about this?"

   Zhu Xi replied: "That is certainly correct."

   The questioner continued: "If this is right, then are there viable ceremonies recorded in the *Rites* regarding things like capping, marriages, funerals, and sacrifices?"

   Zhu Xi replied: "As for the rituals like the ones regarding capping and marriages, how could they not be viable? Just the funeral and sacrificial rituals have troublesome complications."

   The questioner said: "If that's correct then those who lack a thorough and refined understanding of ethics and pattern-principles [*yili* 義理] will be inadequate to participate in the rituals?"

   Zhu Xi replied: "That is certainly correct."

   The questioner said: "What about the institutions and practices of the wellfield and enfeoffment systems?"[13]

   Zhu Xi replied: "Here too there are viable ones. For example, if there is an official who has achieved significant deeds the ruler could give him a township as a fiefdom, as they did for the marquises of townships or precincts in the Han dynasty. If taxes on people's fields must be fair then dividing lines must be made, and outlining them

---

with imperial support, led a series of major political and economic reforms known as the "New Policies." Many Confucians of Zhu's era, including Zhu himself, considered Wang's New Policies to be disastrous.

13. Like the ancient ritual forms recorded in the *Rites*, the wellfield and enfeoffment systems are also endorsed by authoritative Confucian classics. And yet just as some Song Confucians doubt that elaborate ancient rituals can be implemented in later times so too do many doubt that these ancient social systems can be instituted.

successfully lies in making sure that the ditches and moats are correct first. Other examples include the [ancient] virtues of filial piety, fraternal respect, conscientiousness, and trustworthiness, as well as the proper way to conduct ordinary human relationships and daily affairs. These can be disseminated through music by arranging for people to sing about them or by imitating the ritualized reading method of the *Rites of Zhou*, spreading them all over the countryside and replacing the current practice of writing prohibitions on white walls." (*ZZYL*, chapter 108, p. 2683)

16. It was asked: "In his *Essay on the Fundamentals*, Ouyang Xiu said that nowadays the traditional Confucian rites of capping, marriage, funerals, and sacrifices are practiced only at the imperial court, when in fact the Minister of Rites should be ordered to explain and promulgate these rites in the prefectures and counties of the nation.[14] What do you think of this proposal?"

Zhu Xi replied: "These were promulgated in the past although some time later this policy was suspended, after the effort elicited charges of illegally exposing people's private affairs. Moreover, it was difficult to find people who could instruct others in these rites."

It was asked: "We cannot immediately effect a full-scale restoration of the institutions of the Three Dynasties, so maybe in the meantime we should focus on making rough sets of regulations for managing the empire in specific areas like community granaries or the identification of good students."

Zhu Xi replied: "We could say that this is like making a small repair to a metal pot; if you really want to fix it you need to recast the entire thing. Today, from the imperial court down to the hundred departments and prefectures and out to the provinces and counties, without exception all of them have flawed regulations, particularly those concerning the schools and examination system."

He also said: "One can still see some majesty and humility amongst the rites of the present day, but these qualities are completely gone from contemporary music!"

---

14. Ouyang Xiu 歐陽修 (1007–1072) was an influential Confucian philosopher, poet, and political figure in the Northern Song. For a partial translation of his *Essay on the Fundamentals*, see de Bary and Bloom 1999, 591–595.

It was asked: "Perhaps the imperial court should promulgate regulations regarding rites and music, and order people to discuss and practice them."

Zhu Xi replied: "If we look at it from the perspective of recent events in Zhejiang, the provincial and county governments there regarded the ordinary people as akin to animals, and so even in a year with a plentiful harvest many died of starvation![15] Even a hundred master musicians like Marquis Kui could not restore harmony among these people!"[16] (*ZZYL*, chapter 108, p. 2683)

17. When it comes to institutions it is easy to talk. The question is how to get people to put them into action! (*ZZYL*, chapter 108, p. 2683)

18. It is good to establish regulations that are simple and easy so that people can follow them. To be sure, a reason why the regulations of the wellfield system of the Xia and Shang lasted so long was because they were carried on by sagely and worthy rulers. But it was also because the regulations were simple, unlike the complicated and fragmentary regulations of the Zhou. The Duke of Zhou had no other choice at the time, but it was just because of the complexity of those regulations that they were easily abandoned [in later times]. If Kongzi [Confucius] had been able to continue the institutions and regulations of the Zhou he most certainly would have made them simple and easy, without reaching the levels of complexity and fragmentation that they attained. Today's regulations are extremely complex and people are not able to adapt to them. This is the reason the government only concerns itself with building border fortresses.[17] (*ZZYL*, chapter 108, p. 2683)

19. It does no good to address defects [in the current political situation] through short-term fixes. In this respect we could draw an analogy to

---

15. Zhu is likely referring to a period in the early 1180s during which he, as intendant of Zhejiang, was responsible for addressing wide-scale hunger brought about by extreme drought conditions there. Zhu tried to alleviate the crisis by confiscating food stores from wealthy families in the area. He also blamed some local officials for the drought, impeaching and bringing charges against several of them, most famously Tang Zhongyou 唐仲友 (c. 1136–1188), a relative of the Prime Minister.

16. Marquis Kui 后夔 was the mythological inventor of music and dance and the supposed Director of Music for the legendary Emperor Shun.

17. Border fortresses were often garrisoned by conscripts sentenced to military service for committing crimes.

washing clothes. What's needed is an excellent clothes-washer, someone who will carefully and systematically wash each piece of the clothing. Only then will one's efforts not be in vain and will there be a likelihood of improvement. (*ZZYL*, chapter 108, p. 2684)

20. As a sage sees it, it is of course always possible that something could be done in the world [to improve the situation]. But if the power afforded by his position and circumstances does not suffice for him to act, he, too, will be unable to have an effect. (*ZZYL*, chapter 108, p. 2684)

21. To steer the course of future events by carefully examining their subtle incipiencies before they take shape—who other than someone who understands the Way is able to do such a thing! (*ZZYL*, chapter 108, p. 2684)

22. People who are very capable always first assess the circumstances; only when they are certain that there is a pattern-principle for doing something do they go ahead and do it. (*ZZYL*, chapter 108, p. 2684)

23. When not capable [of doing something well on one's own] one should just adhere carefully to the ordinary rules and standards (*fa* 法). (*ZZYL*, chapter 108, p. 2684)

24. Xun Yue said: "Implementing a program of moral education [*jiaohua* 教化] will draw average people into the domain of the noble person. Abolishing moral education will push them down into the streets of the petty person."[18] If people everywhere were to uphold the responsibilities of their offices then even if there were some who were incapable they would still make an effort, fearing what would be said about them publicly. But since there is no public discussion [of the character and behavior expected of people in office] there is nothing for those office-holders to be afraid of! (*ZZYL*, chapter 108, p. 2685)

25. With respect to the people who have talent in this society, if one could reduce their excesses and urge them on when they are deficient, they could perform their tasks. When they take up their responsibilities they would stand above that [grade of public servant who is] conscientious about

---

18. Xun Yue 荀悦 (148–209) was a Confucian thinker and official historian in the Eastern Han dynasty. He thought most people were by nature of mixed moral quality and maintained that both moral education and a system of regulations and punishments were necessary to correct for natural human deficiencies.

trivial matters to the neglect of the big picture. (*ZZYL*, chapter 108, p. 2685)

26. Those who are greedy and corrupt invariably regard those who are incorruptible as wrong, and competitive people invariably think those who contentedly withdraw from the competition are wrong. By inferring from these cases to similar ones we can see that all ordinary people are like this. (*ZZYL*, chapter 108, p. 2685)

27. Huang Gan said: "Once when I was speaking with the Master, I suggested that there is currently a grade of people who are talented at getting their work done, but for whom it would be difficult to guarantee success if they don't understand the ethics and pattern-principles [*yili*] of what they do. The Master didn't agree. He thought that putting it this way suggests that the only employable people are those that take my own side on the matters at hand, that if someone doesn't take my side then he's not a person of talent!" (*ZZYL*, chapter 108, p. 2686)

28. Everything that has gone wrong with people of talent today is due to the slandering and rejection of the proper study of the Learning of the [Confucian] Way [*Daoxue* 道學]. The way of ruling is most certainly rooted in rectifying the heart-mind and cultivating the self. One must truly see this point and then start from there. Instead, today's scholar-officials say that if they do their work as it is convenient for them, they will be able to accomplish it. They think all talk of pursuing the Learning of the Way, all talk of rectifying the heart-mind and cultivating the self, is idle and of no use to themselves. If someone folds his hands in front of his chest and plants his feet together [the sort of ritual expression of respect and deference that one would expect of someone who takes Confucian cultivation seriously], they say he is putting on a superior affectation, that he is seeking to boost his reputation, that he is aloof. One must be as slovenly as a street person to be considered a learned Confucian of true talent! (*ZZYL*, chapter 108, pp. 2686–2687)

29. It is not the Way of the sages and worthies to seek for approval in everything, to strive for success, to always try to gain just the superficial branches of wisdom, or to fail to follow what's correct in the pattern-principle of Heaven. (*ZZYL*, chapter 108, p. 2687)

30. Someone asked: "For those with the power to govern, should they treat leniency as fundamental and severity as playing a supporting role?"

Master Zhu replied: "I say that severity should be fundamental and leniency should play the supporting role. As it says in the 'Quli' ['Summary of Rites' chapter of the *Rites*], 'In conducting the responsibilities of one's office and carrying out the regulations, if one isn't ritually proper then one will fail to effect awe and severity.'[19] One must ensure that the orders are carried out and prohibitions heeded. It would be wrong to claim that there is leniency in allowing orders and prohibitions to be ignored and unheeded." (*ZZYL*, chapter 108, p. 2689)

31. When the ancients governed they made leniency fundamental in all respects. Today this has had to be reversed so that severity is fundamental. Surely this is because things must be straightened out in this manner before there is even the means by which to achieve what's proper. People today have become so lenient that there is no unity or discipline in affairs at all. We have no power to determine how urgent a task should be, what should be given or taken. In the end it is the schemers and the most brazen people who get their wish. Under these circumstances, the common people not only fail to receive the benefits [intended by those who govern] but also have disaster inflicted upon them. (*ZZYL*, chapter 108, p. 2689)

32. Among those who argue for leniency in the use of coercive powers to govern, most are not in charge of anything. I regard them as having ruined this character "leniency [*kuan* 寬]." (*ZZYL*, chapter 108, p. 2689)

33. The foundation of ruling lies in being amiable and close to the people.[20] (*ZZYL*, chapter 108, p. 2689)

34. Of the greatest affairs of the empire that cannot be treated lightly, none are more important than the use of the military and the apportioning of punishments. Carelessness when one is on the brink of deploying troops for battle can result in the accidental deaths of several people. This is why Laozi says, "Fine weapons are inauspicious instruments, the sage uses them only when he has no other choice."[21] When trying criminal charges or hearing litigation it's easy enough to look at events as they are

---

19. *Rites* 1A.8.

20. Here, "ruling" is a translation of *zheng* 政, which refers in particular to the sort of governing done by someone who has (but doesn't necessarily use) coercive powers to compel people's obedience by force.

21. Zhu paraphrases *Daodejing*, chapter 31. For a translation, see Ivanhoe 2002, 31.

presented before one, but when it's hard to determine what is actual and what is fabrication, or when a human life is at stake and both litigants stick to their own accounts with no third parties to corroborate either side, then one must ponder it very carefully for fear of making a mistake. (*ZZYL*, chapter 110, p. 2711)

35. On issues of punishment Zhu Xi said: "Nowadays when people argue for reducing the severity of someone's punishment they only do it out of pity for the criminal, without thinking about the victims, who are deserving of greater consideration. Take those who commit robbery and murder, for example. Many seek to spare their lives and fail to take the innocence of the deceased into consideration. This is to attend to the worth of robbers and thieves while giving no consideration to good people. In cases like cheating on wine taxes or pilfering during a period of famine one also should adjust the severity of punishment in light of the seriousness of the circumstances." (*ZZYL*, chapter 110, p. 2711)

36. Li Gonghui asked: "On the character *shu* 恕 [sympathetic concern, clemency], most of those in earlier generations took this to mean caring for others. What do you think of that explanation?"

    Zhu Xi replied: "In the final analysis, 'caring for others' is the most common sense of the character." He continued: "Human life is supremely valuable, so why do state officials hold executions in marketplaces? Surely it is because the people executed have killed other people, and if the murderers were not executed then there would be no way to uphold justice in the face of the wrong done to them. In this the caring heart-mind comes down on the side of the murder victim. Nevertheless, the ancients did endorse the views that one should 'go light when the crime is in doubt' and that 'it is better to err and permit a judicial irregularity than to kill an innocent person.'[22] So although the caring heart-mind just comes down on the side of the murder victim some of its care does spill over to the other side." (*ZZYL*, chapter 110, p. 2712)

37. The larger the area that one governs, the more difficult it becomes. Being a provincial inspector is not as easy as being a prefect, and being a prefect is not as easy as being a county magistrate. Surely this is because of the types of humane and caring heart-mind required for the positions, with a

---

22. *Book of Documents* 1.3, "The Counsels of Great Yu."

different type needed for each magnitude. If something needs to be done and the official does not do it, then there is no chance that he will be able to reach the people. (*ZZYL*, chapter 112, p. 2733)

38. Regardless of how great or humble one's office is, there is only one standard of public-orientedness no matter what the task. When someone is truly public-oriented what he does will be truly refined. Even if he occupies a humble office, others will gaze upon him with great awe. If he isn't public-oriented then even if he's a prime minister he can do this and that and yet still have no good outcomes. (*ZZYL*, chapter 112, p. 2735)

39. Zhu Xi once lamented that provincial and county officials so busied themselves with unimportant matters that they never allowed people opportunities to bring formal suits or complaints [before them], and, moreover, that it was so difficult to know the true feelings and condition of the people and so hard to find those who could serve as one's eyes and ears, that no matter how clearly they might inquire there was still much they did not know. With these points in mind, how could officials be sure they had gotten everything exactly right when it came time to make a clear and certain decision? . . . (*ZZYL*, chapter 112, p. 2735)

Bibliography

Angle, Stephen C., and Justin Tiwald. 2017. *Neo-Confucianism: A Philosophical Introduction*. Malden, MA: Polity.

de Bary, William Theodore, and Irene Bloom, eds. 1999. *Sources of Chinese Tradition*, Vol. 1. New York: Columbia University Press.

Ivanhoe, Philip J., trans. 2002. *The Daodejing of Laozi*. Cambridge, MA: Hackett.

Song, Jaeyoon. 2011. "Redefining Good Government: Shifting Paradigms in Song Dynasty (960–1279) Discourse on 'Fengjian.'" *T'oung Pao* 97: 301–343.

Tillman, Hoyt Cleveland. 1982. *Utilitarian Confucianism*. Cambridge, MA: Council on East Asian Studies.

Further Readings

Hymes, Robert P., and Conrad Schirokauer, eds. 1993. *Ordering the World: Approaches to State and Society in Sung Dynasty China*. Berkeley: University of California, chapters 4–5.

Schirokauer, Conrad. 1978. "Chu Hsi's Political Thought." *Journal of Chinese Philosophy* 5: 127–148.

Tillman, Hoyt Cleveland. 1992. *Confucian Discourse and Chu Hsi's Ascendancy.* Honolulu: University of Hawaii Press, chapters 5 and 7.

Poetry, Literature, Textual Study, and Hermeneutics

On-cho Ng

Introduction

The translated passages by Zhu Xi in this chapter illustrate the lineaments of his hermeneutics, together with his views on literature and poesy. Zhu's hermeneutics is dedicated to revealing the ultimate, most notably conceived as pattern-principle (*li* 理), and the Way (*dao* 道). Zhu elevated the Four Books as scriptural texts with canonical authority, regarding them as the sages' words par excellence and encasing the cosmological truth of *li* and *dao*. In Zhu's hermeneutics, reading and understanding are charismatic in nature, insofar as the reader can fathom and penetrate the mind of the classics' authors (the sages) through self-cultivation and investigation of things, leading eventually to the apprehension of the ultimate principle of *li*. Zhu's exegesis has been criticized for its latitude, which seems to play fast and loose with the words of the original texts. If indeed this criticism is valid, it is because he identifies the reader with the author in the sense that they share the same heart-mind, such that understanding can be attained outside of the remit of words and texts. Textual investigation, in the end, is merely a means to apprehend the truth of *li*. In other words, reading is the very realization of the Way, and the Six Classics are the works of the Three Dynasties that demonstrate the workings of pattern-principle in the midst of the Way.

Even though our heart-mind is ultimately the same as that of the sages, we still have to work hard in our pursuit of learning through reading. Zhu tells us how we should read in the most meticulous, thorough, unbiased, and exhaustive way. The goal of such unstintingly careful reading is to understand every part and detail of the text at hand, even if we have to read it a hundred times. Procedurally, he exhorts us to focus on the main arguments before moving on to dissecting the details, always seeking to lay bare the coherence of the text by exposing and making clear the multiple meanings of the words as they are situated in varying contexts. He informs us of the right order and sequence of reading, first taking on the Four Books before the other classics and histories. He warns us against just relying on commentaries, which should be consulted only after perusal of the original texts.

But in the final analysis, Zhu does not endorse reading that is primarily reliant and premised on textual components. Reading, as far as he is concerned, is but "one task of the investigation of things," whose goal is to comprehend the *li* and *dao* embodied in the classics and not to wallow in the words and phrases themselves. Zhu posits that the Way is the root and trunk of texts, and texts are the branches and leaves. Accordingly, he shows his displeasure, for instance, with Su Shi's approach to reading, which privileges and luxuriates in the text, therefore missing the profound root, the Way. Zhu's principal concern is with the direct and unmediated apprehension of pattern-principle via reading, which is imminently possible because the readers and the authors (the sages) share the same heart-mind.

Thus, Zhu portrays the act of reading as an experiential act of sensory embodiment and engagement, as it cannot be simply a philological and textual exercise. Reading is really talking directly with the sages, face to face. Zhu also tells us that reading is like eating. In the case of eating a piece of fruit, for instance, the first bites will not fully convey the flavors. But when the process of chewing continues until the fruit is broken down, all the flavor will come out. Since reading is like eating, Zhu cautions against textual gluttony. Just as proper nourishment will only come if one eats appropriately in such a way that the consumed food is fully digested, so too one must read mindfully, prudently, and judiciously, so that pattern-principle is thoroughly understood. Zhu's approach to reading is thus instinctual, like the natural act of eating. He is convinced that the reader has direct access to the *li* embodied in the classics, if only one's heart-mind is untrammeled by private desires and distracted thoughts. It is small wonder that on occasions, Zhu asks us to scrub clean the heart-mind while reading.

In short, Zhu's hermeneutics is religiously inspired, entirely committed to the *dao* and all-pervading *li* that inhere in the classics, whose authors' intents can be apprehended by the charismatic reader in an autogenetic way, eliding textual and intellectual endeavors.

Given Zhu's stress on the deeply instinctual experience as a crucial part of both the act of reading and the experience of understanding, he presumes an intimate relation between poesy, classical studies, and ethical melioration. What gives substance to the poems in the *Odes* is moral pattern-principle, hermeneutically obtainable from the text. They stimulate and bring forth our finer purposes and motives, playing crucial roles in self-cultivation. They exemplify what Zhu calls the "correct/orthodox" poetry, which is educative and inspiring, as opposed to the "altered/heterodox" one, such as Qu Yuan's *Chuci*, even though the latter can be useful in offering instructions and warnings via negative examples. But because of the emotional potency of poesy, it must be treated with care, lest it be misused and abused as distorted expression of our feelings toward reality. Zhu sings the praises of poetry that is not laden with artificial, literary adornment, such as that of Tao Qian and Li Bo and celebrates poems from the Han, Wei, and Western Jin periods, collected in the *Wenxuan* (anthology of select literary works) compiled by Xiao Tong (501–531).

As for literature and belles-lettres, or *wen*, in general, Zhu sees its function and value in terms of the accommodation and encapsulation of the Way (*wen yi zaidao* 文以載道). For this reason, he takes to task Su Shi's famous proclamation that literature must go along with the Way (*wen bi yi yu dao ju* 文必以與道俱). Zhu presumes the mutual identity of literature and the Way, whereas Su only sees their connection. Zhu faults Su for giving literary aesthetics and the attendant emotions an independent ontological niche. To Zhu, accommodation of the Way is the very encapsulation of pattern-principle and moral pattern-principles (*yili* 義理), which is the primary function of literature. As with his stance on poetry, literature must not be defined in terms of verbal adornment (*cihua* 辭花), because its objective is always to convey ideas (*dayi* 達意), in light of the foremost need to carry the Way. The former is a symptom of a degenerate and decadent sociopolitical milieu, while the latter is a manifestation of strength and vigor. In short, he takes substance over style, for *wen*, after all, represents the branches and leaves of learning, not the roots and trunk.

Translations
Hermeneutics

1. The Six Classics are the works of the Three Dynasties and before, and having passed through the hands of the sages, they are in their entirety Heavenly pattern-principle. (*ZZYL*, chapter 11, p. 190)

2. The sages wrote the classics in order to teach later generations. These texts enable the reader to reflect on the ideas of the sages while reciting their words, and hence to understand what is in accordance with the pattern-principle of things, see the entirety of the proper Way itself, practice the Way with all of one's strength, and thereby enter the realm of the sages and worthies. (*ZZWJ*, chapter 82, in *ZZQS*, vol. 24, p. 3895)[1]

3. We rely on the classics to understand pattern-principle. Once pattern-principle is apprehended, there is no need for the classics. If our ideas and intentions are always stuck on them [i.e., the classics and their commentaries], when will we ever attain a liberatingly thorough understanding [of pattern-principle]? (*ZZYL*, chapter 11, p. 192)

4. To read is to observe the intentions of the sages and worthies. To follow the intentions of the sages and worthies is to observe the natural pattern-principle. (*ZZYL*, chapter 10, p. 162)

5. Do our best to study the books of the sages so that we understand their intentions and ideas, like speaking with them face to face. (*ZZYL*, chapter 10, p. 162)

6. Reading is one task in the investigation of things (*gewu yishi* 格物一事). We must now carefully savor the taste of each paragraph, reading it over and over again. In one day or two days, only one paragraph is read, and this paragraph then becomes a part of us. After establishing a solid foothold in this paragraph, we then read the second paragraph. We persist and persevere in this way. After such persistence, we will discern the pattern-principle of the Way in its entirety. Such effort requires reflection while walking and thinking while sitting [i.e., incessantly], every now and again reflecting repeatedly on what is already known. Then understanding will naturally occur, without our making arrangements

1. *ZZWJ* refers to *Hui'an xiansheng Zhu Wengong wenji* 晦庵先生朱文公文集 (*The Collected Writings of Master Hui'an, Zhu, Duke of Culture*). *ZZQS* refers to *Zhuzi quanshu* 朱子全書 (*The Complete Works of Master Zhu*). See Zhu Xi 2002 in the bibliography.

for it. The phraseology and meaning of a text may have been explained this way or that, but each time it is read, there is a new understanding. Therefore, for any text, each individual reading leads to revision. For texts whose explications have been firmly established, each reading leads to firmer discernment, with far greater clarity. Therefore, I have said that in reading, one should not value copiousness; one should only value familiarity with what is read. Nonetheless, the hard work will only yield results if we bravely move forward, not ever thinking about retreating or turning back. Only then will things work. (*ZZYL*, chapter 10, p. 167)

7. In reading, you should just look at the meanings of the words of a paragraph in question. There is surely no need to create side issues. While reading the one paragraph, you must read it over and over again. You have to be totally familiar with it. Only then can the meanings be seen; only then can pleasure be felt. Only if you don't relish the idea of moving on to read another paragraph will you apprehend [the one paragraph you are reading]. People often forge ahead without looking back to reflect, only wishing to look at tomorrow's stuff that has not yet been read, and not ever inquiring about yesterday's stuff that has been read. You must over and over again savor the flavors [of the text]; only then will you attain [understanding]. If the effort exerted is great, understanding is extensive. When understanding is extensive, its utility is lasting and assured.

   He also said, "You must not open your mouth rashly, speaking vaguely and broadly. There must be understanding within the heart-mind." (*ZZYL*, chapter 10, p, 167)

8. In reading to discern the pattern-principle of the Way, one must be open-minded, transparently and plainly tolerant, freely going [to where the reading leads]. The first thing is not to oblige your reading with results, as the obligation for results will result in underlying worries and anxieties. Thus, [worries and anxieties] will congeal into something like a caked object in the mind, which does not break up. Now, just let go of trivial matters and don't think trivial thoughts. You have to only focus your heart-mind to savor the taste of moral pattern-principles, and then your heart-mind will become refined. When your heart-mind is refined, you will become familiar [with pattern-principle] (*ZZYL*, chapter 10, p. 164)

9. When people read a text these days, even when they have not reached a certain point here and now, their heart-minds are already on what comes later. When they do reach the point here and now, they want to abandon it and move

forward. Accordingly, they themselves do not seek thorough understanding. We must linger and love what is being read, as though we cannot bear to leave it. Only then can we understand it in an empathetic and visceral way.

He also said, "Reading is like observing a house here. If we view the house from the outside and say that it has been seen, there is no way for us to get to know it. We must go inside, viewing everything individually, and making inquiry into the size and the layout, and the extent of the latticework and windows. After the first viewing, we need to continue to see it time and again, so that the entire whole is committed to memory. Such is the right way." (*ZZYL*, chapter 10, p. 173)

10. Generally speaking, to read is surely to become familiar with [*shoudu* 熟讀, lit. to thoroughly cook] what is read. After being familiar with what is read, reading is naturally refined. With refined reading, pattern-principle can naturally be discerned. It is like eating a piece of fruit. When it is first bitten into, the flavor is not discerned, but it is eaten anyway. It must be chewed carefully until it is broken down, and then the flavor will come out. Only then will we begin to know if it is sweet or bitter, nectarous or acrid; only then will we begin to know the flavor.

He also said, "Gardeners water the gardens. Those who are adept at watering do so with the vegetables and fruits individually, according to their needs. Before long, the watering is sufficient. The soil and water are well balanced, and the plants, receiving nourishment, will naturally grow. Those who are not adept at watering rush to take care of things, using buckets and buckets to saturate the vegetables in the garden. People may see them tending the gardens but the plants never do get proper watering." (*ZZYL*, chapter 10, p. 167)

11. He also said, "The method of reading is such that one reads with great diligence. Much effort is expended on the initial book but later ones will not require much [effort]. At the beginning, one book will consume every bit of one's energy. The following one will consume eighty to ninety percent, and the following one will consume sixty to seventy percent, and the following one will consume forty to fifty percent." (*ZZYL*, chapter 10, p. 167)

12. Reading must involve focus. Read this one sentence and then understand this one sentence. Read this one chapter and then understand this one chapter. It must be that one chapter is completed before another chapter should be read. Don't think about another chapter and another sentence.

You only need to coolly and calmly read on the side [you are working on], and you also should not exert the heart-mind and think excessively, as before long, you may harm your spirit. The respected ones who came before us said: "In reading, we cannot but exercise reverential attention (*jing* 敬)." With reverential attention comes focused concentration, and the heart-mind will not stray. (*ZZYL*, chapter 10, p. 168)

13. Generally speaking, reading a book must involve intimate familiarity [with it], such that all its words seem to have come from my own mouth. Continuing to reflect intently on it, all its ideas will seem to come from my own heart-mind. Only then is there success. Yet, after intimate reading and focused thinking that lead to understanding, we must question if there is more to this, and then there may be further progress. If you think that this is the end, then there will never be progress again. (*ZZYL*, chapter 10, p. 168)

14. To be a person is just to be a person, to read a book is just to read a book. Usually, a person who does not understand after reading [a book] ten times should read it twenty times, and if [one] still does not understand, [one] should read thirty to fifty times, and then there will surely be understanding. If after fifty times, one is still in the dark without understanding, then it is that one's material nature (*qizhi* 氣質) is not good. People nowadays who have not yet read a book even ten times claim that the book can't be understood. (*ZZYL*, chapter 10, p. 168)

15. Reading cannot do without establishing the limit at the outset. [It] should be managed like farm work, where the farms have boundaries. Such is also the case in the pursuit of learning. Today's scholars do not realize this pattern-principle, so that when they first start, they are tremendously eager. But then they become gradually slothful, and in the end, they pay no attention whatsoever. This is all because there is no setting of the limit at the very outset. (*ZZYL*, chapter 10, p. 174)

16. The method of reading begins with becoming familiar with what is read (cf. section 10 in this chapter). You must look at [the text] front and back, left and right. But even when you think the correct view is attained, it still cannot be said that the Way is there. You must still savor the text time and again. (*ZZYL*, chapter 10, p. 165)

17. Read less but become familiar with [what is being read]; experience and test repeatedly [what is being read]; and refrain resolutely from

calculations of gains [from what is being read]. These are the only three things that should be constantly adhered to. (*ZZYL*, chapter 10, p. 165)

18. In reading, be modest with the design of curriculum but lavish with the exertion of effort. Even if you can read two hundred characters, read only a hundred characters, but exert the fiercest of efforts on the hundred characters. Understand every little detail. Read and recite until what is taught [in the reading] becomes familiar. In this way, even forgetful people will naturally remember, and those who lack the native ability to comprehend will also be able to understand. If you read much but in a general, superficial way, there are no benefits at all. In reading a text, you should not read it alongside [other texts] that you have never read before, but you should read it alongside [other texts] that you have already read before. (*ZZYL*, chapter 10, p. 165)

19. In reading, you should not covet copiousness. Rather, be expert and familiar [with what is read]. If you are able to read a page today, read only half the page. Read the first half of the page with the utmost energy. Only when you read both halves in this manner will you become familiar [with the whole page]. Your reading will be right only if you discern directly the meanings and intents of the ancients. (*ZZYL*, chapter 10, p. 166)

20. In reading, you must know the place where everything connects. Whether [coming at it from] the east or the west, they are all in contact at this pivotal point. Only so is [understanding] achieved. Just focus your head on the task at hand, not thinking about the past or predicting the future, and you will naturally reach the place. But now you say that you did not complete [the task]; you fear that you may be late and tardy; you fear that you are not up to the task; you fear that it is difficult; you fear that you are by nature unintelligent; and you fear you are forgetful. All this is idle talk! Just focus your head on the task at hand, and do not ask if you will be slow or fast. Soon you will get to the place. If you have not done this before, you should now exert effort to make amends. Don't be looking around worriedly at the future or the past, thinking and considering east and west, or before long, you will have frittered away your whole life, not realizing that you have grown old! (*ZZYL*, chapter 10, p. 164)

21. In reading, it is only by focusing attention on and savoring the taste [of the text] that moral pattern-principles can be seen to be emerging from the prose and words. (*ZZYL*, chapter 10, p. 173)

22. In reading, one must discern the rhetorical style and verbal continuity. (*ZZYL*, chapter 10, p. 173)

23. In reading, you must look for an opening in the text, for only then will the moral pattern-principles be found in the most thorough manner. If the opening is not discerned, then there is no way to enter the text. Discerning an opening, the context and continuity of the text will naturally be laid bare. (*ZZYL*, chapter 10, p. 162)

24. When it comes to [reading] long passages of words and phrases, tackle in the most painstaking way three to five points, and what comes next will be easily solved, like a knife splitting [bamboo]. What afflicts scholars is superficial [effort], not being painstakingly immersed [in learning]. (*ZZYL*, chapter 10, p. 162)

25. When people nowadays read, they begin by first setting up their opinions before reading. They gather all the words of the ancients in so as to create their own meanings. This way, merely one's own intentions are elaborated; how can the intentions of the ancients be seen? Humbly place the words of the ancients before you and see where their intentions are going. As Mencius says about poetry, "One meets the aims [of the poet] with one's intention" (5A4). Now "meets" means "awaits." It is as though you are waiting for someone on the road ahead. When he hasn't come, you must wait patiently, and the time will come when he arrives. If when he hasn't arrived and you become impatient and move ahead to find him, then you are not meeting the aim with intention but rather seizing the aim by using your intention. This way, you are just twisting the words of the ancients to suit your own intentions. There will in the end be no progress or gain. (*ZZYL*, chapter 11, p. 180)

26. In reading a text, read a large passage with the utmost appreciation. Rouse your spirit, keep your body upright, and don't fret as though a dagger and a sword were at your back! Be most thoroughgoing in penetrating even one passage. Hit its head and the tail will respond; hit its tail and the head will respond. Only then is reading done right. It should not be the case that you are with the book when it is opened, and you forget it when it is closed. [Nor should it be the case that] when you look at the commentary, you forget the original text, and when you look at the original, you forget the commentary. You must fully penetrate one passage before moving on to later pages. (*ZZYL*, chapter 10, p. 163)

27. What is necessary is to leave one scar with one blow of the truncheon, to have blood on the palm with one slap! This is precisely how to read others' words. How can you ever neglect that? (*ZZYL*, chapter 10, p. 164)

28. Reading words and texts is like a cruel official applying the severest of regulations to the extreme, entirely devoid of pity [lit. human sentiments]. If they are just casually read, then where are the taste and flavor? Whenever there are places in the text that you don't understand, you must exert the utmost effort, not stopping until you thoroughly discern the moral pattern-principles. (*ZZYL*, chapter 10, p. 164)

29. Reading texts and words is like catching a thief. You must reconstruct the details of the crime, including stolen items worth even as little as a penny. If only the general outline [of the theft] is portrayed, even though you know who the thief is, you will still not know where the theft was committed. (*ZZYL*, chapter 10, p. 164)

30. After reading the words, one stops because one thinks that one already attains understanding. In fact, after such understanding, one must ponder if there is more behind [the words]. Moreover, even if one picks up a piece of text and reads it, one may not entirely and thoroughly understand its meanings, let alone the moral pattern-principles. As the respected elders would say, even if [a text] seems easily comprehensible, it is not the case that its meanings are explained and apprehended. It must be read and read again, only focusing on reading and focusing on obtaining the meanings. (*ZZYL*, chapter 10, p. 173)

31. The reader should not be obsessed with the idea of finishing, as once there is this obsession, the mind will be fixated on the blank page at the very end. It is not beneficial. (*ZZYL*, chapter 10, p. 173)

32. If people constantly read books, then most likely, this heart-mind can be controlled, thus constantly being preserved. (*ZZYL*, chapter 11, p. 176)

33. When one first practices reverential attentiveness, one cannot avoid lapses. But once the lapses are felt, one rouses the heart-mind. Where there is this awareness, then there is the resumption [of reverential attentiveness]. What I want is for people, through reading books, to experience moral pattern-principles with their selves. If they read books daily, then this heart-mind will not stray. But if they are involved only in affairs and things, then this heart-mind can easily become submerged. Knowing that it is so, [they] experience moral pattern-principles with their selves

through reading books, and they can be summoned back [to learning]. (*ZZYL*, chapter 11, p. 176)

34. If the original heart-mind (*ben xin* 本心) has long been submerged and moral pattern-principles not thoroughly nourished, then it is necessary to read books to exhaustively explore pattern-principle. In so doing without interruption, the heart-mind of material desires (*wuyu zhi xin* 物欲之心) will naturally not triumph, and the moral pattern-principles of the original heart-mind will naturally be safe and secure. (*ZZYL*, chapter 11, p. 176)

35. Preservation of the heart-mind and the reading of books must be taken as the same thing. Only then will it be right. (*ZZYL*, chapter 11, p. 177)

36. Because the heart-mind is not stable, pattern-principle is not discerned. So now in reading books, the heart-mind must first be stabilized, rendering it like still water and a bright mirror. How can a murky mirror reflect things? (*ZZYL*, chapter 11, p. 177)

37. There is a method to reading books. It is to just scrub clean the heart-mind. If you don't understand [what you are reading], put [the book] down and wait till your ideas and thoughts are clear before picking it up in due time. Now we talk about having an empty heart-mind, but how can the heart-mind be emptied? It is just to place the heart-mind onto the text. (*ZZYL*, chapter 11, p. 177)

Views on Literature

38. Literature (*wen*) carries the Way (*dao*) (*wen suoyi zaidao* 文所以載道) much as a carriage carries things. Therefore, just as one who manufactures the carriage will surely decorate its wheels, so too will one who produces literature make fine phraseology and verbiage, as they both wish people will love and make use of them. But if I decorate them and people do not make use of them, then they are empty decorations, which do not benefit the real world. Furthermore, when it comes to a carriage that does not carry things and literature that does not carry the Way, even if the decorations are beautiful, what are they for after all? (Zhou 1937, chapter 10, p. 180)

39. [Chen] Caiqing asked, "The first sentence of Li Han's preface to Han Yu's collected writings is very good."

[Zhu] replied, "Sir, you say it's good, but I view it as having a fault."

Chen said, "'Literature (*wen*) is an implement that threads together the Way (*wen zhe guandao zhi qi* 文者貫道之器).'[2] Now, even the Six Classics are *wen,* in which all that is said is the pattern-principle of the Way. So how can there be a fault?"

[Zhu] replied, "It's not so. This *wen* flows entirely from the Way, and so how can there be this pattern-principle such that *wen* is on the contrary able to thread together the Way? *Wen* is *wen,* and *dao* is *dao. Wen* is precisely like the side dishes in a meal. If literature is used to thread together the Way, then it is like taking the branch as the root, and the root as the branch. How is that admissible?" (*ZZYL,* chapter 139, p. 3305)

40. People nowadays write prose pieces, but none amount to prose. Generally speaking, most focus on the matters of trivial words, while also developing a liking for newfangled words and phrases. When it comes to explaining moral pattern-principles, they refuse to provide clear illustration. Looking at the prose composed by respected elders like masters Ou[yang Xiu] and Su [Shi], in what ways have they ever been like this? The words of the sages and worthies are plain and easily understood. In accordance with these words, the Way is illuminated. They wanted those of later generations to seek [the Way] through them [i.e., their words]. Had the sages wanted to establish words that were hard to understand, the classics of the sages would surely not have been written. Where moral pattern-principles are recondite and people generally do not understand them, it is just that people have not yet arrived at understanding on their own. Scholars must savor the flavor of and deeply ponder [the text] in a prolonged manner, and in time, understanding will naturally come. Has it ever been like what people nowadays do: wishing to speak about the text but at the same time fearful about speaking of understanding, never knowing what has been discerned? In the final analysis, it is that the people themselves do not understand what is read, and so they do not dare to speak penetratingly, but they nonetheless rashly pounce on what is being said inside [the text] like a hawk. (*ZZYL,* chapter 139, p. 3318)

41. To thoroughly comprehend the hundred philosophers, classics, and histories is to use them to identify and corroborate right and wrong, so that moral pattern-principles are illuminated. How can it simply be the

---

2. This is the sentence from the preface to Han Yu's (韓愈 768–824) collected works, *Changli xiansheng ji* 昌黎先生集, to which Chen referred here.

desire to ensure that one's words and prose are not inelegant? With the illumination of moral pattern-principles, together with tirelessly acting [on them], even those that are preserved [at the core] in the center will become bright and shine forth to reach all four quarters, and they can be applied in any manner. [Moral pattern-principles], manifested as words, proclaim the commitments of the heart-mind, which will naturally grow and spread in extraordinary ways. They can be loved and transmitted. But nowadays, to hold the brush [i.e., to write] is to cleverly investigate and explore elegant prose, bent on pleasing people by dealing only with the exterior. It's really a shame! (*ZZYL*, chapter 139, p. 3319)

42. The Way is the roots and trunk of literature, and literature is the branches and leaves of the Way. As the Way is the roots and trunk, what is manifested through literature is entirely the Way. Writings of the worthies and sages of the Three Dynasties were produced from this heartfelt thought, and so literature was the Way. Nowadays, Su Dongpo says, "What I call literature must go along together with the Way (*wen bi yi yu dao ju* 文必以與道俱)." Accordingly, what is literature is literature, and what is the Way is the Way. So, when it is time to write, one has to readily find the one Way to put it inside the writing. Herein lies the great flaw. It is just that his words are usually so elegant and marvelous that this [flaw] is wrapped up in them, so it does not leak out. Speaking of his root problem, it is that for him, one always starts with literature and gradually addresses the pattern-principles of the Way. It is not that there should first be the explaining and understanding of the pattern-principles of the Way before literature is composed. Therefore, on the great root [of things], he is mistaken. Master Ouyang's prose is closer to the Way, not working with empty words. As the "Treatise on Music and Rites" of the *Tang History* says, "In the Three Dynasties and before, governance came from one source; since the Three Dynasties, governance came from two sources." These discussions are very good, as they know that there should only be one root. If we follow what Dongpo says, there are then two roots and not one root.[3] (*ZZYL*, chapter 139, p. 3319)

43. One day, talking about writing, [Zhu] said, "There is no need at all to focus on prose and verse as such, but it is necessary to illuminate pattern-principle. Upon knowing the essentials of pattern-principle, one's own

---

3. Here, he is borrowing the language of *Mencius*, 3A5.

texts and words will be solid with evidence. The texts and words of [Cheng] Yichuan in his twilight years, such as the *Commentary to the Classic of Changes* (*Yizhuan* 易傳), can truly hold water! Su Zizhan [Shi/Dongpo], even though he has great facilities in composing essays with majestic aura, in the end cannot avoid the flaws of shallowness and omission." (*ZZYL*, chapter 139, p. 3320)

44. While discussing literature, [Zhu] said, "The composition of words and texts must rely on concreteness (*shi* 實), so that what is said is shaped and ordered. Don't fuss with small gimmicks within an empty frame. In general terms, concreteness accounts for seventy percent, while refinement (*wen* 文) should only account for twenty or thirty percent. For example, Master Ou[yang Xiu]'s writings are good precisely because they rely on concreteness, with shape and order." (*ZZYL*, chapter 139, p. 3320)

45. Because [Zhu] was discussing how the literati nowadays loved to compose writings so as to address the question of benefit (*li* 利) and harm (*hai* 害), he talked about both and said, "It need not be like this at all. What is needed is only the understanding of moral pattern-principles. When moral pattern-principles are understood, then [the question of] benefit and harm is understood. Under Heaven, from antiquity to now, there is only this one pattern-principle. The way our contemporaries do things is subtly continuous with that of the ancients, because there is only one pattern-principle." (*ZZYL*, chapter 139, p. 3322)

46. When the respected elders composed texts and words, they did so by relying only on established form and protocol, and so they did it extremely well. Then later, people came to dislike the conventional form and worked with changed and new forms. But the foundation has to be good, and if it is not good, there will be, to begin with, strangeness.

   [Zhu] also said, "When the respected elders employed words, they certainly used what the ancients said, but they also used common and colloquial language. People of later generations all wanted to create a novel language, with the result that all literature became diverse and different, thereby replacing conventional ways of speaking with different ones." (*ZZYL*, chapter 139, p. 3320)

47. When asked about the words used in the "On Encountering Sorrow" (*Lisao* 離騷) and "Divination" (*Buju* 卜居) chapters in the *Songs of Chu* (*Chuci* 楚辭), Zhu said, "I have never understood the meaning at the level of the individual words, but the general meaning is evident. For example,

[the phrase], '... be obliging and unctuous, as yielding as lard and leather,' has the basic meaning of going along in the most yielding and welcoming way with the various wishes of people that come your way. Phrases like this don't present the smallest of obstacles to understanding, in that they are all uttered spontaneously as they become composed words. Lin Aixuan [Lin Guangchao 1114–1178] once said, 'Beginning with Ban Gu (32–92) and Yang Xiong (53 BCE–18 CE), all worked on manufacturing texts and words. But as for those who had come before, such as Sima Qian (145?–86? BCE) and Sima Xiangru (179–117 BCE), they only spoke spontaneously.' Based on my present view [of them], that was the case. The ancients were selected for office based on their ability 'to climb high and compose poetry [there and then].' This means that for certain, they were both quick-witted and knew how to speak most volubly and fluently. Perhaps it was that some of the ancients became renowned for their oral speech, and what they said was put on paper. But people of the later generations only worked with [words that were put on] paper. Since Ban and Yang, for example, worked on [putting words on] paper, they did not measure up to the language before them. At that time, both Su Qin (d. 317 BCE) and Zhang Yi (d. 309 BCE) could speak well. What the *Records of the Historian* (*Shiji* 史記) recorded were the spoken language of that time." (*ZZYL*, chapter 139, pp. 3297–3298)

48. Generally speaking, the writings of the ancients all traveled on the right path, but those who came later made up and added new things, all taking the narrow and treacherous heterodox path. So now, if you follow the orthodox standard and work with the pattern of the path, before long, your writings will naturally surpass those of others. (*ZZYL*, chapter 139, p. 3301)

49. There is the literature of the age of order, the literature of the age of decline, and the literature of the age of chaos. The Six Classics are the literature of the age of order, [whereas writings like] the dispiritingly apathetic and tediously fragmentary *Conversations from the States* (*Guoyu* 國語) are indeed the literature of the age of decline. The language and polemics at the time were such that they accurately suited the fact of the Zhou dynasty's inability to rise up to strength. As for the literature of the age of chaos, it was identified with the Warring States period [403–222 BCE]. But it possessed a heroic and majestic air that cannot be compared to the language of the *Conversations from the States* of the age of decline. Writings from the Chu and Han periods are truly marvelous and

majestic. How can it be easy to reach [their level]? (*ZZYL*, chapter 139, p. 3297)

50. Writings at the beginning of our dynasty were serious and mature. I once took a look at the edicts and related works from before the Jiayou period [1056–1063]. The language has some serious shortcomings even though the talented writers were renowned literati at that time. Notwithstanding the shortcomings of the language, its phraseology is prudent and weighty. It has the sense that it desires to be crafty but does not have the ability [to do so]. Therefore, its style is wholesome and generous. By the time we reach Master Ou[yang Xiu]'s writings, what was good was very good but there were still some very bad [elements], and so the air of peace and harmony had not yet dissipated. When we get to the writings of Dongpo, they had already rushed toward excessive wittiness. By the time of the Zheng-Xuan [Zhenghe (1111–1117) and Xuanhe (1119–1125)] periods, they became extremely grand and beautiful, thus losing the air of peace and harmony. When the sage [Kongzi] claimed that he preferred men of ancient times in matters of rites and music,[4] his idea was simply this. (*ZZYL*, chapter 139, p. 3307)

Views on Poesy

51. I [Zhu Xi] was asked, "Why was the *Odes* written?"

I replied, "That people are born quiescent is the nature (*xing* 性) [endowed by] Heaven. That they feel things and become active is the desires of nature. Once there are desires, they cannot be without aspirations. Once there are aspirations, they cannot be without speech. Once there is speech, what cannot be exhausted by speech will be expressed through sighs that linger, with a natural sound and rhythm that does not stop. That was why the *Odes* was composed."

[I was further] asked, "What is that which [the *Odes*] uses to teach?"

I said, "Poetry is the surplus that [occurs when] people's heart-minds feel things and then give form to them in words. Among what the heart-mind feels is that which is correct and that which is crooked, and so the language that gives shape [to them] can be right or wrong. Only the superior sages feel things in an invariably correct way, and so their words are

---

4. The reference is to *Analects* 11.1.

always sufficient as teachings. Perhaps the things they feel may be mixed, but what they express cannot but have been carefully selected. Thus, a morally superior person must think in order to self-reflect, offering in the process his admonition and condemnation, which become his teachings. . . . Kongzi, being born during this time [of chaos], . . . made a special effort to work on the texts of the *Odes* and develop a discourse on it, expunging the duplications and redundancies, and providing order to what was chaotic and disorganized. In his editing, he removed that which was good but not sufficient as models of virtues, and that which was bad but not sufficient as warnings against transgressions, in order to be succinct and concise, so that the *Odes'* durability and persistence may be demonstrated. [The *Odes*] enabled students to have the means of examining their merits and shortcomings, such that the good will find a teacher in it and the wicked will be reformed by it. . . . This is why the *Odes* is a Classic. With it, human affairs below may be determined, and the Way of Heaven above is replete. There is not one pattern-principle that is not complete in it."

I was still asked, "But how do we go about acquiring its learning?"

I replied, "[You should] base yourself [on the teachings of] the 'Two Souths' [i.e., the odes of 'Airs of Zhou and the South' and 'Shao and the South'] and seek their beginnings. [You should] refer to the 'Airs' of the various states so as to know thoroughly the changes wrought; [you should] rectify yourself with [the teachings of] the 'Elegantiae' so as to expand your horizons; and [you should] go along with [the teachings of] the 'Hymns' so as to establish the bounds. These are the main points about the learning of the *Odes*. Then use the stanzas and lines to create summaries; use philology to establish order; use chanting to give the odes clear voice; and immerse yourself in the *Odes* to embody them. Explore the subtle and hidden emotions in the midst [of the *Odes*], and investigate the guiding power that prompts the beginnings of speech and action. Then, the Way of cultivating the self, regulating the family, and bringing peace to the world can be obtained right here, without needing to wait and to seek it elsewhere." (*ZZWJ*, chapter 76, in *ZZQS*, vol. 24, pp. 3650–3651)

52. The [act] of reading the *Odes* is chanting and reciting. While pondering the elusive twists and turns of its intents, it is as if I myself am composing the poems. Naturally, it is sufficient to rouse a good heart-mind. Now, if in reading the *Odes*, you only use your own ideas to envelop it, then

it is similar to composing contemporary writing. Without ever under-standing the elusive twists and turns of the intents in the midst [of the *Odes*], what have you gained actually? (*ZZYL*, chapter 80, p. 2086)

53. Now that I have glossed the *Odes*, it has been explained and thus is easily comprehensible. But there is still the need to seriously recite and chant, savoring the taste of the moral pattern-principles, and chew on the flavor before one can gain [from reading it]. If you read the *Odes* cursorily and stop after only two or three days, not only will you not get the flavor but [you will] also forget [what you have read], so nothing is accomplished. The ancients said the *Odes* rouses the emotions,[5] so you have to read in such a way that emotions are roused. Only then are you reading the *Odes*. If there is no such arousal, you are not reading the *Odes*. (*ZZYL*, chapter 80, p. 2086)

54. Talking about Qu Yuan's character, his intention and action might have overstepped the bounds of the *Doctrine of the Mean* and so he cannot be a model.[6] But they came from the earnestness of being loyal to the ruler and loving the country, stemming from a wholesome heart. The words and meanings of his writings might be unrestrained and demonic, full of hatred and resentment, so that they cannot be lessons. But they came from genuine sentiments of profound concern and melancholy apprehension, which he could not help feeling. Since he did not know to go north and search for the way of the Duke of Zhou and Kongzi, he galloped around in the dying streams of changed Airs and changed Elegentiae [in a decadent literary tradition]. Therefore, pure Confucians and serious literati might be too ashamed to praise him. But if his writings enabled exiled officials, banished children, estranged women, and divorced wives to sing their laments, once their tears were wiped dry, so that they may have the good fortune of being heard by Heaven, then how could the writings, as far as interpersonal relations and the Heaven-endowed good nature among people are concerned, not promote mutual growth and augment the principles of Three Bonds and Five Relationships? This is why I always savor the flavor of his words and do not dare to view it as the literary composition of a poet. (*Chuci jizhu*, in *ZZQS*, vol. 19, p. 16)

---

5. Zhu is here quoting *Analects* 17.9.

6. Qu Yuan (c. 340–278 BCE), author of the famous *Songs of Chu* (*Chuci* 楚辭), heartbroken at the fall of the capital of his state of Chu, committed suicide by drowning himself in a river.

55. Writing poetry in itself is not a bad thing. That people deeply begrudge and reject it is due to the fear that it drifts into afflictions. But why should poetry be blamed to begin with? When a long separation is about to begin in short time, without poetic words, it will not be possible to write down the feelings that are hard to articulate. . . . Poetry first and foremost speaks of one's commitment and so one should dispel lingering sadness, and be at ease, calm, and centered. But if it drifts too far afield, then commitment will be destroyed. For a community, [poetry] is beneficial for the nurturing of humaneness. Thus, appropriately, its meanings should be refined and its pattern-principle apprehended, thereby animating and pondering the central relationships. Still, some may not be able to avoid drifting. How much more so when one leaves the community and lives apart, when things can change infinitely in split seconds? With what are we to defend against that which throws our eyes and ears into confusion and influences our intentions? (*ZXJ*, chapter 77, 4028–4029)[7]

56. There is no harm in writing a few lines of poetry that appeal to the heart, but there is no need to write much, lest you be mired in it. When one is not engaged in work, being calm and self-composed, what could be better than thinking over some lines of poetry? The true flavor then comes through, and this is different from those who regularly recite and chant [poems]. (*ZZYL*, chapter 140, p. 3333)

57. When I read Chen Zi'ang's (659–700) poem, "Inspired Encounters," I loved the subtlety and abstruseness of its language and intention, and plangency and resonance of its sound and rhythm, which cannot be reached by contemporary poets. . . . Wanting to emulate his style, I composed dozens of pieces. But because of limited imagination and meek writing ability, I failed to do it. However, I also regretted his lack of expertise in pattern-principle and his use of Daoism and Buddhism to create an air of sophistication. When I am not doing anything specific in my studio, I occasionally wrote about what I saw, amounting to some twenty pieces. Although they fail to fathom the subtle and distant, or to follow the steps of the former [poets], they are all relevant to the practicality of daily utility, and so their words are accessible and easily

---

7. *ZXJ* refers to *Zhu Xi ji* 朱熹集 (*Collected Work of Zhu Xi*): see Zhu Xi 1996 in the bibliography.

comprehensible. I use them to caution myself while sharing with the like-minded. (*ZZWJ*, chapter 4, in *ZZQS*, vol. 20, p. 360)

58. Lately, fearing that excessive words would harm the Way, I have absolutely abstained from writing poetry. But having read for two days the chapter, "Making Intention Sincere," in the *Great Learning*, I was moved. In the morning of the winter solstice, I wrote this for self-counsel, for I could not help but speak the words:

> *The spiritual heart-mind penetrates with profound understanding;*
> *Distinguishing good and bad as the fragrant or foul herb.*
> *Why have I been deceiving myself,*
> *And silently wrapping up my shame?*
> *Today is the winter solstice;*
> *I woke up sighing, feeling my hidden worries.*
> *My heart-mind knows that an inch of light*
> *Has come to shine on the dim unfathomable spring.*
> *The friendly will start to come from this point forward,*
> *And the drove of dark forces will remain no more.*
> *I have long been lost on my journey;*
> *Reaching this point, I shall turn my boat around.* (*ZZWJ*, chapter 2,
>   in *ZZQS*, vol. 20, p. 283)

Bibliography

Zhou Dunyi. 1937. *Tongshu* 通書. In *Zhouzi quanshu* 周子全書. Shanghai: Shanghai shangwu yinshuguan.

Zhu Xi. 1996. *Zhu Xi ji* 朱熹集 (*Collected Work of Zhu Xi*). Edited by Guo Qi 郭齐 and Yin Bo 尹波. Chengdu: Sichuan jiaoyu chubanshe.

————. 2002. *Zhuzi quanshu* 朱子全書 (*The Complete Works of Master Zhu*). Shanghai: Shanghai guji chubanshe and Hefei: Anhui jiaoyu chubanshe.

Further Reading

Cheng, Chung-ying. 1986. "Chu Hsi's Methodology and Theory of Understanding." In *Chu Hsi and Neo-Confucianism*. Edited by Wing-tsit Chan, 169–196. Honolulu: University of Hawaii Press.

Fuller, Michael. 2005. "Aesthetics and Meaning in Experience: A Theoretical Perspective on Zhu Xi's Revision of Song Dynasty Views," *Harvard Journal of Asiatic Studies* 65 (2): 311–356.

Lynn, Richard John. 1986. "Chu Hsi as Literary Theorist and Critic." In *Chu Hsi and Neo-Confucianism*. Edited by Wing-tsit Chan, 337–407. Honolulu: University of Hawaii Press.

Ng, On-cho. 2008. "Trans-cultural Reading: Zhu Xi's Classical Exegesis and Hermeneutic Ultimacy." *Zhongguo zhexue yu wenhua* (*Journal of Chinese Philosophy and Culture*) 3: 255–276.

Yang, Zhiyi. 2012. "Zhu Xi as Poet." *Journal of the American Oriental Society* 132 (4): 587–611.

Social Conditions of His Time

Beverly Bossler

Introduction

Zhu Xi wrote in such detail about philosophical and metaphysical concerns that we might easily forget that his ultimate objective was the moral transformation of society. Despite his social concerns, he seldom wrote systematically about social issues, and when he did his pronouncements tended to be abstract and programmatic. That said, we can catch glimpses of Zhu's attitudes to social problems in his directives and exhortations to people in his jurisdiction, promulgated during his stints as a local official, as well as in his letters to disciples and friends addressing concrete issues in family relations, and in his funerary biographies (especially for women), where he exhibited considerable flexibility and accommodation to social custom.[1] The thirteen texts translated below include selections from these three types of documents.

This chapter begins with a set of Zhu's official directives. Texts 1–6 range from general admonishments to behave well and be diligent in agriculture, to specific warnings about officials cheating commoners, illegal family division, and unorthodox religious practices. These straightforward texts reveal Zhu's unshakeable conviction that, if only each person would behave appropriately, all would have sufficient food to eat and clothing to wear and harmony would reign. They also show Zhu's frustration that his repeated admonishments and "sincere intentions" have not had much effect on local practice. Finally, these admonitions give us a fascinating glance at local customs. They reveal some of

---

1. On this point see Bettine Birge, "Chu Hsi and Women's Education," in de Bary and Chaffee 1985, 325–367. See also the chapter on "Chu Hsi's Treatment of Women" in Chan 1989, 537–547.

the ingenious ways that local officials found to extort money from the populace, and indicate that in general the countryside was far less "Confucianized"
than its literati governors liked to admit.

The remainder of the texts translated here deal more specifically with family
issues. Like his writings on society, Zhu's writings on families were largely pre-
scriptive: families needed to be properly "regulated" and interactions among
family members guided by ritual. But he was seldom very specific about what
this meant in practice. Texts 7, 8, and 9 offer a slightly more detailed glimpse
of what Zhu had in mind. Text 7 is a memorial asking that a text on marriage rituals be disseminated to local officials, partly as an antidote to some of
the irregularities that Zhu fulminated against in his exhortations. Text 8 is an
excerpt from a sealed memorial sent to Emperor Xiaozong in 1189, and was
designed to remonstrate with the emperor himself. In Zhu's view, as the Son
of Heaven, the emperor was not only a model for the rest of the realm; his direct connection to Heaven meant that his behavior determined the fate of the
realm, and the regulation of the imperial family was critical to the governance
of the country. Although Zhu couches his argument largely in terms of general moral principles, he specifically if obliquely warns the emperor against
letting power fall into the hands of palace favorites and their relatives. In text
9, a funerary inscription for a woman known as Lady Shao, we get a slightly
more concrete sense of what Zhu means by a properly "regulated" family, in
the form of the family rules that Lady Shao implemented after her husband's
death, which Zhu Xi enthusiastically endorsed. This text also reveals something of the qualities Zhu admired in women, including strictness, dedica-
tion, charity, frugality, modesty, punctiliousness, and filiality.

Texts 10, 11, and 12 reflect Zhu Xi's efforts to reconcile classical rituals
concerning concubines, which emphasized distinctions between wives and
concubines, with his own conviction that a son owed his birth mother filial
respect and remembrance even if she had been a concubine. Zhu's views themselves reflected a major shift in ideas about status that took place between the
Tang and Song dynasties, as well as the growing prevalence of concubinage in
Song society.[2] These texts show that the ubiquity of concubines in the homes
of the Song elite gave rise to much confusion over such issues as how to refer
to a concubine mother, who was owed ritual mourning and to what degree,
and what to do about a birth mother who had left one's father's family to
marry another man (as many concubines did).

---

2. On these developments, see Bossler 2012, 52–128; 208–249.

Finally, text 13 is also concerned with the ritual confusion caused by re-marriage. The rather complicated text is Zhu Xi's response to his disciple Li Hui, who struggled to reconcile three separate interpretations of the proper treatment of a successor wife (a legal wife [not concubine] taken in marriage after the death of the first wife). In the first half of this text, Zhu quotes at length from Li's letter to him. Therein, Li in turn first quotes a passage by Zhang Zai, who had insisted that, since in principle neither a man nor a woman should have more than one spouse, only a first wife may be buried jointly with the husband. Li then quotes Cheng Yi, who agrees that a man's partner (in the grave or on the sacrificial altar) is usually his first wife, but adds that if the son carrying out the sacrifices was born to the second wife, then his birth mother is the partner. Li Hui expresses doubts about Cheng Yi's interpretation, pointing out that a childless first wife would then not receive partner sacrifices at all. Li had previously asked Zhu Xi about this issue, and Zhu had responded that all the legal wives, no matter first or second, should receive sacrifices together. But Li is still bothered by the discrepancy between Zhu Xi's views and those of Zhang Zai, pointing out that the latter were based in "utmost pattern-principle." Zhu Xi's response here is striking, for he essentially refutes Zhang's position that "utmost pattern-principle" would dictate a husband having only one wife. Rather, Zhu argues, a husband can have wives and concubines in life, so why would it be a problem for him to have multiple wives as his partners in death? (We might note that Zhu here ignores the law that said a man could have only one legal wife at a time.) Zhu chides Li Hui for taking Zhang Zai's words to extremes and thereby creating problems where none exist.

Taken together, these texts show us Zhu Xi striving to bring the complex and fractious society around him into conformity with his own vision of moral order.

Translations

1. Instructing customs

The *Classic of Filial Piety* says,
"Utilize the Way of Heaven, follow the benefits of earth"
    This is to say: plow and plant the earth according to the time and season.

"Be cautious in conduct and restrained in consumption . . ."

To be cautious means not to do illegal things: do not break the law. To be restrained in consumption means to be thrifty and frugal: do not spend or consume wildly.

". . . in order to support your parents."

If people can put into practice what is in these three sentences, their bodies will be secure and their energy sufficient; they will have [sufficient resources] to support and nurture their fathers and mothers, making their fathers and mothers secure and happy.

"This is the filiality of the common people."

"Common people" is to say ordinary people [lit., "the hundred surnames"]. If they are able to put into practice what is in these four sentences, that is filial obedience. Even if the father and mother are not alive, it is still necessary to behave like this; then they will be able to protect the patrimony of the father and mother and not be bankrupted: that is filial obedience. If when the parents are alive they cannot support and nurture them, and when the parents are dead they cannot preserve [their legacy], that is to be unfilial. People who are unfilial, Heaven will not accommodate, earth will not sustain; in the underworld demons and spirits will chastise them, in this world the laws of the officials will punish them. You must thoroughly guard against this!

Above are the five sentences making up the main text of the "Commoners" section of the *Classic of Filial Piety*; they are in accord with what was said by the former sage, King Ultimate Sage Transmitter of Culture [i.e., Confucius]. I offer this to encourage the people to keep and recite it daily, and in accord with this explication of the classic, morning and night to think of it, and constantly and assiduously to follow and preserve it. It is unnecessary further to chant the name of the Buddha or the Buddhist sutras: they are of no benefit, and waste your effort in vain. (*ZXJ*, chapter 99, p. 5058)[3]

2. Exhortation placard

Today we provide a list of items that we exhort [the people] to put into practice:

---

3. *ZXJ* refers to *Zhu Xi ji* 朱熹集 (*Collected Work of Zhu Xi*): see Zhu Xi 1996 in the bibliography.

Item: Exhort and instruct the mutual security groups to mutually admonish each other [with regard to] affairs.[4]

We look to the people of the same mutual security group to admonish one another to be filial to their parents, respect their elders and superiors, be amiable to their natal and marital kin, and be sympathetic to their neighbors.[5] Each should accord with his own status, and follow his own profession; do not steal or rob, do not unrestrainedly drink or gamble; do not get into fights; do not sue one another. Publicize the notable deeds of filial sons, obedient grandsons, righteous men, and faithful women, fully reporting them [to the government] so that they can be honored and rewarded according to the statutes. Those who do not abide by these instructions should also be brought up and reported, investigated, and dealt with according to law.

Item: Restrain the mutual security groups to mutually maintain orderly affairs.

Assiduously store water for fire prevention; assiduously be on the lookout for thieves and robbers; assiduously forbid fighting. It is not permitted to buy or sell private [that is, not monopoly] salt; it is not permitted to butcher draft oxen; it is not permitted to gamble your possessions; it is not permitted to transmit or practice demonic teachings.[6] The people of the mutual aid group should monitor one another: if they are aware of [transgressions] and do not report them, they will be sentenced along with the criminals.

Item: Exhort and instruct the literati and commoners: they ought to be aware that one's body derives from one's father and mother, and elder and younger brothers alike derive from the father and mother; thus the Heaven-endowed affection toward parents and brothers is exceedingly deep and exceedingly important. Moreover, people's love for their parents and respect for their elders are all born of the nature of one's

---

4. The *bao wu* 保伍 was a group of five families which served as a basic, village-level unit of government organization. As this passage suggests, members of a *bao wu* were expected to keep an eye on one another and stood as guarantors for one another's behavior.

5. The term translated here as "look to" (*yang* 仰) literally means, "look up to," but in government documents of this period has the sense of "we hope you will . . ."

6. There is an ongoing scholarly debate about whether the term translated in this chapter as "demonic" (*mo* 魔) might in fact be a reference to Manichaeism. For a recent intervention in the debate, see Lin 2004. I am grateful to Ari Borrell for alerting me to this article. See also the discussion in Chan 1989, 308–311.

original heart-mind: it is not forced, and it cannot be exhausted. Today there are people who are unfilial and unbrotherly: they constantly contravene the teachings and commands of their parents, daring to provide for them inadequately; they are careless and argumentative with their brothers, tolerating mutual distance between them. They defy Heaven and are at odds with pattern-principle (*li* 理). This is greatly painful [to observe]. They ought to immediately reform themselves, and not invite great punishment.

Item: Exhort and instruct the literati and the commoners: they ought to know that the marriage of husbands and wives is the beginning of human relations; with regard to the inquiries and arrangements of matchmakers, the rituals and laws are extremely strict. Yet among the customs of this district there is the so-called [practice of] "sheltering and looking after," which is when [a woman] is originally neither wife nor concubine, but lives openly with [a man]. There is [also] the so-called "running-away [together]," wherein without waiting for a matchmaker, they stealthily run away and seduce one another. In offending against ritual and flouting the law, there is nothing worse than this. They ought to immediately reform themselves, and not fall into punishment.

Item: Exhort and instruct the literati and commoners: they ought to be close and amiable with their relatives and neighbors. When there is some minor annoyance, they ought each to think deeply about it, and also [find a way to] compromise and reconcile. They must not easily resort to lawsuits. Even if they are in the right, they will still necessarily injure their finances and undermine their occupation; how much more so if they are in the wrong, unable to avoid being convicted and undergoing punishment! In the end it will certainly be inauspicious, and should be scrupulously avoided!

Item: Exhort and instruct the official households, which is to say the families of those who serve in office: they are different from ordinary commoners. They especially ought to be content in their station and abide by what is right; their responsibility is to overcome their own [interests] to benefit the people. Not to mention that there is no one among their neighbors who is not a relative or old friend: how can they rely on their power to oppress the weak, and use their wealth to swallow the poor? Prosperity and decline goes in cycles: this is something they ought to think deeply about!

Item: Exhort and instruct families who have encountered bereavement to bury [their dead] in a timely fashion. They must not temporarily encoffin [the dead] at home or deposit the coffin at a temple. Those who have been temporarily placed in the coffin encased in lime must also be buried within one month.[7] It is certainly unnecessary to provide feasts for monks or contribute to the Buddha, holding large and imposing ceremonies. Rather, simply bury the deceased as soon as possible in accord with the family's resources. Those who disobey will be beaten one hundred strokes, in accord with the statutes; [if they are] officials they will not be evaluated for appointment and [if they are scholars] they will not be allowed to sit for the examinations. When relatives and acquaintances of the area come to condole and see the deceased off, they ought to cooperate and support the bereaved; they must not castigate them about the food and drink they have provided.

Item: Exhort and instruct men and women: they must not, under the name of cultivating the Way, privately set up hermitages.[8] If there are such people, they should be married off in a timely fashion.

Item: Restrict temples and monasteries. Among the commoners, they must not, under the name of worshiping the Buddha and transmitting the sutras, gather men and women together in mixed company day and night.

Item: Restrict the towns and the villages. They must not, under the name of exorcising disasters or praying for blessings, collect money and goods and create and deploy effigies.

The aim of the above exhortations is simply that the people each will recognize the pattern-principle of the Way and be a good person. Themselves recognizing [what is right], they will not commit [crimes], and the official punishments will have no reason to reach them. They must assiduously observe and follow [these admonitions], in order to preserve peace and harmony. If they are not obedient, and still dare to flout them, the country has clear laws and the clerks will not dare to be partial. Everyone should deeply consider this, so as not to cause later regrets. (*ZXJ*, chapter 100, pp. 5100–5102)

3. Text on promoting agriculture

[Original note]: During the days as Prefect of Nankang prefecture
I humbly observe that the basis of the people's life is food, and the basis of having enough food is agriculture: this is a natural pattern-principle.

---

7. Lime was typically used to preserve the body prior to burial.

8. Hermitages were private religious dwellings.

Among those whose vocation is agriculture, those who are diligent in their efforts and speedy in carrying out work will acquire more; those who do not make an effort and who are not timely will acquire less: this is also a natural pattern-principle. The paddy land of this prefecture is hard and barren, the fertile topsoil is not deeper than three or five inches; even if people and households are diligent and timely in their efforts to manage agricultural affairs, I fear their harvest will still be less than that of other places. But [instead] the local atmosphere and customs are in the main lazy: the plowing and planting are therefore not timely, and [the farmers] do not exhaust their efforts in weeding and fertilizing; the irrigation ponds and channels are neglected and not repaired; the work of cultivating fibers [for clothing] is disregarded and left undone. This is the reason that their plans for making a living and having enough food are sketchy; this is why the fields have become increasingly barren and sterile, and what they take in has become extremely little. Add to this that the taxes [lit., "official property"] are heavy, and they have no other skills with which to subsidize [their livelihoods]. As soon as there are floods or droughts, they are driven to [become] refugees. Below they lose the living passed down to them by their forbears, above they are short on the regular levies [owed] to the state. In letting the people reach this end, how can the functionaries who lead the people and the officials who promote agriculture not bear some responsibility! [I] have long served in the countryside [lit., in the fields and gardens], and I am familiar with agriculture. I have been in [this] office for some time, and have personally seen the harm [this laziness causes]. I regret that, because I am responsible for keeping the seals [that is, regular official duties], I have not been able to go in and out on the footpaths morning and evening, and with the fathers and elder brothers lead the sons and younger brothers to work among the hoes and plows, so that their wives and children would have full mouths and expanded bellies [lit., "drum-bellies"] and no longer [experience] the disasters of hunger, cold, and fleeing, so as to assist the emperor above in loving and supporting the common people. Day and night [I have been] fretful with worry and concern. Last winter I once printed a poster exhorting and instructing the households under my jurisdiction to be filial, brotherly, loyal, and reliable in the work of farming and producing silk. [My instructions were] detailed and complete, comprehensive and thorough: I trust you have all heard and know about them. Yet recently in early spring I went out to examine the outer districts, and in the paddy fields next to the road the earth had still not been broken.

This means that fathers and older brothers, sons and younger brothers, still have not grasped the meaning of work and have not been able to be diligent in being timely. Keeping in mind that they have not clearly understood my instructions, I cannot bear to beat them in punishment. Now I am following the old ceremony of mid-spring and promulgating the virtuous intention of the sage emperor, by again printing and disseminating my previous exhortation as well the [rules for] planting mulberry and other laws by the Xingzi magistrate Wang Wenlin.[9] All of you, my fathers and elder brothers, as well as your sons and younger brothers, must respectfully obey this! If you apply these words and put them into practice day and night, you will certainly see results. Those who govern from now on should even more in a timely fashion go outside the city and make rounds of inspection. If there are those who do not accord with the instructions, punishment must be imposed. Everyone should be informed of the above directive. (*ZXJ*, chapter 99, pp. 5062–5063)

4. Instruction regarding taxes on the monopoly sale of wine to the people and forcing them to acquire wine

I have investigated and determined that, when the common people have gatherings on auspicious or inauspicious occasions,[10] to celebrate a repair or construction project, and the like, if they [wish to] use wine, they are permitted according to law to purchase it according to their means. If they do not [wish to] use it, they are also permitted to follow their preference, and cannot be compelled [to buy]. Recently I have inquired and learned that, whenever people have auspicious or inauspicious [occasions], the various counties and assisting officials have permitted the forcible collection of the people's money under the name of "wine purchase tax," to the point that the [government-run] monopoly markets illegally force commoner households to purchase wine. I am extremely worried that honorable people will be harmed, and that weddings and funerals and construction will not be held in a timely fashion: it is necessary to restrain [such practices].

Accordingly, today I am printing a notice to inform commoner households that henceforth, when they have gatherings for auspicious

9. Xingzi county was one of the districts under Zhu Xi's jurisdiction; virtually nothing is known of Wang Wenlin.

10. "Auspicious and inauspicious occasions" was a standard way of referring to ceremonies like weddings, funerals, birth celebrations, and so forth.

or inauspicious occasions, [or] to celebrate a repair or construction project and the like, if the officials dare to forcibly collect the wine purchase
[tax], or the wine-producing monopoly markets force them to buy wine,
they are requested to establish witnesses, prepare a plaint, and come directly to the prefecture to bring suit. [There they may] eagerly wait for
the perpetrator to be detained, thoroughly investigated, and dealt with
according to the statutes. (*ZXJ*, chapter 99, p. 5071)

5. Directive regarding brothers who fight over property

When we examine the classical texts on rituals, [we see that] anyone who is a son should not collect private wealth; moreover, the text
of the statutes also forbids having separate registrations and separate
funds [from parents]. Indeed, [because] parents are supreme [in status],
sons do not have complete control even over their own bodies: how do
they dare privately to maintain wealth, or arrogate fields and gardens to
themselves as their own property? This is a natural pattern-principle of
[people's] Heavenly nature and the human heart-mind; that the former
kings established ritual, and the later kings set up laws, was in order to
get [people] to conform to this principle and [make them] not dare
to contravene it. When this official recently arrived and first took up
office, I inquired about the people's customs and investigated the local
gazetteers. I once [used the examples of] the filial behavior and righteous
living of Grand Master Sima, Adjutant Sima, Magistrate Xiong, and
the Hong Joint Household to exhort the gentlemen and commoners to
cultivate filality, brotherliness, loyalty, and faithfulness. At home [they
should] serve their fathers and brothers, abroad [they should] serve
their elders and superiors; [they should] be forthright and caring with
their families and kin, and amiable and cordial to their neighbors; [they
should] share with one another and sympathize with one another in
difficulties. [I exhorted them thus] with the intent of respectfully aiding
the sage Son of Heaven to improve customs. It has already been several
months, but my sincere intentions have not been sufficient, and there
has been no obvious result. Recently, in reviewing legal cases, there were
Liu Chong and his brothers of Jianchang county and Chen Youren and
his brothers of Duchang county, both of whom still had mothers at
home, and both of whom without authority directed the division of
family property, made excuses for themselves, did not pay their taxes,
and brought their conflicts to court: it is appalling to hear about! In
addition to promulgating an order for Jianchang county to seek out and

destroy the contracts orchestrated by Chen Youren and the others, there in the courtroom I also orally ordered that Liu Chong, Chen Youren, and their brothers live together and share their wealth as of old, serve their [respective] mothers above and lead their [respective] younger brothers and nephews below, cooperate in the family business, collectively [manage] income and expenditure, and pay their taxes [lit., "official property"]. Moreover, I have reflected that under our jurisdiction there are still people who abandon ritual and law and harm customs and teachings in this way, and the senior officials have not been able instruct [the people] and forbid [such practices] in a timely fashion. [I, who] have taken on the responsibility to transmit good customs and transform the people, on self-examination cannot overcome my trepidation.

Now I am setting out the legal guidelines below, which must be transmitted [to the people]:

> According to the statutes . . . etc., etc. [Remainder of text omitted in the original].

The above, in addition to already being posted in the marketplace and at the gate to Xingzi county, [should also] be posted at the markets in Duchang and Jianchang counties, so as to instruct and inform the populace. If their grandparents or parents are [still living], and sons or grandsons without authority illegally divide land and property and live separately, or separately register property, [their crimes should] immediately be reported in accord with the instructions in the above directives. They should bring to court the contracts they have established, confess [their crimes], destroy [the contracts], and correct [their behavior]. [They should] serve their parents, cooperate with elder and younger brothers, together manage the family business, collectively share income and expenses, and pay their taxes: they must not be behind in their payments. If any persons do not henceforth respect these restraints, but instead disobey and end up in court, they will certainly be sent to prison, and their punishment decided in accord with the statutes (etc., etc.).

Proclaimed on [unspecified] day in the eighth month of the sixth year of the Chunxi reign period [1181]. (*ZXJ*, chapter 99, pp. 5059–5060)

6. Placard Exhorting Female Daoists to Return to Lay Life

To the prefecture: [I have] investigated [and found] that recently the officials of this prefecture have failed to notice that among the people are many who illegally build private hermitages, and that many of them are headed and managed [*zhuchi* 主持] by female Daoists. Formerly, when I first arrived at my post, I determined that this [state of affairs] was inappropriate, and consequently I [have] already issued orders and established a placard to forbid [this practice], [saying] henceforth it is not permitted to privately build hermitages to live in. I [have] repeatedly warned against it: [my words] were nothing if not strict. Recently, in the course of reviewing plaints [in legal cases], I have come to learn that there are still female Daoists living in hermitages, and there have been some who have been sued for fornication. Obviously, they have not obeyed my restrictions, [instead] stubbornly contravening the laws of the land, deceiving their superiors and behaving selfishly, undermining and destroying mores and customs. [Therefore] it is necessary again to issue an exhortation.

The placard to the right now exhorts [all] the soldiers and civilians, men, women and so forth of this prefecture. I have heard that of the important human relationships, [the relationship between] husband and wife is primary; it is the head of the Three Bonds, which in accord with pattern-principle cannot be discarded. Accordingly, during the era of the former kings, men each had their allotted place, women each had a [home to] return to; there were matchmakers and betrothals, so they could be mutually paired. In this manner, men occupied their correct [place] in the outer realm; women occupied their correct [place] in the inner realm; their persons were cultivated and the family regulated, mores and customs were strict and orderly, the succession was clear, people's hearts were peaceful, and the hundred things were obedient and regulated. In the decline of later eras, the ritual teachings were not clear, [and] the Buddhist dharma and demonic sects took advantage of this opportunity to surreptitiously develop and spread their heterodox words, confounding the people's hearts and making it so that men grew up but did not take [wives]; women matured but did not marry. [They] called it leaving the home to cultivate the Way, benightedly hoping for rewards in future lives.

Accordingly, if everyone in the world followed their teachings, in less than a hundred years there would be no human beings, and all between heaven and earth would be open space for animals; the intimacy of father and son, the righteousness of ruler and minister, and the tools that those who have countries use to preserve law and order would have no one to whom they would apply. Fortunately, those who follow them are

few, and morality has not been destroyed. Those who do follow them
are also all dull and lowly types, who are deluded by their doctrines but
cannot penetrate their meaning; who take pleasure in the name ["monk"
or "nun"] but cannot put the reality into practice. When their physical
vigor becomes excessive, their libido daily increases. Although within
they regret having left home [to become celibate], without they are also
embarrassed to return to lay life. As a result, of the unmarried males, there
are none who do not steal others' wives; of the unmarried women, there
are none who do not wantonly engage in illicit behavior. If the officials
indulge them without question, customs and mores daily decline; [but]
if they are all restrained with laws, then the criminals daily become more
numerous. This is because these people are not able to plan for themselves; they blithely believe the heterodox sayings and so come to this.
[It is] also the fault of their parents, who are unable to think ahead for
their sons and daughters. If we consider and investigate the details, the
situation is truly lamentable. This is why my previous placard did not shy
away from repeated warnings. But my previous warnings were not put
into practice, because the approach was not [sufficiently] broad.

Now, on reconsidering in detail, with regard to letting them retain the
name of "female Daoist" and return to their parents' or brothers' homes,
this was also not appropriately handled, and in the end regret was una-
voidable. Wouldn't it be better to have the youthful among them, those
whose looks have not deteriorated, each return to their original homes
and obey the orders of their elders, openly carrying out betrothals and
[celebrating] marriages as appropriate, in order to restore the teachings
of ritual and righteousness of the former kings, respect the constant
moral nature of humanity, end the monstrous doctrines of the demonic
Buddhists (*mo fo* 魔佛), and reform the filthy customs of licentious disorder. Wouldn't it be wonderful! If some say that for getting married
there must be expenses of betrothal presents and dowry, so too does
cultivating the Way have the expense of hermitages, vestments, and beg-
ging bowls. Their parents should, in accord with their means, shift [their
resources] from the latter to the former: what is there to prevent it? How
can they selfishly worry about spending too much, unreasonably maintain the present [situation], and make their sons and daughters be alone
and lonely, with no one to rely on, and decline into improper behavior and [incur] punishments of beating and flogging? All my [people],
young and old, must obey these words, ponder and deeply consider
them: do not pass on regret! Thus I have posted. The [unspecified] day

of the eighth month of the first year of Shaoxi reign period (1190). (*ZXJ*, chapter 100, pp. 5097–5098)

7. Memorial petitioning to strengthen marriage rituals

I respectfully submit that in the rituals and statutes, marriage is extremely important. It is the origin of distinguishing male and female, regulating husband and wife, correcting customs, and avoiding calamity and chaos. Upon inquiry, I have learned that in this county from generation to generation there have been no rituals for marriage. The rural people [lit., "of the lanes and alleys"] are poor and cannot [provide] betrothal [gifts]. In some cases they go so far as to run away and seduce [one another], which they call "attracting a companion to be a wife." This has become so common as to become the custom. The practice has spread to [the point that] even some literati and wealthy households do it, without the slightest scruple. The harm is not only that it is perverse and contrary to ritual, and violates the country's laws: when jealousy arises, it brings on disastrous disputes, such that in some cases because of this they commit murder without remorse. The customs are confused and benighted; this is deeply pitiable. I would like to request that this be prosecuted according to the current statutes, and orders given to prohibit it. I also request that the prefectural officials all be instructed to examine and disseminate the marriage ceremonies for gentlemen and commoners of the *Five Rituals of the Zhenghe Period*, as a basis for preserving [customs] and restricting [this evil] practice. (*ZXJ*, chapter 20, pp. 800–801)

8. Jiyou [1189] Plan for the Emperor, Sealed Memorial (Excerpt on regulating the family)

. . . The second is what is called "cultivate one's person to regulate the family." I have heard that the basis of all under Heaven is the country, and the basis of the country is the family. Therefore, if the family of the ruler of the people is regulated, then there is nothing under Heaven that will not be well-governed. If the family of the ruler of the people is not regulated, then there is no means by which all under Heaven can be well-governed. This is to say, of the flourishing of the Three Dynasties, and the ability of sage rulers to cultivate their administrations, there were none that were not based in regulation of the family.

Now, when the correct position of males is outside, the correct position of females is inside, and the distinctions between husbands and wives are strict, that is regulation of the family. When the wife is of one body [with the husband] above, the concubines receive and carry out [orders] below (*qie jiecheng yu xia* 妾接承於下), so that the distinction between primary and secondary (*di shu* 嫡庶) is defined, that is regulation of the family. When the virtuous are selected and [lascivious] music and sex avoided, when the strict and respected are kept close and the crafty and clever are distanced, that is the regulation of the family. When gossip from the inner [household] is not spread abroad, and gossip from the outside does not enter [the household], when [improper] gifts are not received and [improper] requests are not made, that is the regulation of the family. But within the inner quarters, favor frequently overcomes righteousness: this is the reason that even [men of] heroic talent still can get into trouble with wine and sex, drown in romantic emotions, and be unable to control themselves. If one does not correct one's heart and cultivate one's person, move in accord with ritual and righteousness, and make [others] submit to one's virtue and fear one's power, then by what means can one rectify the back palace, stop [improper] requests [for favor], restrain the imperial affines, and avoid the sprouts of calamity? The *[Book of] Documents* says, "The crowing of the hen in the morning signals the subversion of the family." The *[Zuo] Commentary* says, "The flourishing of good fortune is always based in the household; the decline of the Way always starts within the home." If your sagely intelligence would pay attention to this, all under heaven will be fortunate indeed! (*ZXJ*, chapter 12, pp. 491–492)

9. Grave inscription for Ruren Lady Shao

Mr. Shi Gao of Jinhua carried out the funeral of his mother, née Shao, interring her in the grave of the late gentleman [his father], in the Nine-league plain of Xunli village. He sent his son Yuan with two separate documents, a "Record of Conduct" composed by Ye Shi of Yongjia, as well as a record of additional facts about her life, and informed [me]: "When my late father died, my former teacher Master Donglai honored me with an inscription, and you, Master, wrote it out [in calligraphy]. Now again, due to my lack of filiality I have met with the great disaster [of my mother's death]. Although I have fortunately completed the funeral, there still is the carving on the grave that will be handed down to posterity that not been designated [to anyone]. I dare to presume on your former kindness, and with repeated obeisance ask [that you undertake it]." At the time I was sick in bed out in the countryside, but I stood to receive the document and read it. It said:

"The Lady was a person of Jinhua county in Wu prefecture; her great-grandfather was [named] Xiong, her grandfather was [named] Yue, and her father was [named] Zhicai. She was married to Mister Shi Ruyi of Qingjiang in the same county. Mister Shi's [family] had been prosperous for generations, and he was stalwart and upright. During the Fang La disturbance,[11] the bandits burnt down nearly everything. Mister [Shi] himself rebuilt things one by one, completely excelling his ancestors. The Lady was able to help him astutely, without neglecting anything. As the family became successful, Mister Shi was able to strictly regulate the inner and outer [affairs of the household], educate his sons and grandsons, be reliable in his dealings with others, and become respected in his village. The Lady was also able to serve him scrupulously, without negligence. The Shi family was a good lineage and large family; their sons and grandsons competed in the examinations and elevated [the family] name; everyone respected and loved Mister Shi and Lady [Shao]. When Mister Shi died, Lady Shao was also aging. She called the family together and composed a set of regulations which she personally inscribed on a screen, to ensure that they would live together in accordance with ritual, and share equally in food and clothing, so that they would not forget Mister Shi's rules. To the southeast of Qingjiang there were several hundred salt-producing households, living in grass huts near the water. Frequently floods would overwhelm them; the people would always perch in trees to save themselves, and there were some who were swept away. Madame then ordered a boat with food and rice to save [the survivors] and this became a yearly custom. She prepared and stored up coffins, announcing that she would bury those who died in epidemics; the people were touched by her benevolence.[12] Late in her life, special favor was granted in celebration of the birthdays of the emperor and empress, and she was able to be enfeoffed as Ruren, and in addition a headdress and cape were bestowed. She died on the *gengyin* day of the seventh month in the tenth year of the Chunxi reign period

---

11. Fang La, a disaffected lacquer-tree grower from Zhejiang, led a rebellion against the state in 1120–1121. Although the rebellion was put down, it did considerable damage in the region of Northern Zhejiang. For a recent discussion, see Wu 2017.

12. Proper burial was an important cultural value in China, and helping the destitute be buried properly was a popular charitable activity.

[1183], at the age of seventy-one. She had three sons: Gao, Qi, and Zong, and two daughters, who married Liu Yan and Chen Bao. Her grandsons were [. . . ten names listed]. Of her granddaughters, two married [respectively] Chen Zhiwang and Wang Shuyi; the rest are still young. Her great-grandsons were Ju, Li, and Gao; her great-granddaughters were Zhuang and Fu."

That is roughly what Master Ye wrote; it is quite detailed on milady from beginning to end. But he also recorded the words of her hand-written rules. First, that sons and grandsons should carefully preserve the family rules, and were not permitted to contravene them; second, on arising with the sound of the clapper in the morning, old and young should go to the image-hall for the morning audience, and then go to the central hall to report and pay respects. Third, men or women going in or out, goods or money spent or received, male or female servants added or dismissed, must all be reported to the family head. Fourth, daughters-in-law are not allowed to hoard private funds. Fifth, female servants should not go out the central door without reason, and male servants are not allowed to frequently enter the [main] hall, the [private] chambers, or the kitchen. With this, I knew that what milady taught had grasped the essentials of regulating the family. He went on to say that milady's nature was frugal and simple, that she was not swayed by glitter and extravagance, and that her accessories were ordinary, never changing by chasing after what was fashionable. She was careful with the seasonal sacrifices: once when she was cutting meat for the winter sacrifices, her hands were cold and the knife fell. Her daughters-in-law asked to do it for her, but she would not permit it. Her mother [née] He late in life had a disease of the limbs; [milady] returned home and was so worried she could not bear to leave. When her mother died, [milady] was nearly sixty, but she still ate vegetarian food to complete the mourning.[13] Her elder sister lived as a widow, poor and sickly; milady looked after her thoroughly. She treated her sons and younger brothers with exceptional grace. Mister Shi was assiduous in teaching his sons, and the talented and honorable of the age were often guests in his household. Milady daily arranged the food, and always personally attended them; even when it was difficult she never appeared weary. From this

---

13. The idea is that, given her advanced age and the potential danger to her own health, Lady Shao would not be expected to keep a vegetarian diet. That she did so demonstrates her exceptional filial piety.

I also could see that what milady taught she practiced herself, and was not just words. Ah! This is truly admirable! Since I am ill, in the end I have been unable to write an inscription, so I am just tentatively recording the facts like this to give to Yuan to take back and carve on the stone to erect at her grave. Written by Zhu Xi of Xin'an, on the *wuchen* day of the tenth month in winter of the twelfth year of the Chunxi reign period [1185]. (*ZXJ*, chapter 90, p. 4601)

10. Reply to Li Shouyue

The way that you have explained the term "concubine mother" (*shu mu* 庶母) is also not correct. "Shu mu" is what one calls one's father's concubine who has given birth to sons; gentlemen wear *sima* (緦麻) mourning [for such a concubine], and grandees do not perform mourning for [them at all].[14] With respect to a mother, the *Rites and Rituals* (*Yi li* 儀禮) has the passage, "The sons of the lord regard her as mother." Now, immediately following there is also a clear commentary saying, "This refers to one who has given birth to you"; therefore, without regard to whether she is the father's wife or the father's concubine, either way she receives the name of "mother."[15] That within the commentary there is also language referring to the "legal wife" (*di mu* 嫡母), is also to clarify that the one who has given birth to you [even if she is a concubine] is legitimately called mother. With respect to ranks and enfeoffments, one again only calls her "birth mother" (*suo sheng mu* 所生母) and does not call her "concubine mother." I have not had the leisure to investigate the discourse in the *Complete Ceremonies* (*Tong dian* 通典), but comparing it with [the rule] that "the sons of the lord wear [mourning clothes of] coarse headgear and hempen robes, and remove them as soon as the burial is over," I fear that one who carries on the importance of the lineage temples and dynastic altars [that is, a

---

14. Chinese mourning ritual stipulated five distinct "levels" of mourning dress based on the closeness of the relationship between the mourner and the deceased. "Sima" mourning was the lowest level.

15. According to Chinese law during most of the imperial period, a man could have only one legal wife. A legal wife had to be married with proper ritual, and had ritual responsibilities to a man's ancestors. Concubines could be taken in without any particular ceremony, and could be sent out of the family when the master tired of them, or at his death. Legally, all children were regarded as belonging to the legal wife, regardless of who bore them, and in the Song all were regarded as legitimate sons of the father, as long as he acknowledged them. In this text and others like it, we see Zhu Xi attempting to work out how concubines' sons should balance their ritual responsibilities to their birth mothers and legal mothers.

lineage heir] should not observe the rituals for a grandmother who is one's father's birth mother. At the moment, I am still ill; I will continue to investigate and report back . . . (*ZXJ*, chapter 55, p. 2773)

11. Reply to Sun Jingfu

. . . In the classics on rituals, a father's concubine who has [given birth to] sons is called a concubine mother (*shu mu* 庶母), and when she dies one wears three months of *sima* 緦麻 mourning for her. This is clearly related to her status, and originally one ought not to consider whether she is old or young. But with respect to how she is treated ritually, one also ought to follow the orders of one's elders: this is not something that sons and younger brothers can decide for themselves. (*ZXJ*, chapter 63, pp. 3310–3311)

12. Colophon to 'Discussion of Not Supporting an Expelled Mother'

The *Book of Rites* [says that] one does not wear mourning for a married-out mother, but the laws and statutes say that one does. Someone was dubious of this difference. According to my investigations, the *Ritual* in discussing a "married-out mother" doesn't mention "one's own" and only says "successor," and also does [mention] wearing mourning for an expelled mother: all these bring up the less important to clarify the more important. It shows that for one's own [birth] mother who has been married out, one still must wear mourning. In this initially it is no different from the meaning of the laws and statutes. In addition, [regarding] one who is his father's heir, it only says "one doesn't wear mourning for an expelled mother" and does not extend this to a married-out mother; this also brings up the less important to distinguish it from the more important, and shows that one should still wear mourning for a married-out mother. In looking at Yu Zhengfu's disquisition [about] the tribute student's concubine mother,[16] it was not [a case where] the father died while the children were young, and so she remarried [another], [nor] did she commit one of the "seven crimes deserving expulsion"; but there was still a reason for her to leave. [Therefore] this is in fact a [case of] a married-out mother and not an expelled mother. The mistake in the

---

16. Yu Zhengfu was a disciple of Zhu Xi. He seems to have been something of a specialist in ritual.

discourse of Magistrate Yin of Yueping is precisely in taking a married-out mother for an expelled mother, and saying that [one for whom one should] wear mourning was [one for whom one should] not wear mourning. [In] Zhengfu's rebuttal it was precisely these two points that were of concern. Now, if one only has the words "This is a married-out mother," and does not discuss the reason that she was not expelled and [so] should still be mourned, and [moreover] on the contrary titles the beginning of the essay, "Do not support an expelled mother," and then only says that this is different from the expelled mother of the ancients, and that you can't follow the passage that says not to mourn, then this is also mutually self-contradictory and on the contrary serves to support the incorrect discourse of Magistrate Yin. I fear that those who look at it will inevitably have doubts, and so I am writing this to clarify. ([original note]: Although Zhengfu did not grasp that she was not an expelled mother, he still did not dare to truly regard her as an expelled mother. [Accordingly,] near the end of the essay, one place had the words, "Do not support an expelled mother," and he personally changed the word "expelled" to the word "birth': so we can see his general intent. But if he had given it a bit more effort he could have clarified the whole issue). Still, in Zhengfu wanting the lady to support this mother, in what manner did he want her to support her? I have heard that, if a mother is remarried and a son follows [her to her new household], the stepfather should build a small shrine for him outside the family gate, and have the son worship [his father] there. But the wife [that is, the son's remarried mother] must not dare to participate. The one who said this felt that, even though grace reaches to the parent [and therefore the son should worship his deceased father], [the mother's relationship to her ex-husband's] lineage was extinguished, because a woman cannot have two husbands. By the same token, the remarried mother during her lifetime cannot enter into the ancestral shrine [of her first husband]; when dead she cannot be sacrificed to at the [first husband's] ancestral shrine; and [by the same token] she also cannot be supported in the [son's] home. The son should lead his wife and children to go to his mother's home, or set up a hut next to her to support her; wouldn't this be fulfilling his moral role according to ritual?

Someone said, "Saying this is all well and good if the mother has a home, but if she unfortunately doesn't have a home, then what does one do?" It would be acceptable to build her a room outside [the son's home]. (*ZXJ*, chapter 84, pp. 4356–4357)

13. Reply to Li Huishu (excerpt)[17]

... [Li asks]: "Master Hengqu [Zhang Zai] said, '[With respect to] joint burial and joint sacrifice, if discussed in respect to the utmost pattern-principle, one should only inter one [consort with the husband]. The Way of husband and wife [is that] when they first marry, they never pledge to remarry; that is, a husband ought only to take one wife, and a wife ought only to marry one husband. Today, when a woman's husband dies and she is not allowed to remarry, [this] accords with the great righteousness of Heaven and earth. So how is it that the husband can take another wife? But looking at it [from the point of view of] the most difficult situations, for taking care of the in-laws, carrying on the family, and continuing the sacrifices, one can't do without [a wife]; and so there is the principle of [a man] remarrying. But when it comes to burial and sacrifice, although there are joint graves and joint altars, if you consider it in the light of human feelings, how could one chamber encompass two wives? If one judges this on the basis of righteousness, [a man should be] buried and receive sacrifices[18] with the one he married first, and the successor wife may be [interred and receive sacrifices] in a separate place.' [I], Hui, have just now been looking at Master Cheng's *Sacrifices and Ceremonies*, which says 'generally as a partner there is only one official wife; if the one carrying out the sacrifices was born of a second marriage, then his birth mother is the partner.' I once doubted this, and said, 'It is correct to say that in general for a [sacrificial partner] one only uses the main wife, and if a [woman] who was the second wife has no children, it is also permissible to offer her accessory sacrifices in a different place. [But] if the one who is sacrificing is the son of the second wife, and is permitted to use his birth mother as the grave partner, and the [first] main wife was childless and therefore does not receive partner sacrifices [at all], how can this be acceptable?' [I], Hui, previously once inquired about this of [you,] Master, and later respectfully received your venerable admonishment and instruction: [You said] "I'm afraid this saying by Master Cheng is incorrect. The *Guiding Principles of the Tang* says, 'All who are legitimate wives, without regard to order, should be sacrificed to together.' It is different from the ancient rituals of the nobility." I have

---

17. This passage has been partially translated in Xu 2016, 233–234.

18. There is some ambiguity here, as the term Zhang Zai uses, *fu* 祔, can mean either "joint sacrifice" or "joint burial."

respectfully understood milord's admonishment and instruction, which of itself is extremely compatible with human feeling. But [since] what Hengqu said was like this, [I,] your humble younger brother, have often been uncomfortable about the righteousness of joint burial and joint sacrifice, such that I have secretly agreed with what Hengqu said. [I], Hui, humbly feel that since Hengqu was speaking [from the perspective] of utmost pattern-principle, it cannot be otherwise. If you want to deal with it from the perspective of the feelings of contemporary people, then one can only follow what [you,] Master, have said. If by chance one follows Hengqu's words, and the former wife is sonless and the one sacrificing is the son of the second wife, how should this be handled?"

[Zhu responds:] The righteousness of husband and wife is like the greatness of [the hexagram] *qian* and the extensiveness of [the hexagram] *kun*: each has their own [relative] place.[19] Thus when alive, the husband has wives and concubines, but the wife can only have one Heaven [that is, husband]. How much more so when they have died and are receiving joint sacrifices, which cannot be compared to living? What Hengqu said [you] seem to have extended too far. If you just follow what the Tang people discussed it will be correct. How much more so the problem of "the first wife has no sons, the second wife has sons." On the surface it seems like something very worrisome. But today husbands and wives are not necessarily buried jointly, or separate graves are established for successor wives; this also ought to be acceptable. (*ZXJ*, chapter 62, p. 3253)

Bibliography

Birge, Bettine. 1985. "Chu Hsi and Women's Education." In *Neo-Confucian Education*. Edited by William Theodore de Bary and John W. Chaffee. Berkeley: University of California Press.

Bossler, Beverly Jo. 2013. *Courtesans, Concubines, and the Cult of Female Fidelity: Gender and Social Change in China, 1000–1400*. Cambridge, MA: Harvard University Asia Center.

Chan, Wing-tsit. 1989. *Chu Hsi, New Studies*. Honolulu: University of Hawai'i Press.

---

19. *Qian* and *kun* are the first two of the sixty-four hexagrams of the *Classic of Changes*. *Qian* is correlated with Heaven, the male principle, activity, *yang*; *kun* is correlated with earth, the female principle, receptiveness, *yin*. In some formulations, *qian* and *kun* are seen as complementary; here Zhu Xi highlights a hierarchical relationship between them.

Lin Zhenli 林振礼. 2004. "Zhu Xi yu Moni jiao xin tan 朱熹与摩尼教新探 [A New Probe into Zhu Xi and Moni Religion]." *Quanzhou Shifan xueyuan xuebao (shehui kexue)* 泉州师范学院学报（社会科学 *[Journal of Quanzhou Normal University (Social Science)]* 22: 30–37.

Wu, Junqing. 2017. "The Fang La Rebellion and the Song Anti-Heresy Discourse." *Journal of Chinese Religions* 45 (1): 19–37.

Xu, Man. 2016. *Crossing the Gate: Everyday Lives of Women in Song Fujian (960–1279)*. Albany, NY: SUNY Press.

Zhu Xi 朱熹. 1996. *Zhu Xi ji* 朱熹集 (*Collected Work of Zhu Xi*). Edited by Guo Qi 郭齐 and Yin Bo 尹波. Chengdu: Sichuan jiaoyu chubanshe.

Further Readings

Birge, Bettine. 1985. "Chu Hsi and Women's Education." In *Neo-Confucian Education*. Edited by William Theodore de Bary and John W. Chaffee. Berkeley: University of California Press.

Bossler, Beverly Jo. 2013. *Courtesans, Concubines, and the Cult of Female Fidelity: Gender and Social Change in China, 1000–1400*. Cambridge, MA: Harvard University Asia Center.

Xu, Man. 2016. *Crossing the Gate: Everyday Lives of Women in Song Fujian (960–1279)*. Albany, NY: SUNY Press.

6

Heaven, Ghosts and Spirits, and Ritual

Hoyt Cleveland Tillman

Introduction

The Chinese term *tian* 天, often glossed as "Heaven," has several meanings: the blue sky, the natural world, the pattern-principles (*li* 理) of everything, and a consciousness that presides over all. The concept of Heaven as a sky deity has a long history in Inner Asia and beyond. The Zhou tribal invasion around 1045 BCE introduced this deity to China and justified Zhou rule through the Mandate of Heaven (*tian ming* 天命). Traces of this deity with anthropomorphic characteristics are preserved in China's classics and culture; however, Confucians over the centuries, and especially Zhu Xi's identification of Heaven with pattern-principle, contributed to its gradual transformation into a philosophical concept at the expense of its ancient theistic significance. Modern scholars have generally continued and enhanced this rationalization inherent in Zhu's philosophical system.

Anthropomorphic notions about Heaven were more complex. Responding to questions about Heaven's role, Zhu employed traditional terms: master-governor (*zhuzai* 主宰), master (*zhu* 主), Lord (*di* 帝), Lord on High (*shangdi* 上帝), and the heart-mind of Heaven (*tianxin* 天心). Besides suggesting what Heaven was, he asserted what Heaven wasn't. Although Heaven was not a person sitting on a throne judging wrongdoing, Heaven possessed consciousness that was bound to be faithful to pattern-principles. I surmise that Zhu posited a ruling power over the flux of *qi* (vital energy) because pattern-principle, as moral norm, had no capacity to control *qi*. Thus, he associated pattern-principle with a presiding lord to support the notion of a natural cosmic order underpinning Confucian rituals and values. Confucian philosophers had projected an ideal Triad between Heaven, earth, and humanity, each with unique roles. Zhu strengthened this traditional notion. Especially with his parallels between Heaven's heart-mind and the heart-mind of the Way (*daoxin* 道心) within people, Zhu provided confidence in human ability to become good and enhanced his particular group and version of Confucian values (Tillman 1987).

Zhu Xi used the term *guishen* 鬼神 with different meanings in various contexts. During the middle decades of the twentieth century, senior scholars generally focused on Zhu's usage of the term to refer to the contractive and expansive phases of *qi* in the functioning of all things. Since *gui* (ghosts) was a homophone for *gui* 歸 (returning), and *shen* (spirits) was a homophone for *shen* 伸 (extending), these terms, like *yin* and *yang*, highlighted the functioning of phases of *qi* in nature and in relation to pattern-principles. Many in this senior generation projected Zhu's system as highly rational and compatible with science. During the last quarter of the century, scholars' attention turned to folk religious implications of Zhu's usages of *guishen*, which literally referred to ghosts and spirits. Despite his philosophical explanation of the dispersal of a deceased person's *qi*, Zhu endorsed invoking an ancestor's *qi* to partake of offered food. Although everyone's *qi* eventually disperses completely, sincere offerings of food and wine refreshed the vitality of an ancestor's *qi*. Thus, Zhu augmented philosophical justification for rites to venerate the dead. Furthermore, hungry ghosts and monsters arose when a person's *qi* was strong or enraged by violent death. Such occasions were not ordinary; thus, Zhu argued that Buddhists were wrong to teach that souls were reborn into this world. Late twentieth-century scholars explored tensions inherent in accounts of such strange phenomena, which did not fully accord with Zhu's natural philosophy. Although one could analyze Zhu's statements both as naturalizing (explaining ghosts within a philosophical system) and as spiritualizing (enhancing a sense of awe about nature and ancestors), Zhu did not bifurcate his understanding into such modern categories. Moreover, this second wave of scholars underscored how important Zhu's notions of spirits were to his support for Confucian rites in a society dominated by Buddhism.

Since the turn of the century, a few scholars have enhanced this last emphasis in order to explore how Zhu used prayers to Confucius to augment his own authority (e.g., Tillman 2004). Moreover, in his prayers of supplication to diverse local deities (even ones legal in other places, but with no legitimate connection locally) in Nankang, he set aside his ideological hostility toward temples and deities, which he judged to be illicit, in order to relieve drought and forestall famine. Such diverse efforts were some of the contributing factors first to his ascendancy within the Learning of the Way (*Daoxue* 道學) Confucian fellowship and later (within forty-one years of his death) to his enshrinement in Confucian temples and to official adoption of his commentaries on the Four Books for education and the civil service examinations. In places where he served as teacher and official, there was even an apotheosis of his spirit in special shrines (Chen and Tillman 2014).

As in his discussions of Heaven, Zhu followed and further developed the idea from Cheng Yi that ritual is synonymous with pattern-principle. This integration of ritual into Zhu's philosophical system is the focus of many recent scholars. Nevertheless, Zhu refused to reduce ritual to pattern-principle. For instance, he criticized students of the Cheng brothers who took this reductionist view to advocate embodying, practicing, and submitting to pattern-principle, instead of to ritual. Disparaging their abstract projections of imagined idealistic worlds, Zhu saw flaws in Cheng Yi's penchant to talk too loftily and abstractly, so students were lacking in purposeful practice (*gongfu* 功夫) and only sought what was lofty. Retraining traditional understandings of role differentiations and ritual practice was crucial to family, social, and political communities. The *Family Rituals* (*Jiali* 家禮), ascribed to Zhu, provided prominent ritual guidelines in late imperial China. Ultimately, he regarded ritual norms as grounded in the natural order, and the sages only observed and clarified the hierarchical order and persistent sequential patterns in nature; thus, he enhanced the absoluteness of social and cultural norms.

Translation
Heaven

1. It was asked, "Regarding the phrase in the *Analects* 3.13, 'commit an offense against Heaven,' your commentary says, 'Heaven is pattern-principle.' Is this pointing to making an offense against the blue heavens, or is it an offense against pattern-principle?"

[Zhu Xi] replied, "What makes Heaven Heaven is nothing other than pattern-principle. If Heaven did not have these pattern-principles, it would not be Heaven. Thus, the blue sky is just this Heaven of pattern-principles. Therefore, we say, 'The thing itself (*ti* 體) is called Heaven, and its master-governor (*zhuzai* 主宰) is called the Lord (*di* 帝).' It's like 'parents and children have kinship relations, and ruler and ministers share duty or rightness (*yi* 義)'; even though these pattern-principles are like this, it's also necessary above to have pattern-principles instructing like this to begin with. Nevertheless, it's not like the Daoist claim that there are 'Three Pure Imperial Spirits' attired in robes and seated on their thrones." (*ZZYL*, chapter 25, p. 621)

2. It was asked, "In (Cheng Yi's) phrase, 'the master-governor is called Lord,'[1] who is the master-governor?"

[Zhu Xi] replied, "Naturally, there is a master-governor. Heaven is an absolutely strong and totally *yang* entity, and naturally rotates without ceasing. Since it does so, there must be a master-governor. Such matters must be looked into for oneself, because words are inadequate to explain them." (*ZZYL*, chapter 68, pp. 1684–1685)

3. [Zhu Xi] said, "The blue sky is called Heaven. It is what rotates and revolves without ceasing. It is certainly improper to say that within the heavens is a person judging guilt and immorality; however, to say that the Way (*dao* 道) completely lacks a master-governor is also improper. It's necessary for people to see this for themselves." (*ZZYL*, chapter 1, p. 5)

4. [Zhu Xi] said, "[According to the *Book of Documents*,] 'Heaven mandates the five ranks of official robes and the five office seals to those possessing virtue! Heaven punishes the guilty with five bodily punishments and the five required services!' As for those with great virtue, bestow great blessings of official robes; as for those with little virtue, reward with little blessings; those with great guilt, punish with grave penalties; those with little guilt, punish with slight penalties; all this is completely 'Heaven's mandates and Heaven's punishments.' The sages never add one iota of their own intention to it, but only receive and implement Heaven's model or regulations (*fa* 法), and nothing more." (*ZZYL*, chapter 78, p. 2020)

5. It was asked: "When [the *Book of Documents*] proclaimed, 'Heaven sees as my people see and hears as my people hear,' is Heaven simply pattern-principle?"

[Zhu Xi] replied, "If all were taken to be pattern-principle, why would it also say, 'as my people see and hear'? There is a sense here of a master-governor." (*ZZYL*, chapter 79, p. 2039)

---

1. In commenting on the *Qian* 乾 hexagram in his *Explanations of the Book of Changes* (*Yi shuo* 易說), Cheng Yi made this statement, which Zhu quoted and discussed in the passage just prior to this one in the *ZZYL*.

6. It was asked, "I feel it's also not right for people now to do things like burn incense and worship Heaven."

    [Zhu Xi] replied, "Heaven is simply within oneself, so what is there to make supplications to? Within this one body, all that thinks and moves is Heaven. The one body's activity within Heaven is just like fish in water, everything filling the stomach is water." (*ZZYL*, chapter 90, pp. 2291–2292)

7. [Zhu Xi] said, "According to a [Shang dynasty] legend, there really was a Lord of Heaven who answered Gaozong (King Wuding, r. 1250–1192 BCE) [in a dream] and said, 'I bestow you with a good advisor (Fu Yue).' Today, people explain this Lord in terms of a master-governor and say it is without form; I think this explanation is inadequate. I also consider it unacceptable to say, as is commonly done, that it was the Jade Emperor.[2] In the final analysis, scholars are not able to explain what is going on in this case." (*ZZYL*, chapter 79, p. 2035)

8. [Zhu Xi said], "The finest and most minute things of Heaven and earth also have heart-mind, but there is a range of things having or not having consciousness. For example, as for a blade of grass or a tree, when turned toward *yang* they have vitality, but turned toward *yin* they wither, so they possess inherent likes and dislikes. The utmost greatness of Heaven and earth is providing life to many myriads of things, and revolving and circulating without ceasing; the four seasons, as well as days and nights, just like all kinds of things, come and go according to their natural sequence. Heaven and earth naturally possess a heart-mind that lacks a [deliberate] mind of its own. In the Return (*fu* 復) hexagram [in the *Classic of Changes*], the one *yang* is born below, which represents the heart-mind of giving life to things. It's also like the *Book of Documents* says, 'It is only the august Lord on High that bestows compassion on the masses below,' and 'The Way of Heaven encompasses prosperity and goodness, as well as calamity and licentiousness.' All this makes clear that there appears to be a master-governor within it. The heart-mind is this master-governor's capacity, and feelings are its ideas. . . ." (*ZZYL*, chapter 4, p. 60)

9. It was asked, "Inequalities or differences in mandates are, I feel, not really [due to] someone determining such differences. It's just that the *qi*'s two

---

2. According to ancient Chinese mythology, the Jade Emperor rules in the heavens and can intervene in the earthly world, so he was widely worshiped by the masses.

phases (*yin* and *yang*) in their complexities and unevenness follow and randomly occur, so every instance is not the same. Isn't it because all this is not caused by human efforts that people say these happenings are what Heaven has mandated?"

[Zhu Xi] replied, "These happenings simply flow from the great source. Such occurrences might seem as though there isn't one issuing a mandate for them. Yet, is there [really] one above us who orders these [things to happen]! According to the *Book of Odes* and the *Book of Documents*, it seems that there is a person above, as in such statements as, 'the Lord's wrath.' Nevertheless, this ruler is none other than pattern-principle being so. In the whole world there is nothing higher than pattern-principle; hence, there is the term 'Lord' to refer to it. In the passage from the *Book of Documents* which says, 'Only the august Lord on High bestows compassion on the masses below', the word 'bestows' has the meaning of a master-governor." (*ZZYL*, chapter 4, p. 63)

10. [Zhu Xi said,] "Hengqu (Zhang Zai) wrote, 'If one does not personally engage things, the heart-mind disregards them as extraneous.' He further wrote, 'The heart-mind that disregards things as extraneous is not adequate to unite with Heaven's heart-mind.' It's probably because Heaven is large and encompasses all things, that there is nothing outside of it. With all the things and pattern-principles that exist, if there is one that I neglect, my heart-mind regards that one as extraneous, and thus my heart-mind is not like Heaven's heart-mind." (*ZZYL*, chapter 98, p. 2519)

11. It was asked, "Does the heart-mind of Heaven and earth also have consciousness? Or, does it just indifferently take no deliberate actions (*wuwei* 無為)?"

[Zhu] replied, "It's not right to say that the heart-mind of Heaven and earth does not possess consciousness, but it does not think in the calculating manner that people do." (*ZZYL*, chapter 1, p. 4)

12. It was asked, "Regarding the heart-mind of Heaven and earth and the pattern-principles of Heaven and earth, pattern-principles are the pattern-principle of the Way. Therefore, does heart-mind have the meaning of master-governor?"

[Zhu Xi] replied, "Heart-mind certainly has the meaning of master-governor; however, what is called the master-governor is just pattern-principle, and it's not that there is another pattern-principle outside of the heart-mind, or that there is another heart-mind outside of pattern-principle."

It was further asked, "Is this word 'heart-mind' very similar to the word 'Lord?'"

[Zhu Xi] replied, "The character for 'person' is analogous to the character for 'Heaven', and the character for 'heart-mind' is analogous to the character for 'Lord.'" (*ZZYL*, chapter 1, p. 4)

13. Yang Daofu asked, "Teacher, you earlier taught us to contemplate cases where Heaven and earth have heart-mind and no heart-mind (*wu xin* 無心). Recently considering this, I said that in cases where Heaven and earth have no heart-mind, humaneness (*ren* 仁) is then the heart-mind of Heaven and earth. If one posits that they possess heart-mind, they must also have calculating thought and deliberate actions. How could Heaven and earth ever have calculatingly deliberate thinking! Nonetheless, that by which 'the four seasons revolve and the numerous things are born' probably is their conforming to what ought to be and thus they are as they are naturally. Thus, they don't await deliberate thought before becoming the Way of Heaven and earth."

[Zhu Xi] replied, "If so, then what about what the *Classic of Changes* refers to: 'See the heart-mind of Heaven and earth in the Return hexagram'; or 'centered and enhanced, the feelings of Heaven and earth can be perceived'? If it's like you said, you are referring only to cases where they have no heart-mind. If Heaven and earth really [only] possessed no heart-mind, unnatural phenomena might occur, such as oxen giving birth to horses, or peach trees producing plum blossoms. As Master Cheng said, 'Regard [the term] master-governor as referring to the Lord, and regard nature and feelings to be referring to the Qian 乾 [i.e., Heaven] hexagram.' The meanings of these terms are thus determined naturally, and the heart-mind is the locus of the master-governor; therefore, we say that Heaven and earth take their heart-mind to be giving life to things. At the time, Jingfu (Zhang Shi) thought that it was inappropriate for me to make such statements. Still, I say that Heaven and earth have no dealings other than to regard their heart-mind to be giving birth to things. The *qi* of the one source revolves and circulates, without ceasing for any interval, and all [of this activity] is about giving life to a considerable number of things. As Master Cheng said, 'Heaven and earth have no heart-mind but have transformations, and the sages have heart-mind but no deliberate actions (*wuwei*).'"

[Zhu Xi] added, "This refers to cases where Heaven and earth have no heart-mind. This is rather like, 'the four seasons revolve and the numerous things are born', so in that situation how would Heaven and earth need a heart-mind? When it comes to the sages, they do nothing but follow pattern-principle, so what else would they need to do! Therefore, Mingdao (Cheng Hao) commented, 'The constancy of Heaven and earth is to use heart-mind to universally encompass the myriad things without exercising a heart-mind of their own; the constancy of the sages regards their feelings to be following the myriad things, and so do not have their own [self-centered] feelings.' This says it the best."

It was additionally asked, "When referring to universally encompassing the myriad things, this is none other than the heart-mind being everywhere and thus without self-centeredness, isn't it?"

[Zhu Xi] replied, "Heaven and earth regard this heart-mind as extending to all things, so when people receive it, it becomes the heart-mind of people, and when things receive it, it becomes the heart-mind of things. Grasses, trees, and animals connect with it, and it becomes the heart-mind of grasses, trees and animals. However, there is ultimately only one heart-mind of Heaven and earth. Now, you need to realize situations where they have heart-mind, but also know cases where they have no heart-mind; only in this way can you avoid rigid pronouncements." (*ZZYL*, chapter 1, pp. 4–5)

14. [Zhu said,] "Where did Heaven and earth ever say that they deliberately wanted to give life to a sage or worthy! The birth of a sage was simply a natural process of a quantum of *qi* coalescing; yet, when the birth of a sage did occur, it appeared as though Heaven had an intention about it. . . ." (*ZZYL*, chapter 4, p. 80)

15. [Zhu said], "Only when the heart-mind is set free to be generous and fair will it be expansive, so don't let it be prepossessed with self-centered intentions about divisive barriers, and it will be expansive. With the heart-mind made expansive, it will naturally not be anxious and pressed. If one encounters calamity, one will not panic, or if one reaps a windfall, one will not exuberantly cling to it. Within short intervals, situations also aren't certain, because calamity may turn into prosperity, and prosperity into calamity. As Xunzi said, 'The noble person with an expansive heart-mind will be one with Heaven and the Way. If the heart-mind is constricted, the person will be in awe of rightness and be restrained.'[3] When a noble person's heart-mind is expansive, it is Heaven's heart-mind, but when it is

---

3. See chapter 3 of the *Xunzi*.

constricted, it is the reverently careful heart-mind of [sage-king] Wen of Zhou, and both are good. When an ignoble man's heart-mind is expansive, it is reckless, but when constricted, it is petty and narrow, selfish and miserly, and both are not good." (*ZZYL*, chapter 95, pp. 2447–2448)

16. Teacher [Zhu Xi] said, "Using a person's body as an analogy for discussion: Changes are just like the heart-mind; the Way is just like the nature; the spirit is just like the feelings."

    On a later day, it was asked, "You have used the human body to discuss it (the heart-mind). Is it permissible also to use the human body to explain Heaven and earth?"

    [Zhu Xi] replied, "Heaven's mandate moves and pervades everything, and that which masters and controls these pattern-principles is Heaven's heart-mind; that which possesses these pattern-principles is Heaven's nature, just like the pattern-principles of the seasons—spring, summer, fall and winter; and what produces and nurtures the myriad things is its feelings." (*ZZYL*, chapter 95, p. 2423)

17. [Zhu Xi] said, "To fathom the heart-mind exhaustively refers to knowing all of the pattern-principles of affairs and things and having nothing that isn't fathomed. To know human nature refers to knowing the proper relationships between ruler and ministers, parents and children, elder and younger siblings, husband and wife, and friends—each following its respective pattern-principle. To know Heaven is then to know the naturalness of these pattern-principles." (*ZZYL*, chapter 60, p. 1426)

18. [Zhu Xi commented on a passage from the *Classic of Changes*:] " 'The movements of Heaven and earth have their rhythmic sequences or prioritized order (*jie* 節), and so the four seasons succeed one another.' When the movements of Heaven and earth reach a certain point, they mutually countercheck their own original motion [as the perceived retrograde rotation of some planets]. As this year's winter is finished, there will again be spring, summer, autumn, and winter in the coming year, and beyond a certain point in the interrelated rotation, a season cannot continue. This break makes two section lengths, and the two sections are again broken into four section lengths, which are spring, summer, autumn, and winter. This is a natural rhythm, and from the beginning, there was no person to initiate it [i.e., seasonal succession]. The sages thus followed this natural rhythm to rhythmically sequence or order them (relations among people)—as the *Doctrine of the Mean* says, 'Cultivating the

Way (*dao*) is called teaching,' and the *Book of Documents* says, 'Heaven's order possesses ritual decorum.' Heaven and earth had no deliberate intent in this development, but were spontaneously and naturally so. The sages adopted Heaven as their model and thus set forth these various sequential orders or faithful bonds (*jie* 節) for human relationships to point out [their natural order]."[4] (*ZZYL*, chapter 73, p. 1866)

Ghosts and Spirits

19. Student Chen Houzhi asked: "Ancestors share one interconnected *qi* within Heaven and earth, so isn't it because the descendants offer sacrificial items to be enjoyed that the ancestors converge or disperse?"

[Zhu Xi] replied, "This is like what Shangcai (Xie Liangzuo) said, 'When desiring them to be present, they are present; when desiring them not to be present, they are not present.' This all arises from the people involved. Ghosts and spirits are essentially existent entities. Ancestors are also of one *qi* only with these [descendants here], and there is an inclusive or whole set [of the family]. When the descendants are physically present here, the ancestor's *qi* is also here, and they all share an interpenetrating blood and pulse (i.e., consanguinity). Therefore [as the *Zuo zhuan* 左傳 says], 'Spirits do not enjoy the offerings of those not their kindred and people do not sacrifice to those not their ancestry'; the reason is simply that their *qi* is not related. [According to the classic *Book of Rites*], 'The Son of Heaven (the emperor) offers sacrifices to Heaven above and earth below, and the heads of the various states offer sacrifices to mountains and rivers, and high officials offer sacrifices to the five domestic spirits'— even though these are not one's patrilineal ancestors, the emperor is the host of the Lord of Heaven above and earth below, and the heads of the various states are the lords of the mountains and rivers, and the high officials are the lords of the five domestic sacrifices. When one's hosting reaches the Other (i.e., spirits), then their *qi* also all aggregates summarily

---

4. Zhu is making a parallel utilizing two meanings of the term *jie*, i.e., the sequential order in the heavens and the hierarchical order in human relationships. It is of course common for conservative exponents to ground hierarchical human relationships in the order of nature. However, as more clearly seen in the passages on rituals (especially numbers 30, 34, 35, and 38 in this chapter), Zhu placed an emphasis on the necessary role of sages to embellish the sequential orders in nature with human embellishments or cultural patterns (*wen* 文).

on one's own body; when this happens, there is a locus of interaction." (*ZZYL*, chapter 3, p. 47; translation modified from Tillman 2004, 499)

20. [Zhu Xi said,] "Speaking from the view of Heaven and earth, there is only one *qi*. Speaking from one's own body, my *qi* is the *qi* of my ancestors and simply this one same *qi*, too; therefore, when invoked, they must respond." (*ZZYL*, chapter 3, p. 47)

21. It was asked, "When people die, is it true that their ascending *hun* 魂 and descending *po* 魄 souls then disperse?"

[Zhu Xi] replied, "They certainly disperse."

It was further asked, "When descendants make sacrificial offerings, how is it that there is invoking and connecting with the ancestors?"

[Zhu Xi] replied, "Ultimately, the descendants share the *qi* of the ancestors. Although the ancestors' *qi* is dispersed, their roots (i.e., bloodline) are still right here; if we completely express our sincerity and reverence, we are able to invoke their *qi* to converge right here. It is like waves of water, water in the back is not the water in front, and a later wave is not the same as the preceding wave; nevertheless, they are actually only waves of the same water. The *qi* of the descendants and the *qi* of the ancestors are also like this. There is naturally dispersal, but the ancestors' bloodline is still right here. The bloodline is here, so descendants are actually able to lead the *qi* of the ancestors to converge right here...." (*ZZYL*, chapter 3, pp. 47–48)

22. It was asked, "If descendants are conducting rites to ancestors, it's certainly like this [i.e., what Zhu advocated]. If one is conducting sacrificial rites for other spirits, how should these (rites) be done? Would these include offerings in anticipation of spirits enjoying the sacrificed items?"

[Zhu Xi] replied, "In the case of descendants in relation to an ancestor, there certainly is this obviously unchanging pattern-principle. In offering a sacrifice to the Other (i.e., spirits), one should conduct the rite as it should be conducted. As Confucius said, 'Perform the rites as if present, sacrifice to the spirits as if the spirits were present' (*Analects* 2.4). As in the emperor sacrificing to Heaven, it is what he should sacrifice to, because they are of a similar *qi* category, so why would the spirit not come down to enjoy the offered items? The lords of the various states sacrificed to the spirits of the soil and grain, thus sacrifices in these rites were being conducted by the appropriate *qi* category, so how would the spirits not come down to enjoy the rites? Now conducting rites to Confucius must be based on learning, and thus his *qi* category can be contemplated and known, too. . . ." (*ZZYL*, chapter 3, p. 52; translation modified from Chen and Tillman 2014, 296)

23. [Seeking advice on disciplining students,[5] Zhu Xi prayed to Confucius,] "I, Xi, am unworthy. Recently, I was selected as a county minor official due to the recommendation of the various commoner students, and now have to participate in administering their studies. However, my abilities are few and superficial, so my management of instruction does not inspire confidence. There are certain students under my direction whose bad behavior has stained those in charge. I believe that since I have failed to carry out the Way myself, I have been unable to lead and hone others and have allowed matters to come to this. Moreover, I was unable to impose proper penalties early on to punish and control them. As a result, both virtue and rules were lax, and these disobedient literati ultimately had no restrictions. Therefore, I am reporting to the Former Sage/Former Teacher (Confucius) to request direction in rectifying school rules and in using the punishment of publicly labeling to cause the students to feel ashamed. [According to the *Book of Documents* and the *Book of Rites*,] 'A wooden ruler is to instruct and punish,' and 'the two sticks can be effective in bestowing awe.' All these are models that the Former Sage/Former Teacher bequeathed to later generations for the administration of schools. The Former Sage/Former Teacher is approaching from above, how dare I not put my palms on the ground and kowtow." (*ZZWJ*, chapter 86, in *ZZQS*, vol. 24, pp. 4033–4034, translation modified from Tillman 2004, 502)[6]

24. [In his Cangzhou Study Lodge report to Confucius,[7] Zhu Xi prayed,] "On the thirteenth day of the second month of 1194, I, the later student

---

5. In prayerful report to Confucius's spirit, Zhu confessed his failures and expressed his humility and shame in large part to evoke even greater shame from misbehaving adult students; this stance was a common tactic by Chinese parents to augment children's sense of shame. Importantly, Zhu interjects himself as mediator between his students and Confucius's spirit and thus enhances his own authority.

6. *ZZWJ* refers to *Hui'an xiansheng Zhu Wengong wenji* 晦庵先生朱文公文集 (*The Collected Writings of Master Hui'an, Zhu, Duke of Culture*). *ZZQS* refers to *Zhuzi quanshu* 朱子全書 (*The Complete Works of Master Zhu*): see Zhu Xi 2002 in the bibliography.

7. Zhu echoed his conception of the transmission of the Way, and had students swear allegiance to the Way he transmitted.

Xi, venture prayerfully to entreat the Former and Ultimate Sage, the King of Promoting Culture (Confucius). Respectfully, I acknowledge the legacy of the Way extending back to (primordial sages) Fu Xi and the Yellow Emperor. Its achievements were assembled together by the Original Sage (Confucius), who transmitted ancient teachings, gave instructions, and set standards for ten thousand generations. His three thousand disciples were transformed as if his instructions had been a timely rain. Only (his disciples) Yan Hui and Zengzi were able to obtain Confucius's [complete] legacy. It was not until Zengzi and (Confucius's grandson) Zisi that his legacy was made more lustrous and great. Since then, subsequent followers lost the true transmission in the process of teaching and receiving. The legacy was not continued until more than one thousand years later. What Zhou Dunyi and the Cheng brothers [eleventh-century philosophers] learned and taught was that the myriad principles had one single origin. As for (their contemporaries) Shao Yong, Zhang Zai, and Sima Guang, even though their learning was diverse, they all arrived at the same conclusions about the Way. They facilitated us later generations, as if we were moving from a dark night into the dawning of a new day. When I was a child, I received instruction from (my late father) because of my limited knowledge. In my youth, I was taught by standard teachers, and in my mature years, I have met those who possessed the Way. Gazing upward respectfully, and even though nothing is heard, (I know that) due to the spirit consciousness in Heaven above, we are fortunate that nothing of the transmission has been lost. Now, I am old and retired from government service, and those of us who are fond of the same things have gathered here. Settled on this hill, we have begun living together [at this study lodge]. I looked for the origins and deduced the roots (of our Way) because how could we dare obscure our origins [i.e., neglect the former worthies]? Presenting our offerings and praying respectfully, we trust that the spirits, descending to this place, will draw nigh, communicate, and bless us with illumination. We will then faithfully and untiringly—without rejecting anything— transmit it (our Way) without interruption to those coming in the future. Now, as this is an auspicious day, I will lead the assembled students in celebration, performing the rite of offering food to the spirits (of the sages and teachers named). Please receive these food offerings!" (*ZZWJ*, chapter 86, in *ZZQS*, vol. 24, pp. 4050–4051, translation modified from Tillman 2004, 503–504)

25. [In supplications at the Guangyou Temple,[8] Zhu Xi prayed,] "Great King, You have performed meritorious service to the local people: if natives encountered flood and drought, they all prayed to Great King. None of their prayers ever failed to receive a clear response, just as the shadow always follows the person. For many years, the heart-minds of these people have submitted to Great King just like to their parents, and with complete trust in Great King as toward a venerable personage. Unexpectedly, August Heaven has sent down disaster, the weather became abnormal, so that all living things are suffering from drought. Xi [Zhu humbly using his personal name] and everyone here have been in total disarray and in our supplications for help, we neglected to exclusively beseech Great King. Due to our disrespectful behavior, Great King's retribution descended upon the local people and caused the fields in the whole area to suffer drought, to such an extreme that now the crops have withered and burned. Although Xi sincerely prayed at many temples, the clouds did not produce rain. The autumn sun has become more and more blazing; it has increasingly harmed the crops severely. If it does not rain within the next three days, there will be nothing left for the people to depend upon, and the disaster will be endless; people will have no food, so the elderly and children will be abandoned to die in ditches, and the young will become robbers to struggle for another day's survival. What disaster could be more extreme than this? If Great King does not save the people now, there will be no one to save after three days even if Great King were then to be moved to have compassion. Therefore, Xi and associates will purify ourselves and stay overnight at this temple to await a favorable mandate. If Great King has special sympathy for the people, please pardon our former faults and bestow favor upon us. These three days, Xi and the others will fast and spend the nights here alone to await commands. If within three days, Great King does not respond to us, then it means Great King has forsaken us, so Xi and the others will withdraw, while trembling with fear to await

---

8. While Zhu Xi served as the head of Nankang Prefecture (1178–1181), intense drought required his public prayers at temples pleading for rain. The Song honored the Guangyou Temples in Quanzhou, where Ouyang You had been the administrator (617–618). However, this "border-crossing god" had no legitimate connection to Nankang, so was illicit there; moreover, probably because Zhu's archenemy prime minister, Qin Hui (1091–1155), had bestowed the title "king" on this deity in 1147, Zhu had avoided the temple.

our execution; no one will dare return to make supplications here."
[Fortunately, it did rain within the allotted three days. Zhu returned to
thank the deity for the rain, which lasted six days.] (*ZZWJ*, chapter 86,
in *ZZQS*, vol. 24, pp. 4041–4042, translation modified from Chen and
Tillman 2014, 306)

26. [In endorsing a local petition to the Song court to elevate the spirit of
Tao Kan and to authorize his temples, Zhu Xi wrote,] "This petition is
by the Duchang county tax collector Dong Yi and others: 'Respectfully
we observe that one of the former worthies with a legacy in our prefecture was the awesome Duke Tao from Changsha, an Eastern Jin Palace
Attendant and Defender-in-Chief [Tao Kan, 259–334], who was in-
dustrious, loyal, and obedient. He raised the banner of righteousness
and supported his dynasty throughout his lifetime. According to the
local gazetteers (*Tujing* 圖經), the awesome Duke Tao first resided
in Poyang and later moved to Xunyang [now the city of Jiujiang in
Jiangxi]. His remains were located [here] in Duchang County, and
the temples to the awesome Duke Tao in Duchang County and
the prefectural capital of Nankang have responded to prayers for
averting floods and relieving droughts. Is the record true? Dong Yi
and others are residents of Duchang, and there are two temples in
the south and north of the county. We attest that the deity is intelligent and honest, and he quietly helps the locals. The two temples have
been established for a long time; whenever residents and traveling
merchants make supplications, there is always a response. When the
villagers of Duchang and neighboring prefectures and counties came
to the temples of the awesome Duke Tao to pray for rain in spring
and summer, the deity responded to prayers immediately. At the same
time, the temple of the awesome Duke Tao in Duchang borders on
the river, whose current is turbulent, and ships with bulk goods for
official use frequently pass by. Those on the ships have prayed to the
awesome Duke Tao, so that wind and waves became calm naturally.
Early and later records at the temple have described this clearly. Dong
Yi and others have not hidden the facts, but have stated the deeds of
the awesome Duke Tao in detail. We herewith report to the Throne
and humbly request an enhanced honorary title for him. . . .'" [*ZZWJ*,
chapter 20, in *ZZQS*, vol. 21, pp. 933–934; translation from Chen and
Tillman 2014, 308–309]

Ritual (*li*)

27. [Zhu Xi's commentary on *Analects* 12.1 (about restraining oneself and returning to ritual propriety) quoted Lü Dalin:] "The humane person regards all under Heaven as one body (*ti* or an entity in itself); both Heaven's order and Heaven's sequential seasons are included therein. The reason people are not humane is that they regard the self as only the self and things as only things, and thus do not consider all as the same entity. If one overcomes one's own self-centered interests to return to Heaven's order and Heaven's sequential seasons, then things and the self are simultaneously one entity. Although the world is huge, all belong within my practice of humaneness. If one attains this heart-mind for one day, one possesses this virtue for one day." (*Lunyu jingyi*, chapter 6B, in *ZZQS*, vol. 7, p. 413)

28. [Zhu Xi later made this critical correction:] "Mr. Lü only uses 'same entity' to discuss this (passage) and proclaims that the world's return to humaneness belongs within his own practice of humaneness. He further engages eulogistic praise and extreme language, so does not avoid excessive generalizations or impractical comments, and thus he lost the sage's essential point. If it were really as he says, then the teaching about 'restraining oneself and returning to ritual propriety and the world will return to humaneness' only exists within an imagined ecstasy, rather than the intended effect of actual practice of self-cultivation." (*Lunyu huowen*, chapter 12, in *ZZQS*, vol. 6, p. 801)

29. [Zhu Xi also quoted explanations by Xie Liangzuo on *Analects* 12.1:] Xie said, "Ritual is the established practice for conserving one's heart-mind. If one abides by pattern-principle to follow Heaven, one's movement, action, speech and silence are all from Heaven. If internal and external are in unison, all seeing, listening, speaking and moving are also all from myself."

It was asked, "If speaking and moving are counter to ritual, they can be rectified, but how can seeing and hearing attain agreement with ritual?"

Xie replied, "All four [of these standards] should not be changed, because when changed most [actions] will not accord with ritual decorum; therefore, the humane person is first taken to task and afterwards obtains [the ideal]. Being taken to task includes [being held responsible] for my seeing, my hearing, my talking, and my actions. Looking upward with an insatiable desire to look at birds and turning my head to respond poorly to people would be seeing and hearing without being engaged personally, so in each and every such situation, I would be deviating from the norm."

It was additionally asked, "What about when seeing, hearing, speaking and doing all accord with pattern-principle, but do not conform to ritual prescriptions?"

[Xie] replied, "Speaking and doing can still complete ritual, but seeing and hearing can go beyond ritual. Use this principle in seeing and listening, and they will naturally be in accord with ritual prescriptions, so complying with pattern-principle is returning to submit to ritual decorum."

It was also asked, "In seeking for humaneness, how should we engage in purposeful practice?"

[Xie] replied, "Subduing oneself must come from the locus of one's nature being inclined to engage the tasks, and overcoming one's self-centeredness then requires encountering pattern-principle with a heart-mind that is not preoccupied. Engage, like Confucius's student Yanzi, while seeing, listening, speaking, and doing, and pay attention, like Zengzi, to your facial expressions and appearance, too. In exhaling *qi*, also do like the Buddhists say, 'Let it flow from the center of the heart-mind.' Present-day people sing out, 'Yes, I promise,' but apparently not from the center of their heart-mind because they don't realize the consequences. The old saying, 'The mind wasn't focused in the eyes,' refers to looking without perceiving, hearing without listening, eating without knowing the food's flavor; not perceiving, not listening, and not knowing flavors is like 'not being humane' (*bu ren* 不仁, i.e., paralysis) or a dead fellow with no sense of suffering. But what's proper is just like Confucius's student Ran Yong (Zhonggong) coming through the gate as though greeting an important guest or delegating people as if handling a great ceremony, but retaining the sense of seeing an important guest or being in charge of a great ceremony—all of which is then akin to being able to feel suffering."

[Xie] added, " 'Subduing oneself and submitting to ritual decorum for one day and the world returning to humaneness' is only said from the viewpoint of our inner nature."

[Xie] further added, "Subduing oneself must come from the locus of one's nature being inclined to engage the tasks, and overcoming one's self-centeredness then requires encountering pattern-principle with a heart-mind that is open (*xu* 虛)." (*Lunyu jingyi*, chapter 6B, in *ZZQS*, vol. 7, pp. 413–414)

30. [Commenting on *Analects* 1.12, Zhu Xi highlighted the importance of being at ease when performing rites and adhering to prescribed regulations:] "Rituals are the sequential order or bonds (*jie* 節) and cultural embellishments (*wen* 文) of Heaven's pattern-principles and the ceremonial norms of human affairs. Being harmonious means being at ease and not pressed. This is because although ritual in itself is strict, all of it arises from the naturalness of pattern-principle itself; therefore, in performance of ritual, we must be at ease and unpressured, and it will then be valued. The Way of the former kings in antiquity was grounded in what they recognized as beautiful; thus, all things—whether minor or great— arose from their Way of ritual beauty." (*Lunyu jizhu*, chapter 1, in *ZZQS*, vol. 6, p. 72)

31. [Commenting on *Analects* 2.23, Zhu Xi followed Confucius in seeking to reconcile continuity and change in rituals:] "The Three Bonds refers to the ruler as the bond for his officials, the father as the bond for his son, and the husband as the bond of his wife. The Five Constants refer to humaneness, rightness, ritual decorum, wisdom, and faithfulness. Embellished culture and natural quality refer to the conscientiousness valued by the Xia, the natural qualities valued by the Shang, and the culture valued by the Zhou. The Triad or Three Interconnected System refers to: the Xia using *yin*, the third of the sequential Earthly Branches, as the beginning of the first month of the calendar and the System of Mankind; the Shang using *chou*, the second of the Earthly Branches, as the beginning of the first month and the System of Earth; and the Zhou using *zi*, the first of the Earthly Branches, as the beginning of the first month and the System of Heaven. The great essence of ritual in itself was all continued and unchangeable in the succession of the Three Dynasties. What they increased or decreased did not go beyond areas in the written stipulations where there were excesses or inadequacies, thus the traces of their adjustments can still be observed today. As for the regulations from the past or those rulers succeeding the Zhou dynasty, what they continued and what they removed did not go beyond these adjustments, even if they were a hundred generations from us, and not merely ten generations!" (*Lunyu jizhu*, chapter 1, in *ZZQS*, vol. 6, p. 81)

32. It was asked, "Teacher, you formerly said, 'Ritual is the body or the thing itself (*ti*).' Now you say, 'Rituals are the sequential order or bonds (*jie*) and cultural embellishments (*wen*) of Heaven's pattern-principles and

the ceremonial norms of human affairs.' It seems that this isn't the thing itself (*ti*), but its function (*yong*)."

[Perhaps somewhat frustrated about trying to get the student to comprehend this complexity, Zhu Xi] replied, "You people in the Jiangxi area have a [peculiar] local dialect and a manner of looking at segmenting, just as you say the Way (*dao*) is function, not the thing itself. For instance, speaking of a foot ruler, the wood without inch marks is the thing itself, but one with inch marks is function; or in the case of a steelyard weighing scale, one without markings for differing weights is seen as the thing itself, but one with such markings is function. It's even like a fan held by the handle, you refer to the bone, paper, and paste as the fan itself; when a person moves it, it is function."

When Yang Zhizhi asked about a thing itself, the teacher replied, "What is proper is the thing itself." (*ZZYL*, chapter 6, pp. 101–102)

33. It was asked, "Your commentary says, 'Ritual and music should not be regarded as function.' What about that?"

[Zhu Xi] replied, "Ritual is a matter of being respectful. When one is not respectful in one's heart-mind, outwardly one emptily goes through various patterned formalities; music is a matter of harmonizing with the music, but if one does not harmonize in one's heart-mind with the music, outwardly trying to force oneself won't get it. If one isn't so within one's heart-mind and only tries to force it outwardly, one will in the end make a lot of slip-ups, and even if one gets by with no slip-ups, the internal and the external will not correspond—which is not [true] ritual and music." (*ZZYL*, chapter 25, p. 605)

34. [Commenting on *Analects* 9.11, Zhu Xi said,] "[In Yanzi's statement that Confucius] 'broadened me with culture, and restrained me with ritual,' we see that the Sage taught only these two things: The effort involved in broad cultural discipline is certainly great, and the restraining rituals are only these few. If this [side] is Heaven's pattern-principles and that is human desires, then not engaging human desires is siding with Heaven's pattern-principles. 'Rituals are the sequential order or bonds and cultural embellishments of Heaven's pattern-principles.' Differentiating roles refers to sequences, and culture refers to ornamental refinement. Differentiating roles are not all the same and must have cultural embellishment to perform them properly. All passages in the tenth chapter, 'Community Relations,' of the *Analects* record occasions when the Sage Confucius was emotionally moved

while interacting with people through appropriate rituals." (*ZZYL*, chapter 36, p. 963)

35. It was asked, "[According to the *Book of Rites*,] 'When ritual surpasses (or exceeds), it departs from (or transgresses the norm), and when music surpasses, it degenerates.' At such extremes of excess, ritual and music not only digress and degenerate, but can they also perish?"

[Zhu Xi] replied, "Here, the word 'surpasses' (*sheng* 勝) is crucially important. Only when there is deviation from the norm does ritual lose its restraint and music lose its harmonization. In fact, these [restraints] are precisely the shorelines between life and death."

[Zhu Xi] added, "Ritual and music are all the natural spontaneity of Heaven's pattern-principles. Restraint and cultural embellishments are aspects that Heaven's pattern-principles naturally possess; harmonious music is also an aspect that Heaven's pattern-principles naturally possess. However, these pattern-principles of Heaven were originally transmitted crudely and rustically, so the sages established boundaries for them and separated them into sequential sections, designating what their beginning and ending should be. Having set forth what was outside and within, it was not permissible to differ from (or make mistakes regarding) these boundaries. Transgressing these limits was not in accord with Heaven's pattern-principles. Only if what is called ritual and music accords with the naturalness of the pattern-principles of Heaven will there be nothing that is inappropriate to perform."

[Zhu Xi] also added, "Restraint without ritual decorum will then be without music's harmony. Only when there is first restraint will harmony follow." (*ZZYL*, chapter 87, p. 2253)

36. Teacher [Zhu Xi] asked students, "People performing rituals, like greetings, nowadays are only stern, so how can they attain a harmonious relationship with others?"

The respondents all disagreed.

[Zhu Xi] replied, "You only need to know ritual decorum and how to perform a ritual in the proper way, and it will then be harmonious and re-laxed and not forced. Even when Confucius talked with higher officials, he was naturally respectful, and when he spoke with lower officials, he naturally possessed self-assurance. Educated persons should know how to be suitably respectful when talking with higher officials and how to possess suitable self-assurance when talking to lower officials, and then there will naturally be harmony. Once Lü Yushu (Dalin), made the following excellent statement: 'From coarse hemp to fine silks, if clothing differentiates ranks, there will be no regret felt by anyone within the entire nine lineages of the family. From princes and dukes to the lowest local messenger boys, if their ceremonial regulations and signifiers differentiate regulatory systems, none from the highest to the lowest will dare to dispute their status. All this is because ritual decorum arises from what their own nature possesses, and so none will fail to hit the proper mark in abiding by and carrying out their roles.' This statement highlights that decorum comes from the natural order and does not have even one restraint that is forced upon people; therefore, you must know these pattern-principles, and you will then be naturally harmonious."

Huang Youkai raised Teacher Zhu's old viewpoint, saying, "It's just like how much strictness is involved when the father sits and the sons stand, or when the ruler is honored and the officials are humble. If it appears that the father is agreeable to sitting and the sons to standing, or the ruler is agreeable to being honored and the officials to being humble, then everyone is at ease." [Zhu Xi] replied, "Just so." (*ZZYL*, chapter 22, pp. 513–514)

37. [Zhu Xi said,] "On the basis of their birth and rank, placing them into the position they ought to occupy is called assessment or arranging in order. Based on assessment and participation, bestowing them with what they ought to receive is called order. Heaven's order is thus a natural sequential order. If he is a ruler, teach him to occupy the ruler's position, and if he is an official, teach him to occupy an official's position, and if he is a father, teach him to occupy the father's position, and if he is a son, and teach him to occupy the son's position. The order refers to the matters within Heaven's order, such as the imperial Son of Heaven makes offerings to Heaven and earth, the regional lords make offerings to the mountains and streams, the great officials make offerings to the five deities, and the literati and commoners make offering to their ancestors. The emperor as [associated with the number] eight, the feudal lords as six, the great officials as four, all have sequential order, which is grounded in this natural order." (*ZZYL*, chapter 78, p. 2019)

38. [Zhu Xi said,] "The *Book of Documents* says, 'Heaven's order possesses regulations to encourage or to induce our five regulations and five courtesies! Heaven's order possesses rituals and gives rise to our five rituals having the Mean!' The number of rituals derive from Heaven's regular order, and the sages only followed and augmented them and made

them central, and so simply set forth their usefulness. In all the rituals for what is called capping, marrying, mourning and revering ancestors, participating in the institutions of husband's regulations, cultural objects for rituals and music, chariot ornaments and human clothing— none of these were created by the sages. All of these [institutions] were transmitted by Heaven, and the sages only assisted in the emergence of Heaven's pattern-principles. It's like pushing a cart that was originally moving along on its own: we do no more than merely provide a little assistance." (*ZZYL,* chapter 78, p. 2020)

Bibliography

Chen, Xi, and Hoyt Cleveland Tillman. 2014. "Ghosts, Gods, and the Ritual Practice of Local Officials during the Song: With a Focus on Zhu Xi in Nankang Prefecture." *Journal of Song-Yuan Studies* (44): 287–323.

Tillman, Hoyt Cleveland. 1987. "Consciousness of *T'ien* in Chu Hsi's Thought." *The Harvard Journal of Asiatic Studies* 47 (1): 31–50.

_____. 2004. "Zhu Xi's Prayers to the Spirit of Confucius and Claims to the Transmission of the Way." *Philosophy East and West* 54 (4): 489–513.

Zhu Xi 朱熹. 2002. *Zhuzi quanshu* 朱子全書 (*The Complete Works of Master Zhu*). Shanghai: Shanghai guji chubanshe and Hefei: Anhui jiaoyu chubanshe.

Further Readings

Gardner, Daniel K. 1995. "Ghosts and Spirits in the Song Confucian World: Chu Hsi on *Kuei-shen.*" *Journal of the American Oriental Society* 115 (4): 598–611.

Chen, Xi, and Hoyt Cleveland Tillman. 2014. "Ghosts, Gods, and the Ritual Practice of Local Officials during the Song: With a Focus on Zhu Xi in Nankang Prefecture." *Journal of Song-Yuan Studies* 44: 287–323.

Kim, Yung Sik. 2000. *The Natural Philosophy of Chu Hsi* (1130–1200). Philadelphia: American Philosophical Society.

Tillman, Hoyt Cleveland. 2004. "Zhu Xi's Prayers to the Spirit of Confucius and Claims to the Transmission of the Way." *Philosophy East and West* 54 (4): 489–513.

7

Criticisms of Buddhism, Daoism, and the Learning of the Heart-Mind

Ellen Neskar and Ari Borrell

Introduction

Throughout the Song dynasty, Confucian scholar-officials, Buddhist monks, and Daoist priests belonged to a single social network, in which they formed friendships, studied, traveled, shared intellectual work, and corresponded with one another. Indeed, many literati promoted a syncretic vision based on the notion that the three teachings formed a single Way.

Throughout his life, Zhu Xi maintained friendships with both Daoist and Buddhist elites. Despite (or perhaps because of) this, he came to be a vocal opponent of both Buddhism and Daoism. The first part of the translation in this chapter deals with three main areas of Zhu Xi's critique: his distinction of the neo-Confucian concept of pattern-principle and virtuous governance from seemingly similar Buddhist notions of emptiness and Daoist ideas of non-being and governance by non-action; his concern with what he saw as both schools' lack of social and political engagement and their rejection of ethical norms; and the practice of Buddhist meditation and Daoist quietism.

But, as these selections demonstrate, Zhu did not hold equally negative views toward Buddhism and Daoism. He had a certain respect for Zhuangzi, and believed that Laozi and the later Daoists were "better than" the Buddhists. While Zhu was critical of earlier forms of Buddhism, he reserved a special disdain for the Song dynasty version of Chan and, in particular, for its interpretation of the heart-mind and practice of sudden enlightenment. Significantly, a large portion of his attacks against Chan focus on what he saw as its pernicious influence on scholars in the Learning of the Way and Learning of the Heart-Mind movements. These attacks are taken up in part two of the translation.

Zhu Xi's vehement attacks against Chan Buddhism should be understood within the context of the sociopolitical milieu of literati in the early twelfth century. After the fall of the north to the Jurchens in 1126, neo-Confucians continued to attack former Grand Councilors Wang Anshi 王安石 (1021–1086) and Cai Jing 蔡京 (1046–1126), mainly for their promotion of Wang's New Policies and his interpretation of the Confucian Classics.[1] Perhaps most egregious to them were Wang's and Cai's censures of opponents, including the Cheng brothers and their followers. Ultimately, neo-Confucian literati blamed both councilors for the loss of the north.

These criticisms were not simply a rehashing of old factional struggles. When Qin Hui 秦檜 was Chief Councilor (1138–1155), he reinstated Wang Anshi's commentaries as part of the civil service examinations and renewed earlier criticisms of Learning of the Way, banishing many of its proponents from government service. Qin Hui was also responsible for a policy of appeasement with the Jurchens and the signing of several peace treaties. Zhu Xi and his colleagues in Learning of the Way opposed these treaties and urged the court to retake the north. They came to be known as the pro-war faction.

In this they were joined by a number of Buddhist monks, most prominent among them Dahui Zonggao 大慧宗杲 (1089–1163). Because of his political activism, Dahui was charged with treason, defrocked, and sentenced to fifteen years of exile in the south. That did not stop him from promoting his form of socially engaged Buddhism, which he targeted to Learning of the Way scholars and members of the pro-war faction. Dahui is best known for his rejection of the more quietistic forms of Chan in favor of the *kōan* [*gong'an* 公案] method, a practice he believed was best suited to the active lifestyle of the scholar-official. In short, he believed that *kōan* practice was the key to the self-realization of the literati class, the victory of the pro-war party at court, and the full resuscitation of the Song.

Dahui's outreach was successful. Second and third generation disciples of the Cheng brothers were drawn to his teachings, became his disciples, practiced *kōan* meditation, and freely incorporated his Chan ideas into their writings on Confucian texts.

---

1. Wang Anshi's *New Meaning of the Three Classics* (*Odes, Book of Documents,* and *Rites of Zhou*), along with his son's commentaries on the *Analects* and *Mencius*, became the orthodox interpretation used in the civil service examinations.

Zhu Xi was not immune to Dahui's influence. In his teens and twenties, he spent over ten years studying Chan, first with Dahui's disciple, the monk Daoqian 道謙 (1105?–1152?), who was also involved with the pro-war faction and was exiled for his political activities. During this period, Zhu also corresponded with Dahui.

In 1154 Zhu Xi began to study with Li Tong 李侗 (1093–1163), whose intellectual genealogy could be traced back to the Cheng brothers. Li urged Zhu to turn away from Chan and return to studying the Confucian classics and the Cheng brothers' writings. Thus began Zhu's gradual conversion to Learning of the Way.

In 1164 Zhu began a concerted effort to attack the influence of Chan on neo-Confucianism, an effort that would continue throughout his lifetime. That year he composed his "Critique of Adulterated Learning" (*Zaxue bian* 雜學辨), the bulk of which forms part three of the translation. The work is comprised of passages Zhu selected from four commentaries on classical texts written by Northern and Southern Song literati. To these, Zhu Xi provided his own line-by-line critique. This chapter's translation contains selections from three of these: Su Che's "Commentary on the *Laozi*," Lü Benzhong's "Commentary on the *Great Learning*," and Zhang Jiucheng's "Commentary on the *Doctrine of the Mean*."[2]

Zhu selected these commentaries, in large part, because they were written by renowned literati who enjoyed a wide following. Su Che 蘇轍 (1039–1112) was primarily known as a literary figure and poet, but his philosophical writings were also well regarded. In addition to his "Commentary on the *Laozi*," Su Che wrote commentaries on the *Odes, Mencius*, and *Analects*. In these, Su argued that Confucianism, Daoism, and Buddhism were not antithetical but, rather, formed a single Way. Although Zhu Xi did not consider Su Che to be a neo-Confucian, he saw his mixing of the three teachings to be symptomatic of the eclecticism favored by Northern Song literati and a continued danger to those in his own generation.

Zhang Jiucheng 張九成 (1092–1159) and Lü Benzhong 呂本中 (1084–1145) were neo-Confucians who had studied with first-generation disciples of the Cheng brothers and were considered by their contemporaries as leading figures in the Learning of the Way and pro-war movements. Both were also disciples of Dahui Zonggao. They freely incorporated Chan notions into their interpretation of Confucian texts and imbued core Cheng-school teachings

---

2. The fourth commentary, "An Explanation of the *Classic of Changes*," was written by Su Che's elder brother Su Shi 蘇軾 (1036–1101).

on the heart-mind, pattern-principle, and "investigation of things and extension of knowledge" with a particularly Chan flavor. Zhu was also troubled by the ways in which Zhang and Lü applied these concepts to *kōan* meditation that would lead to a sudden and transcendental enlightenment (something Zhu admitted he never attained). To Zhu Xi, Zhang and Lü represented a liability to the purity and integrity of the Cheng teachings. He used his "Critique of Adulterated Learning" to replace their ideas with a distinctively neo-Confucian praxis and epistemology.

Zhu's attacks on Zhang and Lü are personal and rancorous. One can see them as a kind of rejection of, and coming to terms with, his own Buddhist past. Nevertheless, he remained proud of the time he spent studying Buddhism, for he believed it allowed him to detect both the deceptions promoted by monks like Dahui and the slightest Buddhist influences in the writings of his contemporaries.

Translation
Part One: On Buddhism and Daoism

1. Sacrificial Essay for Chan Master Dao[qian] of Kaishan

In the past I pursued learning and read the *Classic of Changes, Analects,* and *Mencius.* I examined the way the ancients had become sages and, not realizing my own limitations, sought to emulate them. But all my paths were blocked and my Way impeded. And, in the end, I was unable to make progress. Then, I asked my elders how to proceed. They all told me that it is essential to gain awakening and that nothing surpassed Chan teachings for understanding enlightenment. It was then that I became determined to study Chan. . . .

In the fall of 1146 the Master [Daoqian] came to Gongchen Mountain, and it was at this point that we developed a relaxed and intimate daily relationship. One day I burned incense before him and asked for instruction on this matter [Chan]. The Master had a dictum: "Definitely not this."[3] And for the first time I understood that my separation from the Way, which was growing day by day, was because I lacked proper instruction. . . .

---

3. Daoqian used this phrase, "definitely not this" (*jueding bu shi* 決定不是), to indicate that nothing conceived by the rational heart-mind is capable of expressing the deeper truths of Chan. See Xiaoying 曉瑩 (1128–1220), *Luohu yelu* 羅湖野錄, chapter 2 in the Taishō (Tripitaka) 83.386c.

Oh the grief! He was taken from us too soon. My revered Master, his wisdom was so comprehensive and complete. It is I who failed to gain awakening, without even a glimpse. Presenting the rich offerings, my tears fall on his spirit tablet. Bereft, I bow my head. He has transcended it all. (*ZXJ* [*yiji*], chapter 3, p. 5698)[4]

2. Letter to Chan Master [Dao]qian of Kaishan

Previously, I was instructed by Miaoxi [Dahui Zonggao] to not allow even the slightest iota of my book learning or cogitation to remain in my heart-mind but only to constantly raise-up the *kōan* phrase "A dog has no Buddha-nature." May I receive a word of advice to alert me to my deficiencies. (*ZXJ* [*yiji*], chapter 1, p. 5619)

3. Someone was talking about the harm done by Zhuangzi, Laozi, Chan, and Buddhism. [Zhu Xi] said, "Chan teachings do the greatest harm to the Way. Zhuangzi and Laozi did not destroy moral pattern-principles completely. Now Buddhism had already broken with human relations. But Chan, right from its start, completely eradicated moral pattern-principles, leaving no trace. Because of this I say that Chan has done the greatest harm." After a moment, he added: "If you're asking about their substance [*shi* 實], then they're all the same. But there are degrees of harm. . . .[5] When Buddhism first entered China, it only discussed the practice of cultivation. It didn't yet have all the Chan talk." (*ZZYL*, chapter 126, p. 3014)

4. Mo asked, "Ordinarily, I worry about lapsing into heterodox teachings and so I have never read such works as *Zhuangzi* and *Laozi*. Now, I wish to read them. Is that okay?"

[Zhu Xi] replied, "As long as you master [your heart-mind], how can reading them be harmful? The important thing is to understand how their ideas differ from those of the sages." (*ZZYL*, chapter 97, p. 2498)

5. [Zhu Xi said,] "Zhuangzi said, 'Each thing has its norm; this is called the nature.'[6] This phrase, 'Each thing has its norm,' is similar to our saying,

---

4. *ZXJ* refers to *Zhu Xi ji* 朱熹集 (*Collected Work of Zhu Xi*): see Zhu Xi 1996 in the bibliography.

5. Editor's footnote: what follows after the ellipsis picks up in the subsequent section of Zhu Xi's text.

6. *Zhuangzi*, chapter 12.

'When there is a thing, there is a norm.'[7] Compared to other thinkers, Zhuangzi is somewhat better." (*ZZYL*, chapter 125, p. 3000)

6. [Zhu Xi said,] "'Bringing peace to the world' is the most important matter and so there have been many discussions promoting it."[8] . . . He further said, "As for Zhuangzi, I do not know from whom he received the transmission, but he himself had insight into the Way itself. Now, after Mencius, neither Xunzi nor other gentlemen could measure up. For example, [Zhuangzi said,] 'If we speak of the Way but not of its sequence, then it is not the Way.'[9] Comments such as this are excellent. I think that the source [of his ideas] must have been received from a follower in the Confucian school. Later, any of the good points in Buddhist teachings all came from Zhuangzi. However, Zhuangzi's knowledge was not perfected, because his practice lacked a certain refinement. Within a short time, all his teachings degenerated. This is what is called 'The worthy go beyond [the Way].'"[10] (*ZZYL*, chapter 16, p. 369)

7. It was asked, "What is the difference between Buddhist non-being and Daoist non-being?"

   [Zhu Xi] replied, "The Daoists still have being. This is seen in the line, 'Be without desires to see its mysteries; have desires to see its manifestations.'[11] The Buddhists, however, take Heaven and Earth to be an illusion and the Four Elements [earth, water, fire and wind] to be transitory and unreal. That is complete non-being." (*ZZYL*, chapter 126, p. 3012)

8. Qian Zhi asked, "Nowadays, everyone considers 'emptiness' (*kong* 空) to be a Buddhist doctrine and 'non-being' (*wu* 無) to be a Daoist doctrine. What is the difference between emptiness and non-being?"

   [Zhu Xi] replied, "'Emptiness' is a term that encompasses both being and non-being. The Daoist doctrine splits being (*you* 有) and non-being in two. Before things come into existence, all is non-being. [When

---

7. Zhu Xi is citing Mengzi 6A6, which is citing the *Odes*, Mao #260.

8. "Bringing peace to the world" is the last of the eight steps described in the opening section of the *Great Learning*.

9. *Zhuangzi*, chapter 13.

10. *Doctrine of the Mean*, chapter 4.

11. *Daodejing*, chapter 1.

things] appear before our eyes, it is being. And so, they call [the former] non-being. But, in Buddhist doctrine everything is non-being. Before things come into existence, it's non-being. [When things] appear before our eyes, it is also non-being. [Thus, they say,] 'Form is emptiness; emptiness is form.'[12] From the great matters of the myriad affairs and things down to the hundred bones and nine apertures [of the body] everything is equally non-being. [The Buddhists have a saying:] 'To eat all day yet not chew a single grain of rice; to be fully dressed but not wear a single thread of silk.'" (*ZZYL*, chapter 126, p. 3012)

9. [Zhu Xi said,] "To understand the teachings of Buddhism and Daoism, we do not need a detailed analysis. Their greatest crime is just one thing: they reject the Three Bonds and the Five Constants.[13] There is no need to speak of anything else." (*ZZYL*, chapter 126, p. 3014)

10. It was asked, "[Confucius said,] 'Govern through virtue.'[14] Isn't this similar to Laozi's idea of non-action (*wuwei*)?"

[Zhu Xi] replied, "It was not only Laozi who spoke of non-action. Confucius once replied, 'Was Shun not someone who governed through non-action? What did he need to do other than make himself reverent and sit facing south?'[15] What Laozi meant by *wuwei* was truly to do nothing at all. What the Sage meant by *wuwei* was not 'to do nothing,' since he also added, '[Shun] made himself reverent and sat facing south.' This means 'rectifying oneself to rectify others'[16] and 'being serious and reverential to bring peace to the world.'[17] Those in later generations who were unable to govern the world were all unable to be seriously respectful and thoroughly reverential." (*ZZYL*, chapter 23, p. 537)

11. [Zhu Xi said,] "The Way is the pattern-principle universally followed throughout time. The compassion of a parent, filiality of a child,

---

12. *Heart Sutra* (*Xin jing* 心經). Included in *Mahāprajñāpāramitā sūtra* (*Da boreboluomiduo jing* 大般若波羅蜜多經). See Taishō 8.848c.

13. The Three Bonds refer to the relationships between ruler and subject, parent and child, husband and wife. The Five Constants are humaneness, rightness, ritual, wisdom, and trustworthiness.

14. *Analects* 2.1.

15. *Analects* 15.5.

16. *Mengzi* 7A19.

17. *Doctrine of the Mean*, chapter 33.

humaneness of a ruler and devotedness of a minister—each of these is an ethical pattern-principle of our public weal. 'Virtue' is precisely the attainment of the Way within a person. . . . Laozi said, 'When the Way is lost, there is virtue.'[18] Understanding neither [Way nor virtue], he divided them into two different matters and so regarded the Way as an empty thing. We Confucians speak of them as one thing. We call it 'Way,' when we refer to this universally shared [pattern-principle] and not simply in regard to a single person. 'Virtue' is the full attainment of this Way within oneself. Laozi said, 'When the Way is lost, there is virtue. When virtue is lost, there is humaneness. When humaneness is lost, there is rightness.'[19] If one departs from humaneness and rightness, then one is without moral pattern-principles. How can this be the Way!" (*ZZYL*, chapter 13, p. 231)

12. Hu [Shuqi] asked about the proper method for quiet sitting (*jingzuo* 靜坐)

[Zhu Xi] replied, "Quiet sitting means to sit quietly as follows: don't have idle concerns and don't have idle thoughts. But there is no [special] method."

It was asked, "When practicing quiet sitting and one thinks of something, then the heart-mind focuses on that thing. But if one has no thoughts, the heart-mind doesn't have anything on which to focus. What is your view?"

[Zhu Xi] replied, "There is no need to focus on something. If one were to focus on something, then it would be like the Daoists who count the inhalation and exhalation of breath and focus their gaze on the white spot on the tip of the nose. They require a prop because their heart-minds are unfocused. If you cannot cut off thoughts it is better to just let it be; there is no harm in that." . . . [Zhu] further said, "In quiet sitting, when you put a stop to idle and scattered thoughts, then your self-cultivation will go more smoothly." (*ZZYL*, chapter 120, p. 2885)

13. [Zhu Xi said,] "Chan is only a method of obstinately guarding [the heart-mind]. Take, for instance, the *kōan*s 'three catties of hemp' or 'dried shit-stick.' Initially there is no meaning attached to these phrases. They simply teach [practitioners] to deaden their heart-minds, to mull over these phrases continuously, and to focus on them for a long time. Suddenly they have an insight, which is 'enlightenment.' The general idea

---

18. *Daodejing*, chapter 38.

19. *Daodejing*, chapter 38.

is to fix the heart-mind and not let it scatter or become confused and, after a long time, illumination naturally will shine forth. This is how illiterate people are suddenly able to write *gathas*[20] after they achieve enlightenment. Although the experience of enlightenment is the same, there are different depths [of understanding]. I used to enjoy talking to Chan practitioners and this is what they told me. Some of them could really talk it up, but they were extremely boastful and full of hot air. Those like Dahui Zonggao were imposing and charismatic and so were able to stir up an entire generation, including men like Zhang Jiucheng and Wang Yingchen,[21] who both revered him." (*ZZYL*, chapter 126, p. 3029)

14. Treatise on Buddhism, Part One

It was asked, "Mencius speaks of thoroughly exercising the heart-mind to know the nature and preserving the heart-mind to nourish the nature. Buddhist teachings also take as their basis knowing the heart-mind and seeing the nature. Isn't this an area where we happen to have similarities?"

Master Zhu replied, "The difference between Confucianism and Buddhism can be summed up in a few single words."

It was asked, "What are they?"

[Zhu Xi] replied, " 'The nature' is what Heaven bestows on humans and is replete within the heart-mind. 'The feelings' are what arise from the heart-mind when the nature responds to things. 'The heart-mind' is the master of the person and unifies nature and feelings. Humaneness, rightness, ritual, and wisdom are the nature and constitute the heart-mind itself. Concern, shame and disdain, reverential attention, and deference and yielding are the feelings and constitute the function of the heart-mind. Therefore, the [*Book of Documents*] says, 'Bestow good on the people,'[22] and the [*Odes*] says, 'Where there is a thing, there is a norm.'[23] . . .

---

20. *Gatha*s are Buddhist verses written upon attaining enlightenment.

21. On Zhang Jiucheng, see the "Introduction," and the translation, section 20 in this chapter. Wang Yingchen 汪應辰 (1118–1176) was a prominent member of Learning of the Way. Among his teachers were Lü Benzhong and Zhang Jiucheng. He was also a practitioner of Chan, under the guidance of Dahui, with whom he exchanged numerous letters. Zhu Xi and Wang met in 1162 and thereafter carried on a lively correspondence debating the influence of Buddhism on neo-Confucianism.

22. *Book of Documents*, "The Announcement of Tang" (*Tang gao* 湯誥). After overthrowing the Xia dynasty, King Tang announced the victory and the founding of the Shang dynasty to his people, claiming that the August Lord (Shangdi) conferred good on the people.

23. *Odes*, Mao #260.

"The way [the Buddhists] 'know the heart-mind' is to establish another separate heart-mind to know this heart-mind. And, their so-called 'seeing the nature' never comprehends the good bestowed upon the people or the norms inherent in things. Having failed to understand the basis of the nature, none of their responses to things or their expressions of feelings ever accord with moral pattern-principles. Thereupon, they consider these [things and feelings] a burden and cut them off completely. . . .

"The heart-mind is the master of the person and is what unites nature and feelings. It is one, not two; it is host, not guest; it directs things rather than being directed by things. . . .

"Now, when the Buddhists talk about knowing the heart-mind, it means to shut off seeing and hearing in order to seek to know [the heart-mind] itself while in a trance. This is like using the eyes to see the eyes and using the mouth to bite the mouth. Although their goal is impossible to achieve, it inevitably results in internal discord. Isn't this setting up a separate heart-mind? Now if one sets up a separate heart-mind, then the one becomes two and the host becomes guest. . . . They blankly guard themselves, destroy feelings, and abandon affairs. By cutting themselves off from the relations of ruler and minister, father and son, their heart-minds cease to function. . . .

"The so-called *kōan* method of recent years is, moreover, a shortcut [to enlightenment]. The source of these is Zhuangzi's discussion of the cicada catcher and bell-stand carver.[24] But [*kōans*] are more ingenious and intricate. However, being ignorant of the pattern-principle of Heaven and yet selfishly indulging themselves in these practices—how could they deserve praise within the school of the noble person!"[25] (*ZXJ* (*bieji*), chapter 8, pp. 5525–5527)

Part Two: Criticism of Contemporaries for Mixing Confucianism, Buddhism, and Daoism

15. Memorial to the Throne

In recent years, your majesty [Xiaozong r. 1162–1189] has focused his heart-mind on seeking the essentials of the great Way, and has paid

---

24. *Zhuangzi*, chapter 19.

25. The final phrase—"How could they deserve praise in the school of the noble person"—is a paraphrase of *Xunzi*, chapter 7, "On Confucius."

considerable attention to the works of Laozi and the Buddhists. These may be rumors, which I don't know whether to believe or not. If they are true, then I personally believe that this is not the way to transmit the Heavenly endowment of the sacred sages and attain the glory of Yao and Shun. To record and recite flowery rhetoric is not the way to explore the source of, and to bring forth, the Way of governing. Emptiness and quiescence are not the way to unite root and branch and establish the great Mean. (*ZXJ*, chapter 11, p. 440)

16. [Zhu Xi said,] "When I saw the discussion about Confucianism and Buddhism between Lu Xiangshan and Wang Shunbo, I laughed to myself.[26] The difference between Confucianism and Buddhism lies only in the distinction between emptiness and concreteness. . . .[27] [Lu wrote] that the Buddhists and we Confucians are similar in outlook and that the only distinction is [that we] differentiate rightness and profit, being public-oriented and self-centered. His idea is wrong. If it were [as Lu says], then we Confucians and the Buddhists would have the same basic pattern-principles. And, if that were so, then how could Lu trace our difference to a distinction between rightness and profit? The very sources of our doctrines are different: we Confucians hold that the myriad pattern-principles are real, while the Buddhists hold that the myriad pattern-principles are all empty." (*ZZYL*, chapter 124, pp. 2975–2976)

17. Someone said, "Lu Xiangshan says that 'to restrain oneself and return to ritual'[28] does not simply mean that one must rid oneself of desires and resentment. [It also means that] one should not have even a single thought of becoming a sage or worthy."

    [Zhu Xi] responded: "This sort of comment is just like a little child at play. [Lu's] only concern is to sound lofty. Has there ever been this kind

---

26. Lu Xiangshan 陸象山 (1139–1193) was a contemporary of Zhu Xi's. Although he held a competing view of neo-Confucianism, which came to be known as Learning of the Heart-Mind (*xinxue* 心學), the two were friends. They debated their different approaches to metaphysics and epistemology in numerous letters and debates. Ivanhoe has a translation of Lu's letter to Wang in Tiwald and Van Norden (2014, 257–259).

27. Editor's footnote: what follows after the ellipsis picks up in the subsequent section of Zhu Xi's text.

28. *Analects* 12.1.

of talk in the school of the Sage? If people wish to learn to be a sage or worthy, that's excellent. What could be wrong with that! . . . One can see that Lu's ideas are simply Chan. [The Buddhist monk] Bao Zhi 寶誌 (418–514) wrote:

> Do not allow the heart-mind to have the slightest thought of self-cultivation.
> Eternal freedom is within the formless light.[29]

[Lu] wanted to be like this, but how is that possible? . . .

"As I always say, if someone must study Chan, it is far better to be clear about it and go study the [the kind of] Chan with the shouting and beating. But, here Lu mixes the words of the sages and worthies with Chan and produces nothing worthwhile—it's like a dragon without horns or a snake with feet. In the old days, Lu was not like this. Later, he really changed. Now his teachings have ruined the youth (who follow him): they won't read books, they're all confused and don't understand a thing. What a shame! What a shame! It's just like Xunzi's unconscionable and reckless criticisms, which led to Li Si who went so far as to burn books and bury Confucians![30] If Xunzi had lived to see Li Si's actions, he would certainly have regretted it. If Lu were still alive and saw the younger generation all confused like this, he would surely regret his past errors."

[Zhu Xi] also said, "Lu's teachings were always clear at the two ends but vague in the middle."

It was asked, "How were they vague?"

[Zhu Xi] replied, "There were things he couldn't explain. The reason why he couldn't explain them was because of Chan. His infatuation with Chan was like the saying: 'When the mandarin duck embroidery is done,

---

29. From Bao Zhi's "Song of the Twelve Hours" (*Shiershi song* 十二時頌) in *Records of the Transmission of the Lamp* (*Jingde chuandenglu* 景德傳燈錄), chapter 29. See Taishō 51.450b.

30. Li Si 李斯 (280?–208 BCE) was the Prime Minister to the Qin dynasty (221–207 BCE). He is best known for having implemented the Legalist philosophy of Han Fei Zi (280?–223 BCE). His most famous acts include writing the edict ordering the burning of all books of philosophy, history, poetry, etc., and putting to death a number of Confucian scholars. Zhu Xi's link between Xunzi and Li Si is based on the putative notion that Xunzi taught both Han Fei and Li Si.

one may look at it, but no one is given the golden needle.'[31] When I was fifteen or sixteen, I too was interested in Chan. One day I met a monk at Liu Zihui's place and talked with him.[32] He just went along with whatever I said, never saying whether I was right or not. But, he told Liu that I understood Chan's brilliance and spirituality. Later, when Liu told me this, I suspected that this monk had something wondrous about him and so I asked for his instruction. I thought what he had to say was excellent. . . . Later I was sent to serve in Tong'an. At the time I was twenty-four or twenty-five, and I first met Mr. Li [Tong].[33] When I spoke with him, Mr. Li just said I was wrong. I, however, doubted Mr. Li had any real understanding and repeatedly questioned him. Mr. Li was a solemn person and wasn't a glib talker. He instructed me to read only the words of the sages and worthies. Consequently, I set Chan aside for the time being. I thought that, in my practice of the Way, Chan would always be present even as I came to read the works of the sages and worthies. Reading and reading, day after day, I gradually came to savor the words of the sages and worthies. And when I went back to the Buddhist teachings, I gradually saw them to be riddled with flaws and defects." (*ZZYL*, chapter 104, pp. 2619–2620)

18. Letter to Wang Yingchen[34]

. . . Generally speaking, those who discuss the Learning of the Way in recent times err in being too lofty. When they study books and discuss their meaning, they typically delight in taking an easy shortcut and leap ahead without passing through an orderly sequence. They always neglect and disdain the complex and subtle points—precisely those places they should ponder—regarding these to be too lowly and trifling to be worthy

---

31. This phrase, or variations on it, appears often in Chan literature. The translation here is from Thomas and J. C. Cleary, *The Blue Cliff Record*, p. 244. See Yuanwu Keqin 圜悟克勤 (1063–1135), *Foguo Yuanwu chanshi Bi yan lu* 佛果圜悟禪師碧巖錄 in Taishō 48.178a.

32. Liu Zihui 劉子翬 (1101–1147) was one of the four men who became guardians to Zhu Xi after his father died in 1143. Liu was intellectually eclectic, freely synthesizing the Cheng brothers' teachings with Buddhism, Daoism, and the anti-Wang Anshi politics of the pro-war faction. Liu Zihui invited Daoqian to give a Dharma lecture at the temple in his village and that is when Zhu Xi met Daoqian. Another of Zhu's guardians was Liu's brother, Ziyu 劉子羽 (1086–1146), who was a disciple of Dahui's.

33. Li Tong 李侗 (1093–1163) traced his intellectual lineage directly back to the Cheng brothers and was also a member of the pro-war political faction. Although he was a fierce opponent of Buddhism, Li promoted a neo-Confucian form of quiescent practice known as quiet sitting.

34. On Wang Yingchen (1118–1176), see note 20 in this chapter.

of their attention. Consequently, although some are scholars of broad learning, they inevitably fail to fully understand moral pattern-principles of the world. . . .

Having failed to come to a full understanding of pattern-principles, [such scholars] cannot but harbor doubt and uncertainty in their breast. And yet, instead of reflecting on and seeking what is nearby, they become deluded by heterodox [Chan] doctrines. They ensconce themselves in a state of dark unknowingness and all day long blankly chew on meaningless [*kōan*] phrases, waiting for that single, all-encompassing enlightenment. They simply do not know that only after things are investigated will they become clear; that only after moral relationships are closely examined will they be fully understood.

> ("The investigation of things" simply means "to thoroughly probe pattern-principles"; "things have been investigated" is when these pattern-principles are clear. This is the beginning of self-cultivation practice in the *Great Learning*; by pondering and reflecting over a long period, each [person] will [progress from a] shallow to deep [understanding]. There is no precipitous point of sudden enlightenment. Discussions by recent Confucians scholars on this point, it seems to me, are also too lofty. . . .)

Since they believe themselves to have had this "single, all-encompassing enlightenment," they remain utterly ignorant about this [investigation of things]—so how could they take themselves to be enlightened? . . .

And yet, they wait for [enlightenment]—something they may never get—making themselves cling to an irresolvable doubt, fracturing their will, depleting their energy and passing years and months aimlessly and in vain. How can this compare to our [Confucian] teaching, which follows an orderly sequence of learning that begins from an elementary level and progresses to an advanced level. [Our learning] engages in discussion, thought, personal practice, and rigorous examination; it prefers difficulty to negligence, the lowly to the lofty, the shallow to the deep, and clumsiness to artifice. By pondering over things in a relaxed manner and gradually understanding them over a long time, the myriad pattern-principles will become transparent and the sequence of things will become clear and unobscured. . . . Fundamentally, there is no other extraordinary state to attain. (*ZXJ*, chapter 30, pp. 1268–1269)

Part Three: "Critique of Adulterated Learning"

19. Su Che's "Commentary on the *Laozi*" (*Laozi jie* 老子解)

Su Che wrote this book late in life to harmonize our Confucianism with Laozi. And, thinking that insufficient, he went even further and supplemented it with Buddhism. How misguided! . . . I truly fear [Su] will disrupt the transmission of our learning and cause the correctness of the human heart-mind to be lost.

[Su wrote:] Master Kong uses humaneness, rightness, ritual, and music to govern the world. Laozi cuts off and abandons these. Some people consider these incompatible. The *Classic of Changes* says, "What is above form is called the 'Way'; what is below form is called 'concrete things (*qi* 器).'"[35]

I [Zhu Xi] comment: Although the names "Way" and "concrete things" are different, they are really one thing. Therefore [Confucius] said, "My Way has one thread running through it."[36] This is why the Way of the Sage is the height of the great Mean and perfect rectitude and has never been vanquished through the myriad generations. Mr. Su recites the words [of the *Classic of Changes*] but does not grasp their meaning. Therefore, his explanation does not have a single word that accords with [the *Classic of Changes*]. In this, students should first seek it in my explanation so that the meaning of the Sage will be clearly beyond doubt.[37] Thereafter, when they next read Mr. Su's words they will have a clear grasp of his errors.

[Su wrote:] Confucius was profoundly concerned about future generations. Therefore, he taught people using concrete things while obscuring the Way.

I [Zhu Xi] comment: The Way and concrete things are one. If one teaches people using concrete things, then the Way is included within them. Why would the Sage obscure it? Confucius said, "I conceal nothing."[38] How could the Sage have it in his heart-mind to obscure

---

35. *Classic of Changes* (*Yijing* 易經), "Xici zhuan" ("Commentary on the Appended Phrases"), part one.

36. *Analects* 4.15.

37. It is unclear to which of his explanations Zhu Xi is referring. Long after this was written, Zhu did write explanations of the *Classic of Changes*.

38. *Analects* 7.24.

the Way? In general, when Mr. Su speaks of the "Way" being separate from "concrete things," I don't know what he is referring to with such names. . . .

[Su wrote:] Therefore, [Laozi] teaches people using the Way, while downplaying concrete things, thinking that if students only understood concrete things, then the Way would remain obscured. Therefore, he discards humaneness and rightness and abandons ritual and music in order to illuminate the Way.

I [Zhu Xi] comment: The Way is the general name for humaneness, rightness, ritual, and music, and these four are the substance[39] and function of the Way. When the sages cultivated humaneness and rightness and created ritual and music, it was all for the purpose of clarifying the Way. Now here, [Su] says that [Laozi] discarded humaneness and rightness and abandoned ritual and music in order to illuminate the Way. That is like giving up two times five but seeking ten. How perverse!

[Su wrote:] Now the Way cannot be spoken of;[40] what can be spoken of is a semblance of it. Those who attain [the Way] rely on its semblance to realize its truth. Those who are hazy about it hold on to the semblance and get trapped by falsehoods.

I [Zhu Xi] comment: When the sages spoke of the Way, they discussed rulers and ministers, fathers and sons, husbands and wives, elder and younger siblings, and the relations between friends. I don't know whether Mr. Su thinks these words refer to the Way or only to its semblance? And, if one practiced by holding to these, would they really become trapped [in falsehoods]? Still, is it really true that the Way cannot be spoken of? The reason why such a statement exists is because people themselves do not realize that the Way and concrete things have never been separated from each other. And, so instead, they seek [the Way] in the midst of obscurity and formlessness.

[Su wrote:] There were people in later generations who held onto Laozi's doctrines and caused disorder in the world, while those who followed Confucius were free of serious flaws.

---

39. The word translated "substance" here is rendered "the thing itself" or "thingness itself" throughout most of this volume. It refers to the Way itself prior to any operation of the Way in the world.

40. Su is paraphrasing the opening lines of the *Daodejing*.

I [Zhu Xi] comment: There are those who were good at studying Laozi, such as the Han emperors Wen (r. 179–157 BCE) and Jing (r. 156–139 BCE) and Cao Shen (d. 190 BCE).[41] Indeed, they did not bring complete disorder to the world. But Mr. Su's doctrines are certain to bring disorder to the world. Among the followers of Confucius, some were superficial, some profound, some flawed, some flawless—we cannot overgeneralize. One like Mr. Su certainly has read Confucian texts, yet his writings and sayings confuse and mislead later generations in this way. How could we call them flawless?

[Su wrote:] There are quite a number who follow Laozi's words and attain the Way; but those who seek it in Confucius often suffer from not having a place to start [on the path].

I [Zhu Xi] comment: I don't know what people he is referring to when he says, "There are quite a number who follow Laozi's words and attain the Way." How did they attain it? And what Way is it that they have attained? Moreover, when he says "quite a number," it can't be only one or two people. Are there really such multitudes who have attained the Way? Confucius "methodically led students on"[42] and "encouraged people without tiring,"[43] so they entered the path of virtue, calmly and with understanding. Yet when Mr. Su says "They often suffer from not having a place to enter," we can know that he has never undertaken this [teaching] for even a single day and has not been able to enter the gate. Of course, [Su] splits the Way and concrete things and, thus, does not consider humaneness, rightness, ritual, and music as related to the Way. Granted, Su's words concerning "not having a place to enter" cannot harm Confucius's Way or break students' intentions [to learn]; with them he simply declares his own lack of knowledge of the Way. . . .

Mr. Su's "Postface" says: The Sixth Patriarch's saying, "not thinking of good; not thinking of bad," refers to [the state] before the feelings arise.[44]

---

41. Emperors Wen and Jing are remembered for supporting the Huang-Lao school of Daoism. The same is true of Cao Shen 曹参, who served under the first three emperors of the Han. When Emperor Hui (r. 194–186 BCE) appointed Cao to the post of chancellor, Cao instituted Huang-Lao policies as the state ideology.

42. *Analects* 9.11.

43. *Analects* 7.2 and 2.34.

44. Su Che wrote this Postface in 1090. The full statement of the Sixth Patriarch (Huineng 惠能) is: "Not thinking of good, not thinking of evil, just at this moment what is your original

I [Zhu Xi] comment: Although the sages and worthies speak of [the state] before the feelings arise, still goodness is always preserved and there is no bad. The Buddhist saying seems the same but is in reality different. One must be more discerning.

[Mr. Su's "Postface"] also says: Now the Mean is another name for the Buddha-nature; and "harmony" is a general term for the Six Paramitas and their myriad practices.[45]

I [Zhu Xi] comment: When happiness, anger, sorrow, and joy are all balanced and regulated, that is called "harmony." Moreover, harmony is the universal Way for all in the world. As for the Six Paramitas and the myriad practices, I don't know what [Su] refers to; but they destroy and cut off [the relationships between] ruler and minister, father and son and are great impediments to the Way of humankind. Can that really be called the "universal Way"? . . . (*ZZWJ*, chapter 72, in *ZZQS*, vol. 24, pp. 3469–3472)[46]

20. Zhang Jiucheng: "Commentary on the *Doctrine of the Mean*" (*Zhongyong jie* 中庸解)

His Honor Zhang [Jiucheng] began his studies as a disciple of Yang Guishan[47] but left the Confucian school for Buddhism, believing himself to have achieved realization. Then Zhang's Buddhist teacher [Dahui Zonggao] told him: "You have grasped the main point [of Chan]. Now, when you instruct others you should present your teaching in a variety of guises and preach the Dharma as you think appropriate to the circumstances. Make it so that those on different paths end up arriving at the same place. Then there will be no ill feelings between those who have left the world [Buddhists] and those still in it [non-Buddhists]. But

---

face before your mother and father were born?" It appears in a Song dynasty edition of *The Platform Sutra of the Sixth Patriarch* (*Liuzu tan jing* 六祖壇經) and in other Chan texts, including the *Gateless Barrier* (*Wumen guan* 無門關) and *The Records of the Transmission of the Lamp* (*Jingde chuandenglu* 景德傳燈錄). For the quote in *The Platform Sutra*, see *Liuzu dashi fabao tan jing* 六祖大師法寶壇經, Taishō 48.349b.

45. The Six Paramitas are: charity, precepts/morality, patience, diligence, meditation, and wisdom. The myriad practices refer to the actions required to achieve the paramitas.

46. *ZZWJ* refers to *Hui'an xiansheng Zhu Wengong wenji* 晦庵先生朱文公文集 (*The Collected Writings of Master Hui'an, Zhu, Duke of Culture*). *ZZQS* refers to *Zhuzi quanshu* 朱子全書 (*The Complete Works of Master Zhu*): see Zhu Xi 2002 in the bibliography.

47. Yang Guishan 楊龜山 (1053–1135) was the pen name (*hao* 號) of Yang Shi 楊時, a leading student of the Cheng brothers and Zhang Jiucheng's teacher.

you must not let the crude and common sort learn about what I say here; otherwise, they are sure to question what we are doing."[48] . . . As a result of this, all of Zhang's writings are outwardly Confucian but secretly Buddhist. When he moves in and out of [Buddhism and Confucianism] his purpose is to confuse the world and lull men to sleep so that they enter the Buddhist school and cannot extricate themselves from it even if they want to. . . .

[In his Explanation,] Zhang writes: "What Heaven decrees is called the 'nature.'"[49] This merely states how precious the nature is; but the person has not yet taken it as their own. "Complying with the nature is called the 'Way.'" This means that one has embodied the nature as one's own and entered into humaneness, rightness, propriety, and wisdom. However, one has not yet put them into application. "To cultivate the Way is called 'teaching.'" This means that humaneness is practiced between parent and child, rightness is practiced between ruler and minister, propriety is practiced between guest and host, and wisdom is practiced among the wise. From this the degrees and gradations of the Way may be known.

I [Zhu Xi] comment: "What Heaven decrees is called the 'nature'" means that the reason why the "nature" is so named is because it is what Heaven bestows. It is the original source of the moral pattern-principles that human beings have received. It does *not* merely mean to praise the preciousness [of nature]. And why should the nature require the esteem and approval of people? . . . Moreover, calling it "[human] nature" clearly means that people have already received it. Yet here [Mr. Zhang] says "one has not yet taken the nature as one's own." This would mean that when Heaven gives birth to this person it has yet to bestow [the nature] on him but rather puts it in some other place; this would require the person to stand up, go over and get [his nature] and only then "make it his own." I do not understand, then, prior to taking possession of the nature, what it was that allows a human being to breathe, eat, live, and exist in the world and then get the nature? How can this "nature" be an object that is in a specific location that can then be taken and inserted into the human body? The nature possesses humaneness, rightness, propriety, and wisdom; they are the very substance of the nature. Here [Mr. Zhang] says

---

48. This letter is no longer extant.

49. This and the following two quotations are from the opening passage of the *Doctrine of the Mean*.

that one embodies [the nature] and only afterwards enters into humaneness, rightness, propriety, and wisdom. This would mean that the four [virtues] have been pre-established over here and afterwards the nature comes to them. I do not understand where the four [virtues] could possibly come from before this nature has entered the person/body. These are all erroneous and forced words that fail to understand the great source. When an intelligent person sees this, he will not need to read the text in its entirety; its errors and aberrations will be clear from this section alone. To practice humaneness between father and son and to practice rightness between ruler and minister—this *is* the "Way that complies with the nature." But Mr. Zhang rashly takes it to be "the teaching of cultivating the Way" and thus loses the [proper] order and sequence....

[In his Explanation,] Zhang writes: Everyone uses their knowledge to judge right and wrong. But they don't know how to apply their knowledge to being cautious [over what is not seen] and apprehensive [over what is not heard]. If they would shift the heart-mind that judges right and wrong toward being cautious and apprehensive, they would know which is greater.

I [Zhu Xi] comment: The existence of approbation and disapproval is a normative pattern-principle for all under Heaven, and all people possess the heart-mind of right and wrong. This is why it is considered the beginning of knowledge and if one were to lack it, one would not be human.[50] Therefore, to judge approbation and disapproval is to engage in the thorough examination of pattern-principles and is a priority for students. Mr. Zhang rejects this. We now see how he gives full rein to his idiosyncratic and forced speculations. He is incapable of according with the correctness of Heavenly pattern-principle. But aren't his words what the Buddhists call "directly grasping hold of the unexcelled Bodhi without concern for approbation and disapproval"?[51] Alas! Don't these words show the fundamental difference between Confucianism and Buddhism!...

[In his Explanation,] Zhang writes: If, in this way, people see into their nature, then they will naturally accord with the Mean and all their prior baseless talk and aberrant actions will be swept away without a trace.

---

50. This is paraphrasing *Mengzi* 2A6.

51. This phrase is used by Dahui Zonggao in *Dahui Pujue Chanshi fayu* 大慧普覺禪師法語, Taishō 47.890b, 890c, and elsewhere in Chan literature.

I [Zhu Xi] comment: "To see into the nature" is originally a Buddhist term; it implies that a single glimpse is sufficient. Confucians, on the other hand, speak of "understanding the nature." When one understands the nature, one must cultivate and develop it until it reaches full completion. The effort is gradual and certainly not the achievement of a day or two. . . .

[In his Commentary,] Zhang writes: . . . Only when one understands *who* it is that loves learning, *who* it is that practices vigorously, and *who* it is that knows shame, will one have knowledge, humaneness, and courage. What one understands through words and writing merely comes near to these. When you experience them directly and comprehend [*who*] it is that experiences them;[52] when you illuminate them in every moment and comprehend them in every affair—only then is it knowledge, humaneness, and courage. There's nothing to do other than this! . . .

[I (Zhu Xi) comment:] . . . The way he writes his explanation drags it into the preposterous and far-fetched. He simply cannot stop himself. Now, "to love learning," "to practice with vigor," and "to know shame" simply depend on one's self. To insist that one must then further seek to know who it is that is doing this is to assert that there is another body outside this body and another heart-mind outside this heart-mind: if bodies and heart-minds proliferate on and on, where will it end? . . . (*ZZWJ*, chapter 72, in *ZZQS*, vol. 24, pp. 3473–3479, 3484)

21. Lü Benzhong: "Commentary on the *Great Learning*"

[In his Commentary on the *Great Learning*,] Mr. Lü writes: The extension of knowledge and investigation of things is the basis of self-cultivation. "Knowledge" is "innate knowledge" (*liang zhi* 良知);[53] it is what we have in common with Yao and Shun. When pattern-principle has been thoroughly probed, then knowledge is naturally attained, what we have in common with Yao and Shun suddenly appears on its own, and one tacitly comprehends it.

I [Zhu Xi] comment: The extension of knowledge and the investigation of things is the starting point of the *Great Learning* and the first task of students. When one thing has been investigated, then one [aspect] of

---

52. In this phrase, Zhang's original *Commentary on the Doctrine of the Mean* (*Zhongyong shuo* 中庸說) has the additional word "who" (*shei* 誰), which Zhu Xi has omitted. We have decided to translate this phrase as it appears in the original.

53. Citing *Mengzi* 7A15.

knowledge is attained. The achievement is gradual. . . . Since the knowledge attained necessarily has gradations of depth or shallowness, how could [Lü] think that in a single moment one transcendently perceives what we have in common with Yao and Shun? This is just the empty Buddhist talk of "a single hearing [brings forth] a thousand awakenings" and "to enter directly [into enlightenment] with one leap."[54] It is not the concrete work in the Confucian school of "clarifying the good and making one's person sincere."[55] . . .

Mr. Lü writes: The subtle qualities of plants and the different features of objects constitute the pattern-principles of things. The "investigation of things" means to seek the pattern-principles that make plants and objects what they are. The phrase "things have been investigated" refers to one's sudden grasp of the pattern-principle of plants and objects when one's heart-mind is focused on them.

I [Zhu Xi] note: . . . As to the way students ought to apply themselves, they must have an order of priority and importance and a method for gauging their own experience. Only then will they gradually develop themselves fully through the integration of cumulative practice. How can [Lü] believe that by merely focusing the heart-mind on a single plant or object he will suddenly, and without cause, know what we have in common with Yao and Shun? This again is the Buddhist doctrine of "hearing a [single] sound and awakening to the Way" or "seeing a form and enlightening the heart-mind."[56] It is certainly not the original intention of the Confucian canon. . . . [Lü] instead wants to place his heart-mind amidst plants and objects and await his single [sudden] awakening. . . .

[In one of his later letters] Mr. Lü wrote: It is right where empirical knowledge cannot reach that one should "take enlightenment as one's standard."[57] This is precisely what we call "the extension of knowledge

---

54. Both phrases appear many times in the Chinese Buddhist canon. See, for example, the Tang master Yongjia Xuanjue's 永嘉玄覺 (665–713) *Song of Enlightenment* (*Zheng dao ge* 証道歌) and *Records of the Transmission of the Lamp* (*Jingde chuandenglu* 景德傳燈錄) compiled by the monk Daoyuan 道原.

55. Citing the *Mean* 20:17 and *Mengzi* 4A13.

56. These are common Chan Buddhist phrases. For examples of Dahui's use of them, see *Dahui Pujue Chanshiyulu* in Taishō 47.854a.

57. This is another common Chan phrase. See, for example, Dahui's use in *Dahui Pujue Chanshi shu* 大慧普覺禪師書 in the Taishō 47.839b.

and the investigation of things." Recently, I temporarily dispensed with the written word and have devoted myself solely to introspection. Still, I am troubled by the confusion of miscellaneous affairs and am unable to devote myself to single-minded practice. . . .

I [Zhu Xi] comment: "To take enlightenment as a standard" is a Buddhist method that we Confucians do not have. Yet Mr. Lü takes it to be the "extension of knowledge and the investigation of things." This is how he made mistakes in his explanation above, and never realized his error. . . . In our Confucian teaching, "the extension of knowledge and investigation of things" consists in reading books to discover merit and deficiency; and we engage in affairs to examine right and wrong, because there is nowhere that this pattern-principle is not present. Now [Mr. Lü] says he has dispensed with the written word and devoted himself to introspection. Yet he is still troubled by the confusion of miscellaneous affairs and unable to concentrate. This is because he divides pattern-principle and affairs into two. Then, he insists that pattern-principles can be thoroughly probed only when one completely withdraws from worldly activities. . . . Thus, I entirely do not understand what pattern-principles Mr. Lü is [investigating] in his introspection and self-examination! (*ZZWJ*, chapter 72, in *ZZQS*, vol. 24, pp. 3493–3494).

Bibliography

Cleary, Thomas, and J. C. Cleary, trans. 1992. *The Blue Cliff Record*. Boston and London: Shambala.

Tiwald, Justin, and Bryan Van Norden, eds. 2014. *Readings in Later Chinese Philosophy: Han Dynasty to the 20th Century*. Indianapolis, IN: Hackett.

Zhu Xi 朱熹. 1996. *Zhu Xi ji* 朱熹集 (*Collected Work of Zhu Xi*). Edited by Guo Qi 郭齐 and Yin Bo 尹波. Chengdu: Sichuan jiaoyu chubanshe.

———. 2002. *Zhuzi quanshu* 朱子全書 (*The Complete Works of Master Zhu*). Shanghai: Shanghai guji chubanshe and Hefei: Anhui jiaoyu chubanshe.

Further Readings

Buswell, Robert Evans Jr. 1999. "The 'Short-cut' Approach of *K'an-hua* Meditation: The Evolution of a Practical Subitism in Chinese Ch'an Buddhism." In *Sudden and Gradual: Approaches to Enlightenment in Chinese Thought*. Edited by Peter Gregory, 321–377. Honolulu: University of Hawaii Press.

Chan, Wing-tsit. 1989. *Chu Hsi: New Studies*. Honolulu: University of Hawaii Press.

Ching, Julia. 2000. *The Religious Thought of Chu Hsi*. Oxford: Oxford University Press.

Fu, Charles Wei-hsun. 1986. "Chu Hsi on Buddhism." In *Chu Hsi and Neo-Confucianism*. Edited by Wing-tsit Chan, 377–407. Honolulu: Hawaii University Press.

Gregory, Peter N., and Daniel Aaron Getz, eds. 1999. *Buddhism in the Sung*. Honolulu: University of Hawaii Press.

Tillman, Hoyt Cleveland. 1992. *Confucian Discourse and Chu Hsi's Ascendancy*. Honolulu: University of Hawaii Press.

Schlütter, Morten. 2008. *How Zen Became Zen*. Honolulu: University of Hawaii Press.

8

Science and Natural Philosophy

Yung Sik Kim

Introduction

Zhu Xi's conversations and writings covered not only subjects like classics and history that were traditionally important for the Confucian learning but also various other subjects, including what would correspond to "science" and "natural philosophy." These subjects came up in Zhu Xi's sayings and writings in various different contexts. First, there were isolated bits of knowledge about the natural world—and objects and phenomena in it—scattered all over his writings and conversations. His discussions on such basic concepts as pattern-principle (*li* 理), *qi* 氣, *yin-yang* 陰陽, the five phases (*wuxing* 五行), etc., also amounted to what we might call "natural philosophy." In addition, he wrote and commented upon various scientific subjects, such as calendrical astronomy, harmonics, geography, medicine, and mathematics. This chapter presents selections from Zhu Xi's writings and conversations showing his knowledge of these different kinds of topics and his attitude toward them.

For Zhu Xi, the world consisted of three basic constituents: heaven and earth (*tiandi* 天地), the myriad things (*wanwu* 萬物), and human beings (*ren* 人). These three stood in various relations to one another. Heaven (or heaven and earth) produces human beings and the myriad things. Human beings and things dwell between heaven and earth. They partake of the *qi* that makes up heaven and earth, and receive the heart-mind (*xin* 心) of heaven and earth as their heart-mind. Of all that is produced by heaven and earth, human beings are most numinous (*ling* 靈), for they are endowed with the *qi* that is most correct, clear, and complete. Human beings, therefore, form a triad with heaven and earth and complement the activities of heaven and earth.

The natural world—what exists in it and what happens in it—was "natural" for Zhu Xi; he took these phenomena for granted, and did not feel any need to explain them. In fact, they were so "natural" and obvious to him that he frequently alluded to common and familiar natural phenomena in discussing moral and social problems, which were considered more problematic. Rarely did he mention such common natural phenomena for their own sake.

Qualities and activities of *qi* were considered innate by Zhu Xi. Thus, once certain phenomena had been attributed to certain qualities and activities of *qi*, they were deemed sufficiently accounted for, without further need to look for external causes or hidden mechanisms. His acceptance of qualities of life as inherent to *qi* had a similar consequence. It was not necessary for him to look for an external agent that created life.

Such concepts as *yin-yang*, the five phases, etc., that Zhu Xi used in discussing things and events of the natural world are usually sets of categories. And as categories, they are associated with various sets of characteristics. Different characteristics associated with a given category are connected to one another, thus giving rise to a network of mutual associations. Such associations were what made these schemes useful as conceptual tools for understanding and explaining many complex phenomena and difficult problems. Indeed, the principal use of the *yin-yang* and five-phase schemes, for Zhu Xi, was in this mode of transfer and extension.

Yin-yang and the five phases form cycles that repeat fixed sequences. Various *yin-yang* characteristics follow each other continuously, forming cycles that have no beginning or end: movement and rest, contracting and expanding, day and night, hot and cold, and so on. Many sets of five-phase characteristics also repeat their fixed sequences endlessly. For him, such endless cyclical repetition was a universal feature of natural phenomena.

Zhu Xi showed considerable interest in "scientific" subjects and achieved substantial knowledge about them. A few aspects of these subjects made them inherently important for a Confucian scholar like him. For example, some scientific subjects were touched upon in passages of ancient classics, and were thus discussed in many commentaries and sub-commentaries of the classics. Knowledge of some scientific subjects was also present in other standard texts widely studied by Confucian scholars. The official dynastic histories (*zhengshi* 正史), for example, almost always included treatises devoted to astronomy, calendars, harmonics, geography, and astrology, as well as to rites and music. Confucian scholars like Zhu Xi could find knowledge of some of these subjects useful for the welfare of the people and the country. In particular, knowledge of them was actually needed for performing official duties.

Zhu Xi's doctrine of the investigation of things (*gewu* 格物) provided a solid philosophical ground for all the above aspects of Confucian scholars' interest in scientific subjects. Interpreted to mean "investigating the pattern-principle of things," the doctrine led him to stress studying things and events in all areas of human concern. Thus, Zhu Xi's basic position about scientific subjects was that they also should be studied, and should not be ignored. Yet, Zhu Xi did not hide his feeling that there were more important subjects, namely moral and philosophical matters. Zhu Xi did not hold a very high opinion of specialists in these scientific subjects, either. For him, they were merely functionary experts in specialized areas which he did not master himself.

In dealing with these scientific subjects, Zhu Xi not only studied them, and tried to explain them, but also sought to show how they should be studied, and especially what should be read. He evaluated available texts, commentaries, and other earlier works, and identified proper texts and commentaries to be used for studying a given subject. He also wrote his own commentaries. In fact, this kind of work was what Zhu Xi must have felt he needed to do, for having asserted the importance of scientific subjects and the necessity to study them, he had to decide which texts were the best or correct, just as he did for moral and social philosophy. What he did was to prepare a program of study for these subjects for scholars and students to follow.

Translation

The Natural World of Zhu Xi
Heaven and Earth

1. At the beginning of heaven and earth, there was only the *qi* of *yin* and *yang*. This one *qi* moved and turned around continuously. When the turning became rapid, various sediments of *qi* were compressed. Within, there was no outlet [for the sediments], and so they congealed to form the earth at the center. The clear portions of the *qi* became heaven, the sun and moon, and the stars. They constantly turn around and move on the outside. The earth is at the center and does not move. It is not that [the earth resides] down below. (*ZZYL*, chapter 1, p. 6)

2. [Zhu Xi said,] "At the beginning of heaven and earth when it was in a state of chaos and not yet differentiated, I suppose that there were just the two, namely water and fire. The sediments of water formed the earth. Now if you climb up high and look, mountains are all in the shape of waves. It must have been that water floated [the sediments] like this, but I do not know when it congealed. It was extremely soft in the beginning but later congealed to become hard."

   It was asked, "I guess it is similar to tides heaping up sand."

   [Zhu Xi] said, "Yes, it is so. The extremely turbid [portions] of water formed the earth. The extremely clear [portions] of fire formed wind, thunder, lightning, the sun, the stars and the like." (*ZZYL*, chapter 1, p. 7)

3. Heaven moves without ceasing. It turns day and night. Therefore, the earth is placed at the center. If [heaven] stopped for a moment, the earth would necessarily fall down. Heaven's rotation is rapid, and thus can congeal various sediments at the center. The earth is the sedimentation of *qi*. Thus, it is said [in the *Huainanzi*], "The light and clear portions [of *qi*] become heaven; the heavy and turbid portions, the earth."[1] (*ZZYL*, chapter 1, p. 6)

4. [Zhu Xi] also said, "Since ancient times no one has reached as far as the northern sea. I think that the northern sea passes, touching the vault of heaven, and because the land on the north side is long, the northern sea is not very broad. Below the earth and on its four sides is all sea water flowing around. The earth floats on water, touching heaven. Heaven surrounds water and the earth."

   It was asked, "Does heaven have physical form and tangible quality?"

   [Zhu Xi] said, "No. It is merely rotating *qi* that became tense, like rapid wind. Above, at the highest place, it rotates and becomes more tense. If it rotated a little slower, the earth would fall down."

   It was asked, "Do stars have physical form and tangible quality?"

   [Zhu Xi] said, "No, they are merely congelations of the refined portions of *qi*."

   It was asked, "Are they like the candlelight?"

   [Zhu Xi] said, "Yes." (*ZZYL*, chapter 2, pp. 27–28)

5. Heaven, the sun, the moon and the stars all rotate leftward. It is just that there are [differences of being] slower and faster. Heaven moves

---

1. See chapter 3, "The Patterns of Heaven" (*Tianwen xun* 天文訓), *Huainanzi* 1927–1936.

relatively fast: in one day and one night it circles the earth once for 365 plus 1/4 degrees[2] and proceeds still one degree farther. The sun moves a little more slowly: in one day and one night it circles the earth exactly once, and lags behind heaven by one degree. After one year [the sun] meets heaven at an exact place. This is called "one rotation around heaven in one year." The moon moves still more slowly: in one day and one night it cannot circle the earth completely but always lags behind heaven by 13 7/19 degrees. After somewhat more than 29 1/2 days, [the moon] meets heaven at an exact place. This is called one rotation in one month." (*ZZYL*, chapter 2, p. 17)

6. It was asked, "Why does the earth have deviations?"

   [Zhu Xi] said, "I think that the movement of heaven has deviations, and the earth rotates following heaven, and has deviations. Now we sit like this and just believe that the earth does not move. How can we know that [while] heaven moves outside, the earth does not follow it and rotate? As for the deviations of heaven's movement, the difference in the past and present [locations of] the central stars at dawn is [an example]." (*ZZYL*, chapter 86, p. 2212)

7. The body of the moon is always round without any defects. But it constantly receives the sunlight and is bright. On the third or fourth day, the sun shines from below, and the moon is bright on the west side. Human beings look at it from here, and only see the light [in the shape] of a crescent. On the fifteenth or sixteenth day, the sun is below the earth, its light issues forth from around the four sides of the earth, and the moon is bright because of that light. (*ZZYL*, chapter 2, p. 19)

8. The moon does not wax and wane. [It is just that] human beings see it as waxing and waning. On the first day of a lunar month, the moon and the sun pile up on each other. Reaching the third [day] they begin to separate from each other gradually. When human beings below look at [the moon] aslant, its light wanes. Reaching the full-moon day, the moon and the sun are exactly opposite to each other. When human beings in the middle look straight at [the moon], its light is a full circle. (*ZZYL*, chapter 2, pp. 19–20)

---

2. Before they adopted the Western system of 360 degrees, traditional Chinese, including Zhu Xi, counted the circumference of heaven as 365 plus 1/4 degrees, equivalent to the number of days in a year. (The daily movement of the sun in the heaven amounted to 1 degree.)

9. The eclipse of the sun [is caused as the sun] is blocked by the moon. The eclipse of the moon [is caused when the moon] competes with the sun. When the moon partially yields to the sun, there is no eclipse. (*ZZYL*, chapter 2, p. 21)

10. Hengqu 橫渠 [Zhang Zai] said, "When *yang* is entangled with *yin*, then they hold up each other, become rain, and fall." [This means that] when the rising *yang qi* suddenly encounters *yin qi* they hold up each other, fall and become rain. In general, *yang qi* is light and *yin qi* is heavy. Therefore, *yang qi* is pressed by *yin qi* and falls down. [Zhang Zai said,] "When *yin* is helped by *yang*, then it floats, becomes clouds and rises." [This means that] when the rising *yin qi* suddenly encounters *yang qi*, it is sustained [by the *yang qi*], ascends, and becomes clouds. [Zhang Zai said,] "When *yin qi* is congealed and the *yang* inside cannot come out, it is aroused and becomes thunder and lightning." [This means that] the *yang qi* is buried inside *yin qi* and cannot come out, and thus it bursts open and becomes thunder. [Zhang Zai said,] "When the *yang* outside cannot enter, then it turns around ceaselessly and becomes wind." [This means that] the *yin qi* is congealed inside, and *yang qi*, unable to get inside, just turns around outside ceaselessly and becomes wind. When it blows and disperses *yin qi* completely, it stops. [Zhang Zai said,] "Dispersed harmoniously, it becomes frost, snow, rain and dew; dispersed disharmoniously, it becomes perverse *qi* and dim mist." The "perverse *qi*" refers to things like flying hail. "Dim mist" refers to things like yellow fog. They are all *yin* and *yang qi* that are deviant and incorrect. Thus, water of such hail is dirty and turbid, and sometimes blue and black in color. (*ZZYL*, chapter 99, pp. 2534–2535)[3]

11. When it snows, it is simply that rain encounters cold and becomes congealed. Therefore, in high and cold places snow is formed first. (*ZZYL*, chapter 2, p. 23)

The Myriad Things

12. Among the things that heaven produced, there are those which have blood-*qi* (*xueqi* 血氣) and perception (*zhijue* 知覺): humans and animals are examples. There are those which do not have blood-*qi* or

---

3. Zhang Zai's words originally appeared in the "Sanliang" 三兩 chapter of *Dispelling Youthful Ignorance* (*Zhengmeng* 正蒙).

perception but have life-*qi* (*shengqi* 生氣): grasses and trees are examples. There are those whose life-*qi* has already been extinguished but have physical form, tangible quality, smell and taste: dried and withered [things] are examples. . . . Humans are the most numinous and completely possess the nature of the five constant virtues. Birds and beasts are muddled and cannot completely possess [the five constant virtues]. As for grasses, trees, and dried and withered things, [the five constant virtues] have, along with the perception, been lost. (*ZZWJ*, chapter 59 in *ZZQS*, vol. 23, p. 2854).[4]

13. It was asked again, "Humans, birds, and beasts certainly have perception, but their perception has [differences of being] open or blocked. Do grasses and trees also have perception?"

   [Zhu Xi] said, "They also do. For example, if a flower in a pot has a little water sprayed on it, it blossoms. If you cut or press it, it dries up. Is it possible to say that it does not have perception? . . . It is simply that the perception of birds and beasts is different from that of humans, and the perception of grasses and trees is still different from that of birds and beasts. For another example, the rhubarb, when eaten, can cause diarrhea; wolfsbane, when eaten, can cause fever. It is simply that their perception works only in these single respects."

   It was asked again, "Do rotten and decayed things also have perception?"

   [Zhu Xi] said, "They also do. For example, if you burn them with fire and make ashes, cook them in a soup and eat, [they] also [taste] hot and bitter." (*ZZYL*, chapter 60, p. 1430)

14. As for the saying, "Heaven and earth take producing things as their heart-mind,"[5] [this can be] compared to a cauldron for cooking rice. *Qi* turns from the bottom to the top and turns down again. It just keeps turning inside, and steams [the rice] to the point of being cooked. Heaven and earth just contain much *qi* inside, for which there is no way

---

4. *ZZWJ* refers to *Hui'an xiansheng Zhu Wengong wenji* 晦庵先生朱文公文集 (*The Collected Writings of Master Hui'an, Zhu, Duke of Culture*). *ZZQS* refers to *Zhuzi quanshu* 朱子全書 (*The Complete Works of Master Zhu*): see Zhu Xi 2002 in the bibliography.

5. Zhu Xi frequently asserted this, often in discussing the phrase from the "Great Appendix" to the *Classic of Changes*, "The great virtue of heaven and earth is called 'producing [things]' (*tiandi zhi da de yue sheng* 天地之大德曰生)."

out. When it turns once, then it produces one thing. . . . It is like a mill-stone, which just keeps grinding out these things. (*ZZYL*, chapter 53, p. 1281)

15. It was asked, "It has not been ten thousand years since the beginning of heaven and earth. I wonder what it was like before that."

    [Zhu Xi] said, "It is clear that it must have been like it is now."

    It was asked again, "Can heaven and earth decay?"

    [Zhu Xi] said, "They cannot decay. It is just that when people become extremely bad, then everything becomes struck together in one chaotic state; humans and things are all extinguished and come up anew again."

    It was asked, "What was it like when the first human being was produced?"

    [Zhu Xi] said, "[The first human being was produced] by the transformation of *qi* (*qihua* 氣化), as the essences of the two [i.e., *yin* and *yang*] and the five [phases] combined and took physical forms. The Buddhists call it birth by transformation (*huasheng* 化生). [Even] now, many things are born by transformation, lice for example." (*ZZYL*, chapter 1, p. 7)

16. For example, a single seed produces a seedling; the seedling then produces flowers; the flowers then mature into grain which produces seeds again, returning to its original form. One stalk has a hundred seeds, each of the seeds complete in itself. Planting these hundred seeds again, each of them produces a hundred seeds; the production just goes on without stopping. In the beginning, it was only this one seed which continued to divide [itself into many]. [Likewise,] each and every thing has its pattern-principle, which in sum is just one single pattern-principle. (*ZZYL*, chapter 94, p. 2374)

17. A tree begins in spring and spreads out in summer; by autumn there is fruit, and by winter it is complete. Even though [the tree] is said to form fruit, if it does not pass through winter, seeds will not form. Only if it receives sufficient *qi* will there be a time when they [i.e., the tree and the fruits] are ready to be separated from each other. Moreover, if one plants a thousand pieces of fruit, they will form a thousand trees. . . . Throughout its life, each [tree] possesses the life intent (*shengyi* 生意). When winter comes, it appears as though trees have no life intent, and there is no knowing whether [the life intent] has been stored down below. But each fruit has the pattern-principle of life (*shengli* 生理), which still shows the intent to live on endlessly. (*ZZYL*, chapter 69, p. 1729)

Human Beings

18. A human being is a small creature, and "heaven and earth" is a large creature. The head of a human being is round in the image of heaven, the feet are square in the image of the earth. The space in between contains much life-*qi*. (*ZZYL*, chapter 53, p. 1281)[6]

19. Human beings reside between heaven and earth. Although [they share] one pattern-principle, heaven and humans have their own roles in terms of what they do. There are things that humans can do but heaven cannot do. For example, heaven can produce things but must use human beings for sowing seeds. Water can moisten things, but [heaven] must use human beings for irrigation. Fire can burn things, but [heaven] must use human beings for [gathering] firewood and cooking. (*ZZYL*, chapter 64, p. 1570)

20. Heaven can only produce various human beings and things, and provides them all with various pattern-principles of the Way (*dao li* 道理). Nevertheless, heaven cannot do these on its own, and thus produced the sages, who cultivate the Way and establish the teachings on behalf of heaven and in order to edify the people. The saying, "To fulfil the Way of heaven and earth and to support the appropriateness of heaven and earth,"[7] refers to this. What heaven cannot do, the sages must do for [heaven]. (*ZZYL*, chapter 14, p. 259)

21. It was asked, "[There is a saying that] 'the Way of heaven blesses the good and harms the wicked.' Is this pattern-principle fixed?"

    [Zhu Xi] said, "How can it be not fixed? Naturally, the pattern-principle of the Way ought to be like this. [Heaven] rewards the good and punishes the bad. The pattern-principle surely must be like this. If things are not like this, it is simply that the constant pattern-principle (*changli* 常理) has been lost."

    It was asked again, "Sometimes there are [cases of things] not being like this. Why?"

    [Zhu Xi] said, "Blessing the good and harming the wicked is the constant pattern-principle. If things are not like this, then heaven does not have a firm grasp [of the situation]."

---

6. This passage is a continuation of passage 14 in this chapter.

7. See the *tai* 泰 hexagram in the *Classic of Changes*.

[Zhu Xi] also said, "Heaven never does [things] by acting. How can heaven have an intention? It is simply that the pattern-principle is naturally like this. For example, winter is cold and summer is hot. This is because the constant pattern-principle must be like this. If winter is hot and summer is cold, it is simply that the constant pattern-principle has been lost."

It was asked again, "As for cases where the constant [pattern-principle] has been lost, are all of them brought about by human conduct, or are [some of them] mere coincidence?"

[Zhu Xi] said, "There are some that are brought about by human conduct, and there also are some that are like this by mere coincidence."

[Zhu Xi] also said, "Great events cannot be altered (like the sun and the moon for example).[8] Only small events can be altered (like winter's cold and summer's heat. Great heat in winter and snow-fall in the sixth month are examples)." (*ZZYL*, chapter 79, p. 2030)

22. As for the birth of human beings and things, there are differences between them in terms of being refined and coarse. To speak about it from [the viewpoint of] the one *qi*, both human beings and things receive this *qi* and are born. To speak about it from [the perspective of] refinement and coarseness, human beings receive the *qi* that is correct and penetrating, while things receive the *qi* that is one-sided and blocked. Only human beings receive the correct [*qi*], and therefore their pattern-principle is penetrating and not blocked. Things receive the one-sided [*qi*], and therefore their pattern-principle is blocked and without knowledge. For example, the head of human beings is round in the image of heaven, their feet are square in the image of the earth, and they are balanced and erect. Because human beings receive the correct *qi* of heaven and earth, they comprehend the principles of Way, and have knowledge. Because things receive the one-sided *qi* of heaven and earth, birds and beasts live horizontally, and grasses and trees live with their heads downward and tails upward. Among things, those that have knowledge grasp how to do only one task—e.g., ravens knowing filial piety, and otters knowing sacrificial service. Dogs know only how to stand guard, while oxen know only how to till the lands. [But] as for human beings, there is nothing they do not know and nothing they cannot do. The reason why

---

8. Text inside the parentheses translates interlinear commentary that appears as smaller characters in the original Chinese.

human beings are different from things and are to be distinguished from them lies in just this. Nevertheless, to speak of the endowments of individual human beings, there also are differences among them in terms of being muddled and bright and being clear and turbid. (*ZZYL*, chapter 4, pp. 65–66)

23. It was asked, "If one receives clear and bright *qi*, one becomes a sage or a worthy; [if one receives] dark and turbid *qi*, one becomes stupid or unworthy. If one's *qi* is thick, one becomes wealthy and noble; if it is thin, one becomes poor and lowly. This is certainly so. Since the Sage [i.e., Confucius] received the clear, bright, balanced and harmonious *qi* of heaven and earth, he should have been free of any deficiency or want, and yet the Master [Confucius] to the contrary was poor and lowly. Why was this so? Did the fate of the times make this so, or was his endowment still lacking in some way?"

[Zhu Xi] said, "It was because his endowment was lacking. The clearness and brightness of his [endowed *qi*] could only make him a sage or worthy, but could not bring him wealth and nobility. If one is endowed with such lofty [*qi*], one is noble; endowed with the thick [*qi*], one is rich; endowed with the extended [*qi*], one enjoys longevity. Poverty, low position, and early death are the opposites of these. Although the Master [Confucius] received the clear and bright [*qi*] needed to become a sage, he nevertheless received low and thin [*qi*], and was thus poor and lowly. Yanzi [i.e., Yan Hui] was not even equal to Confucius. [He] was endowed with shortened [*qi*], and thus died young."

It was further asked, "As for the alternation of *yin* and *yang*, it ought to be in a fixed balance, and so the worthy and the unworthy ought to be in balance as well. Why then are great people always so rare and petty people always so numerous?"

[Zhu Xi] said, "Naturally, those things [i.e., the *qi* of people] are impure and mixed. How can they be equally distributed? Compare it with minting coins. Pure ones are always rare, and impure ones are always abundant. Naturally their *qi* is impure and mixed. Sometimes it comes to the fore and sometimes it lags behind: thus, one cannot get it to fit exactly. How can one make it balanced and even? Talking about it in terms of a day, it is sometimes dark and sometimes clear, sometimes windy and sometimes rainy, sometimes cold and sometimes hot, sometimes pleasant and sometimes muggy. [From the fact that] there are many changes even within a single day one can see [why this is so]." (*ZZYL*, chapter 4, pp. 79–80)

24. It was asked, "What is your view about the human heart-mind (*xin* 心) in regard to [the dichotomy between] what's above form (*xing er shang* 形而上) and what's within form (*xing er xia* 形而下)?"

[Zhu Xi] said, "As for the *xin* that is one of the five viscera like the lungs and the liver, in fact there actually is such a thing. If it is the *xin* of which scholars nowadays speak, [which can be] 'held or abandoned, preserved or lost,' then it is naturally mysterious, bright, and unfathomable. And so, if the *xin* of the five viscera is diseased, then one can use medicine to help it; but if it is is this [latter] *xin* [that is diseased], then [even such medicinal herbs like] calamus and tuckahoe cannot replenish it."

It was asked, "If so, is the pattern-principle of the *xin* above form?"

[Zhu Xi] said, "Compared with nature (*xing* 性), the *xin* has slight traces. Compared with *qi*, it is naturally more numinous."[9] (*ZZYL*, chapter 5, p. 87)

25. Human beings simply have an abundance of *qi*, but there must be a time when it is exhausted. When it is exhausted, *hun* 魂 and *qi* return to heaven, physical form and *po* 魄 return to earth, and [a person] dies. When a person is about to die, hot *qi* comes out above; thus, it is said that "*hun* ascends." The lower part of the body gradually becomes cold; thus, it is said that "*po* descends." . . . When people die, although [their *qi*] eventually disperses, there also is [some part that is] not completely dispersed. Therefore, there is the pattern-principle that the sacrificial service moves and affects [the ancestors]. Whether the *qi* of an ancestor of a generation far removed [still] exists or not, it is not possible to know. But since the person who offers the sacrificial service is his descendant, their *qi* must be the same, and therefore there is the pattern-principle of moving and communicating with [the ancestor].[10] (*ZZYL*, chapter 3, p. 37)

26. When people exhale *qi*, contrary to what one might expect, the belly swells; when they inhale *qi*, the belly contracts. It is correct to claim that having exhaled the belly swells and having inhaled the belly contracts.

---

9. In this cryptic remark, Zhu Xi seems to be suggesting a descending order of corporeality, concreteness (or ascending order of abstractness, numinousness): *qi* → *xin* → *xing*.

10. Editor's note: see chapter 6 of this volume for further passages from Zhu Xi discussing this subject.

Now [the reason why] it is like this is because when one exhales *qi*, although one mouthful of *qi* has come out, a second mouthful of *qi* is produced, and therefore the belly swells. When one inhales, the *qi* that has been produced rushes out from inside, and therefore the belly still contracts. In general, from birth to death one's *qi* keeps coming out. When it has come out completely, one dies. When one inhales *qi*, it is not that one inhales outside *qi* into [one's body]; it is simply that [the exhaling of *qi*] has been halted for a moment. [Afterwards,] the second mouthful of *qi* comes out. When it cannot come out, one dies. (*ZZYL*, chapter 1, p. 8)

Analogical Uses of Natural Phenomena

27. Observing the movements of heaven and earth, day and night, cold and hot weather, there is not a moment of rest. The sages' exertion in learning is just like this all throughout life till death. There is no way to stop. (*ZZYL*, chapter 34, p. 889)

28. Scholars should be diligent and consistent, and must not stop. If they can be like this, they will naturally carry on without exerting much effort afterwards. It is like pushing a wheeled cart. Once it is pushed and [its wheels] start rolling, then it will naturally move forward on its own. (*ZZYL*, chapter 31, p. 787)

Basic Concepts, Assumptions, and Methods

29. Between heaven and earth, there is pattern-principle and *qi*. Pattern-principle is "the Way that is above form," and is the basis of the birth of things. *Qi* is "the concrete things that are within form," and is that whereby things come into being.[11] For this reason, in coming into being, human beings and things are necessarily endowed with this pattern-principle, and only then have their nature. They are necessarily endowed with this *qi*, and only then have their physical form. (*ZZWJ*, chapter 58 in *ZZQS*, vol. 23, p. 2755)

---

11. The two quotes are from chapter A12 of the "Great Appendix" to the *Classic of Changes*.

30. Whereas *qi* can congeal and operate, pattern-principle does not have feeling, does not plan, and does not operate. Wherever this *qi* congeals and aggregates, pattern-principle exists within it. It is like [the fact that] when people and things, plants and animals come into being between heaven and earth, there are none that do not have seeds. It is definitely impossible to produce a single thing without a seed. That is all *qi*. As for pattern-principle, it simply is a clean and spacious realm. It has no physical form or traces, and it cannot operate. As for *qi*, it can brew, congeal, and aggregate to produce things. But if there is this *qi*, pattern-principle is inside it. (*ZZYL*, chapter 1, p. 3)

31. Although *yin* and *yang* are two characters, nevertheless they are merely the withering and flourishing of the one *qi*. Advancing and retreating, withering and flourishing: where [the *qi* is] advancing it is *yang*, where retreating it is *yin*; where flourishing it is *yang*, where withering it is *yin*. It is merely the withering and flourishing of the one *qi* that brings about the infinite things of past and present between heaven and earth. Therefore, it is all right to say that *yin* and *yang* act as one, and it is also all right to say that [*yin* and *yang*] act as two. (*ZZYL*, chapter 74, pp. 1879–1880)

32. Grasses and trees all receive *yin qi*. Land animals and birds all receive *yang qi*. To divide each [further], grasses receive *yin qi* and trees receive *yang qi*: therefore, grasses are soft and trees are hard. Land animals receive *yin qi*, birds receive *yang qi*: therefore, land animals lie upon the grasses and birds live in the trees. Yet, among land animals there also are those that receive *yang qi*: like gibbons and monkeys. Among birds there also are those that receive *yin qi*: like grouse and pheasants. Though all grasses and trees receive *yin qi*, nevertheless there are those with *yin* inside *yang* and those with *yang* inside *yin*. (*ZZYL*, chapter 4, p. 62)

33. As for the *qi* of the five phases—as seen, for example, in the categories of warm and cool, cold and hot, wet and dry, hard and soft—these apply to all the things that fill up the space between heaven and earth. Pick up anything. There is none that does not have these five. It is only that among them there are different portions—more or less—of them. (*ZZWJ*, chapter 47, in *ZZQS*, vol. 22, p. 2178)[12]

---

12. Editor's note: the translator punctuates differently from the *ZZQS* text.

34. In general, heaven and earth, in producing things, began with what are light and clear and then reached what are heavy and turbid. Heaven firstly produced Water; Earth secondly produced Fire. [These] two things are the lightest and the clearest of the five phases. Metal and Wood are heavier than Water and Fire; Earth is still heavier than Metal and Wood. (*ZZYL*, chapter 94, p. 2382)

35. It was asked, "Why does the appearance (*mao* 貌) [of human beings] belong to Water?"

[Zhu Xi] said, "Their appearance should be lustrous and therefore belongs to Water. Speech comes out from *qi* and therefore belongs to Fire. Eyes govern the liver and therefore [seeing] belongs to Wood. The sound of metal is clear and bright and therefore hearing belongs to Metal."

It was asked, "In general, the above four items all originate in thought, and this is like [the fact that] Water, Fire, Wood, Metal all come from Earth."

[Zhu Xi] said, "Yes, it is so."

It was asked again, "Why does propriety (*li* 禮) belong to Fire?"

[Zhu Xi] said, "Because of its brightness."

It was asked, "Does rightness (*yi* 義) belong to Metal because of its seriousness?"

[Zhu Xi] said, "Yes, it is so." (*ZZYL*, chapter 79, p. 2043)

36. If there is day, there must be night. If it were day for a long time with no night, how could [one] rest? If there were [only] night and no day, how could there be this brightness? The *qi* of spring is harmonious of course. But if there were only spring and summer with no autumn or winter, how could things be completed? If there were just autumn and winter with no spring or summer, how could [things] come into being? . . . Spring, summer, autumn, and winter are just one stimulus-response (*ganying* 感應). What has responded (*gan* 感) in turn becomes stimulus (*ying* 應); what has stimulated in turn becomes response. Spring and summer is one big stimulus. Autumn and winter must respond to it. Autumn and winter also become the stimulus for spring and summer. To speak about it in detail, spring is the stimulus of summer; summer responds to spring, and also is a stimulus for autumn. Autumn is a stimulus for winter; winter responds to autumn and also is a stimulus for spring. Thus, it is endless. If the inchworm does not bend, it cannot stretch; if the dragon and snake do not hibernate, they cannot safeguard

their bodies. Nowadays, in forests winter is warm, and many snakes that come out die. This is the necessary pattern-principle of contracting and expanding, going and coming, and stimulus and response. (*ZZYL*, chapter 72, pp. 1815–1816)

37. I have seen on high mountains the shells of conches and oysters, some of them living in the rocks. These rocks were soils in earlier days, and the conches and oysters are things [that live] in water. What was low has changed and become high, and what was soft has changed and become hard. (*ZZYL*, chapter 94, p. 2367)

"Scientific" Subjects
On the Need to Study Scientific Subjects

38. It was asked again [about Zhu Xi's statement in the *Questions on the Great Learning* (*Daxue Huowen* 大學或問)], "Things must have pattern-principles, and all [things] are to be investigated exhaustively, and so forth."

    [Zhu Xi] said, "This point is extremely important. Scholars must know, in general, how heaven can be high, how the earth can be thick, how ghosts and spirits become hidden and manifest, and how mountains can be congealed. This just is the investigation of things (*gewu*)." (*ZZYL*, chapter 18, p. 399)

39. Scholars should study every affair under heaven. And as for those [affairs] whose pattern-principles are recorded in the classics, each has its main [point] and cannot be interchanged. . . . [If one] discards what is difficult and just takes up what is easy, and looks only at one thing but does not get to the rest, [then] among events under heaven there will necessarily be those whose pattern-principles cannot be thoroughly understood. As for the learning of the various masters [of the ancient times], they all come from the sages: each has its strong points, but none is free of shortcomings. Their strong points must certainly be studied, but their shortcomings also must be identified. When it comes to the histories, the changes of flourishing and decline, order and disorder, and success and failure of the past and present must all be studied. As for major affairs of the times like rites, music, institutions, astronomy, geography, military strategy, and criminal justice, these are all needed by the world and

cannot be left out. All [of these] must be studied. (*ZZWJ*, chapter 69 in *ZZQS*, vol. 23, p. 3359)[13]

40. The arts (*yi* 藝) also must be understood. If any one of them, such as rites, music, archery, charioteering, calligraphy, and computation is not understood, then *this mind* (*cixin* 此心) will feel obstructed. Only when each and every one of them is understood will every one of these pattern-principles of the Way and their circumstances start to flow and circulate without such obstruction. (*ZZYL*, chapter 34, p. 866)

Calendrical Astronomy

41. Heaven is the fastest: it turns one rotation plus one degree a day. The speed of the sun is next to heaven: it moves exactly 365 plus 1/4 degrees a day, but compared with heaven this amounts to retreating one degree. The moon is far slower than the sun: compared with heaven it amounts to retreating 13 plus degrees. Yet, the calendar specialists only compute the degrees of retreat, and say that the sun moves one degree, and that the moon moves 13 plus degrees. This is an expedient method. Therefore [although] there is the theory of the rightward movement of the sun, moon, and the five stars, in fact it is not a rightward movement.[14] Hengqu [Zhang Zai] said, "Heaven rotates leftward. Those that are in it [i.e., heaven] follow it [and rotate leftward]. If [their rotation is] a little slower, it [appears as though they rotated] rightward." This theory [of Zhang Zai's] is the best. The sub-commentary of the [*Book of*] *Documents* on [the expression] *jiheng* 璣衡, the sub-commentary of the [*Book of*] *Rites* on [the phrase,] "The stars turn around heaven," the [calendrical] treatise of the *History of the Han Dynasty* on heaven itself (*tianti* 天體), and Shen Gua's 沈括 *Discussion of the Armillary Sphere* (*Hunyi yi* 渾儀議)—all these can be consulted. (*ZZYL*, chapter 2, p. 13)

42. [Zhu Xi said,] "If it were supposed that heaven makes [exactly] one rotation a day, how would one explain the fact that the position of stars

---

13. This passage is from a work entitled "A Personal Proposal on Schools and Recruitment" (*Xuexiao gongju siyi* 學校貢舉私議), written in 1187 but never officially submitted.

14. On the "rightward movement" theory of the calendar specialists versus the "leftward rotation theory" of Zhang Zai and Zhu Xi, see Kim 2000, 257–259.

[at the same time of the day] differs over the four seasons? Furthermore, if this were how things are, [the position of stars] would be the same every day: how would one count the year; which seasonal point would one take as the definite boundary [of the year]? If it were supposed that heaven does not exceed [one full rotation a day] and that the sun does not reach [one full rotation, but lags] one degree [per day], then it would keep lagging so that in the future it would [become] midnight at noon."

Thereupon, [Zhu Xi] took up the sub-commentary on the "Yueling" [chapter] of the *Book of Rites*, and pointed to the two places in it on "the difference of being fast and slow" and on "move further one degree," and said, "This account is very clear. No other book on the calendar explains it as well as this." (*ZZYL*, chapter 2, p. 15)

43. Studies of calendars and [celestial] images naturally are one school. If one wants to investigate pattern-principle exhaustively, one must also study them. Nevertheless, what is great must be established first. If one moves on to them [i.e., the studies of calendars and images] afterwards, then they will not be very difficult to understand, and there will be nothing that is not comprehended. (*ZZWJ*, chapter 60 in *ZZQS*, vol. 23, p. 2892)

44. As for the calendrical method, I suppose it may still be all right only to discuss the general outlines. If one wants to know the details, one must make observations so that one can verify them. But now lacking the [proper] instruments, it would be difficult to make a complete investigation. (*ZZWJ* (*xuji*), chapter 2, in *ZZQS*, vol. 25, p. 4674)

45. Even though it is a matter of physical form and concrete things, if one has not understood it exhaustively, one should not begin discussions lightly. It is necessary to exert effort to "study what is below (*xiaxue* 下學)."[15] Even if it is astronomy or geography, one may discuss them only after completely understanding them. (*ZZYL*, chapter 101, p. 2593)

46. Calendar makers of today do not have a "determinate method," but merely increase or decrease the degrees of the movement of heaven to seek agreement [with the calendar]. If [the degrees] exceed [the movements], they reduce [the degrees]; if [the degrees] fall short, they augment [the degrees]. Therefore, there are frequent errors. . . . In my view, the ancient calendars must have had a determinate method, but it

---

15. *Analects* 14.37.

has been lost now. Since the Three Dynasties, the calendar makers have been confused and had no determinate view. The more refined and minute [their computations became], the more errors there were. This was because they did not get the determinate method of the ancients. Jitong 季通 [Cai Yuanding 蔡元定] once said, "The movements of heaven are not constant. The sun, the moon, and the stars are accumulations of *qi*, and are all moving things. The degrees of their movements are slow or fast, sometimes exceed and sometimes fall short, and they naturally are not uniform. If our method is applied to heaven and is not moved by heaven, then the gaps between the coarse and the dense, the slow and the fast, and what is exceeding and what is falling short do not come from our [method]. Although these vastly large numbers may have deviations, they can all be inferred and computed without missing any. How? Because our determinate method can regulate the lack of determination in them [i.e., the movements of heaven] and so naturally, there will be no error." What Jitong said was not that the movements of heaven are not determinate but that the degrees of the movements are so [i.e., not determinate].[16] In the deviations of the movements, there still are constant degrees. But the [range of] numbers that the calendar makers of later times dealt with were too narrow and were not sufficient to cover them. (*ZZYL*, chapter 2, p. 25)

47. It was asked, "The fixed stars rotate leftward, and the planets and the sun and the moon rotate rightward. Is this right?"

[Zhu Xi] said, "Now many [calendar] specialists explain it in this way. But Hengqu [Zhang Zai] said that heaven rotates leftward and the sun and the moon also rotate leftward. It seems that Hengqu's explanation is the best. I was just afraid that people might not understand it, and so I included only the old theory [of right rotation] in the [*Collection of*] *Commentaries on the Odes* (*Shi [ji]zhuan* 詩[集]傳)."

Someone said, "It is also easy to show. Suppose that a large wheel is outside and one small wheel carrying the sun and the moon is inside, and that the large wheel rotates rapidly and the small wheel rotates slowly. Even though both are rotating leftward, albeit fast and slow, it is felt as though the sun and the moon rotate rightward."

[Zhu Xi] said, "Right. But if it is so, the character *ni* 逆 (retrograde) of the calendar specialists should all be changed to the character *shun* 順

---

16. Editor's note: the translator punctuates differently from the *ZZYL* text.

(conformable) and the character *tui* 退 (retreat) should all be changed to the character *jin* 進 (advance)." (*ZZYL*, chapter 2, p. 16)

48. An armillary sphere system has been in the capital for a short while, but because I had a foot ailment again, I could not go to see it. Nevertheless, I heard that it is extremely coarse and simple. Since they cannot make the waterwheel, they approved [making it] like this for the time being. . . . The system of Yuanyou 元祐 [period (1086–1094)] was extremely refined. But the book [describing it] is incomplete, and in the most essential places at that. It must have been that the makers kept that one section secret, not wishing to tell people completely [about it]. (*ZZWJ*, chapter 44, in *ZZQS*, vol. 22, p. 2051–2052)

Harmonics and Music

49. The Grand Historian's [Sima Qian's 司馬遷 discussion on the] five-note numbers said, "Nine times nine, eighty-one, is taken as [the length for the musical note] *gong* 宮. Dividing this into three parts and subtracting one [of the three parts], one gets fifty-four to make a *zhi* 祉.[17] Dividing [this] into three parts and adding one [of the three parts], one gets seventy-two to make a *shang* 商. Dividing [this] into three and subtracting one [of the three parts], one gets forty-eight to make a *yu* 羽. Dividing [this] into three and adding one [of the three parts], one gets sixty-four to make a *jiao* 角." (*ZZWJ*, chapter 66, in *ZZQS*, vol. 23, p. 3240)[18]

50. The pitch of *huangzhong* is the longest, and the pitch of *yingzhong* is the shortest. The sound of a long pitch is turbid, and the sound of the short pitch is clear. The twelve pitches "rotate, each one becoming the *gong* [note] in turn." *Gong* is [associated with] the ruler, and *shang* with the minister. What is to be avoided most in music is ministers abusing their rulers. Therefore, there are the four clear sounds (*qingsheng* 清聲). . . . The clear sound is [obtained by] reducing the pitch by one half. If *yingzhong* is *gong*, its sound is the shortest and the clearest. It

---

17. Although the text here gives the name of the note with the character 祉, that is a homophone of the character 徵, which is what is usually used to refer to this note.

18. Quoting the "Explanation of Strings and Pipes (*Qinlüshuo* 琴律說)" section of Sima Qian 1959, chapter 25, p. 1249.

happens that *ruibin* would become *shang* in this case, and then the *shang* note would become higher [i.e., greater in length] than the *gong* note, which would become [a case of] ministers abusing their rulers and cannot be used. Consequently, one handles [the problem] by reducing the pitch of *ruibin* by one half. Although it is reduced by one half, the [same] pitch comes out, and so naturally they can also respond to one another. This is what is recorded in this section of the *Comprehensive Institutions* (*Tongdian* 通典).[19] (*ZZYL*, chapter 92, pp. 2338–2339)

Geography

51. When Yu regulated the rivers, I think he had not traveled throughout all under heaven. For example, Jingzhou, the country of the Sanmiao 三苗 [people] was not one of the places Yu had visited. Often, he had officials go to a place, observe the mountains and rivers there, and prepare pictures and descriptions before returning. Afterwards, he wrote this book. Therefore, the mountains and rivers of the southern region recorded in the *Yugong* [chapter of the *Book of Documents*] often are different from those that are [actually] on the surface of the earth now. (*ZZYL*, chapter 79, p. 2027)

52. It is not necessary to pay too much attention to the geography in the *Yugong*, because today's mountains and rivers all are different. Understanding the *Yugong* is not as good as understanding today's geography. Regulation of rivers [recorded in] *Yugong*, for example, is now all changed and has disappeared. The [Yangtse] river no longer overflows, nor does it reach Feng [Hao]. There is no way to find the Nine Rivers [recorded in the *Yugong*], either. . . . None of these can be understood [anymore]. Yet one must understand the *Yugong*. It is also not necessary to pay too much attention to the geography of today. What people today say about the mountains and rivers of China is nothing but child's talk. If one cannot observe them, there is no way to examine them. (*ZZYL*, chapter 79, p. 2025)

---

19. A Tang dynasty institutional history and encyclopedia written by Du You 杜佑 (735–812).

Medicine

53. Now, what is important in reading is to see what are the things that the sages taught people to exert efforts on. It is like using drugs to cure a disease: one must see how this disease began, which prescription to use to cure it, which medicinal materials to use in the prescription, what weight to use, what proportion to use, how to refine, how to roast, how to mix, how to divide, how to boil, and how to take it. It is just like this. (*ZZYL*, chapter 10, p. 162)

54. If a man has a disease and a doctor uses medicines appropriate for the disease, then they can relieve the disease, and I too follow the way of being a doctor. If the medicines are not appropriate for the disease, then they can even harm other people, and I stray from the way of being a doctor. (*ZZYL*, chapter 73, p. 1851)

55. If one discusses the expedients (*quan* 權) entirely apart from the norms (*jing* 經), it is not right. In general, expedients are those methods that are not used constantly. For example, when man has a disease, one who has a "hot disease" must take a "cold medicine," and one who has a "cold disease" must take a "hot medicine." This is the constant pattern-principle. Nevertheless, there also are times when having a hot disease, then contrary to expectation, one uses a hot medicine to cure the disease; and also, when having a cold disease, one uses a cold medicine to cure the disease. All these are methods that cannot be used[20] constantly. (*ZZYL*, chapter 37, p. 991)

56. In curing disease by using medicine, in general, one takes medicine only if rest is not sufficient [to cure the disease]. If rest is sufficient, naturally there is no disease. Why would one waste medicine by taking it?[21] (*ZZYL*, chapter 9, p. 151)

57. If something is planted in the soil, life-*qi* spontaneously gathers around it. If it has already been uprooted, the life-*qi* has no place to which to attach itself: where can it come into contact [with the life-*qi*]? It is like a man who has a disease. If he has life-*qi* himself, the *qi* with medicinal strength will rely on it, and the life intent will grow. If [his condition] has

---

20. Editor's note: Reading 用 instead of 論, which mistakenly appears in the *ZZYL* text.

21. Editor's note: the translator follows an emendation to the *ZZYL* text here.

already become critical, the life-*qi* will scatter away and not gather again. (*ZZYL*, chapter 63, p. 1552)

58. As for Mr. Xia's [book of] medicine, the prescriptions and uses of drugs are remarkable and absolutely unparalleled. Some appear counter-intuitive, but they are very effective after all. If it is asked why they are so, [the answer is] that all are based on the [medical] classics and study of the ancients: and there are none that do not have [a proper] source. About these, I have personally appreciated [his work] and so am sending the book in order to communicate his techniques to the present age, and also to deride those of our group who do not respect the ancients but use their own [ways]. (*ZZWJ*, chapter 76, in *ZZQS*, vol. 24, p. 3649)[22]

Mathematics

59. [Zhu Xi said,] "As for the method of *tugui* 土圭,[23] erect a gnomon of 8 feet, and extend a template of 1 foot 5 inches horizontally upon the ground. When the sun is at the center [of heaven] and its shadow [exactly] covers the template, this is considered to be the earth's center. Junyi 浚儀[24] is there. Now I do not know whether Junyi really is the earth's center or not."

It was asked, "Why does one make the gnomon 8 feet?"

[Zhu Xi] said, "This, one must compute using the *gougu* 勾股 method."[25] (*ZZYL*, chapter 86, p. 2214)

---

22. Zhu Xi's brief introductory comment to a medical book by a certain Mr. Xia 夏, which he sent to someone along with the book (*Song Xia yixu* 送夏醫序).

23. The *tugui* method of determining the earth's center by measuring the shadow of an eight-foot gnomon is mentioned in the "Diguan 地官" chapter of the *Rites of Zhou*. See Needham 1959, 286ff.

24. Name of the ancient county in present-day Kaifeng area.

25. The traditional Chinese method of calculating various relations among the three sides of a rectangular triangle, often compared to Pythagoran theorem, can be traced back to the *Mathematical Classic on the Zhou Gnomon* (*Zhoubi suanjing* 周髀算經). See Chen, Cheng-Yih 2012.

Images and Numbers

60. Have you seen the numbers of the *Hetu* 河圖 and *Luoshu* 洛書?[26] They are worth looking at when there is nothing to do. Although they are not the most important matters, when one plays with these one will be able to get one's mind to flow, change, and move. (*ZZYL*, chapter 65, p. 1610)

61. As for the image of the *zhongfu* 中孚 [hexagram ䷼], if one speaks about it in terms of the hexagram, four *yang* [unbroken lines] are outside, and two *yin* [broken lines] are inside. Being solid outside and empty inside, it has the image of the egg. Accounts suggesting that the image of the *ding* 鼎 [hexagram ䷱] is the shape of a cauldron (*ding* 鼎) and the image of the *ge* 革 [hexagram ䷰] is the shape of a cooking stove are like this. These and similar explanations have some meanings. But if one [takes up] the [*Classic of*] *Changes* and wants to exhaust all it contains in this forced and far-fetched [manner], then in a while one's understanding will become loose and disconnected. Scholars must first understand the proper principles of the Way. (*ZZYL*, chapter 66, p. 1643)

62. In reading a hexagram and a line, approach it just as a prognosticator would: empty your mind to seek what the words and meanings indicate, and consider it as a decision regarding what is good or bad, proper or improper. Then, examine how the image has been interpreted earlier, seek for that which makes the pattern-principle the way it is, and then extend this to the affair [you are considering]. [This will] allow [everyone] from kings and nobles above and down to common people below to use it for self-cultivation and governing the state. (*ZZWJ*, chapter 33, in *ZZQS*, vol. 21, p. 1465)

Bibliography

Chen, Cheng-Yih 程贞一. 2012. *Translation and Annotation of the Zhoubi Suanjing or the Arithmetical Classic of the Zhou Gnomon and the Circular Paths.* Shanghai: Shanghai guji chubanshe.

Huainanzi 淮南子. 1927–36. Shanghai: Zhonghua shuju.

---

26. *Hetu* and *Luoshu* are charts of mysterious and obscure origin that arrange numbers from one to ten in patterns of dots. See Needham 1959, 56–69.

Kim, Yung Sik. 2000. *The Natural Philosophy of Chu Hsi (1130–1200)*. Philadelphia: American Philosophical Society.

Needham, Joseph. 1959. *Science and Civilisation in China*. Vol. 3. Cambridge: Cambridge University Press.

Sima Qian 司馬遷. 1959. *Records of the Historian* (*Shiji* 史記). Beijing: Zhonghua shuju.

Zhu Xi 朱熹. 2002. *Zhuzi quanshu* 朱子全書 (*The Complete Works of Master Zhu*). Shanghai: Shanghai guji chubanshe and Hefei: Anhui jiaoyu chubanshe.

Further Readings

Kim, Yung Sik. 2014. *Questioning Science in East Asian Contexts: Essays on Science, Confucianism, and the Comparative History of Science*. Leiden: Brill.

Needham, Joseph. 1956. *Science and Civilisation in China*. Vol. 2. Cambridge: Cambridge University Press.

_____. 1959. *Science and Civilisation in China*. Vol. 3. Cambridge: Cambridge University Press.

Zhu Xi's Commentarial Work

ABIDING IN THE MEAN AND THE CONSTANT

Daniel K. Gardner

Introduction

The sages wrote the classics in order to teach later generations. These texts enable the reader to reflect on the ideas of the sages while reciting their words and hence to understand what is in accordance with the pattern-principle (li 理) of things. Understanding the whole substance of the proper Way, he will practice the Way with all his strength, and so enter the realm of sages and worthies.

(ZZYL, chapter 10, p. 173)

It's best to take up the books of the sages and read them so you understand their ideas. It's like speaking with them face to face.

(ZZYL, chapter 10, p. 173)

THE CONFUCIAN CLASSICS have a sacred quality for Zhu Xi. Written by the venerated sages of antiquity they reveal the timeless truths of the Confucian tradition. But these truths will be revealed only to those who approach the texts with a reverential attitude, who take the time and care to reflect meaningfully on what they read.[1] Zhu Xi was critical of the general reading habits of the age: "Nowadays, when people read a text, their minds

---

1. Editor's note: See chapter 4, "Poetry, Literature, Textual Study, and Hermeneutics," in this volume for more on Zhu Xi's views on reading and literature.

(*xin* 心)[2] are already on some later passage even before they have read what's here in front of them. The moment they read what's here in front of them, they want to move on and leave it behind" (*ZZYL*, chapter 10, p. 173). He called instead for unhurried, ruminative reading: "... Pass the words of the sages and worthies before your eyes, roll them around and around in your mouth, and turn them over and over in your mind" (*ZZYL*, chapter 10, p. 162). Readers were to make the words of the sages their own: "We must first become intimately familiar with the text so that its words seem to come from our own mouths. We should then continue to reflect on it so that its ideas seem to come from our own minds" (*ZZYL*, chapter 10, p. 168). When the words of the sages truly become the readers' own, their minds will be transformed—and become one with the minds of the sages.[3] They will thus be poised to "enter the realm of sages and worthies."

For Zhu Xi the entire canon of the so-called Thirteen Classics was precious.[4] But he was aware that reading the canon and apprehending its message were not necessarily easy matters. The texts were old and hence difficult to understand, particularly for "young novices" (*ZZWJ*, chapter 82, in *ZZQS*, vol. 24, p. 3895).[5] To make the canon less formidable, and less incomprehensible, he developed a graded curriculum for it. At the top of this curriculum he placed the *Great Learning* (*Daxue* 大學), the *Analects* (*Lunyu* 論語), the *Mengzi* (孟子), and *Abiding in the Mean and the Constant* (*Zhongyong* 中庸).[6] Their appeal, he wrote, was their "ease, immediacy, and brevity" (*ZZWJ*, chapter 82, in *ZZQS*, vol. 24, p. 3895). Pattern-principle, he told disciples, could be more readily investigated and accessed in these four works than in any other text, or in any other thing (*ZZYL*, chapter 14, p. 249). He wrote an acquaintance, "If we wish pattern-principle to be simple and easy to understand, concise and easy to

---

2. Editor's note: The standard translation for the word translated here "mind" and later in the chapter "mind-and-heart" is "heart-mind."

3. Editor's note: As discussed in the Introduction and chapter 1 of this volume, Zhu believed that the *li* in all things is identical, and so for him as well as other neo-Confucians, there is a relatively literal sense in which one can share the same mind with the sages.

4. For a full discussion of Zhu's program of learning and method of reading, see chapter 3 of Gardner 1990 and Gardner 1989.

5. *ZZWJ* refers to *Hui'an xiansheng Zhu Wengong wenji* 晦庵先生朱文公文集 (*The Collected Writings of Master Hui'an, Zhu, Duke of Culture*). *ZZQS* refers to *Zhuzi quanshu* 朱子全書 (*The Complete Works of Master Zhu*): see Zhu Xi 2002 in the bibliography.

6. The *Zhongyong* is conventionally translated as the *Doctrine of the Mean* and is so translated throughout most of this volume. To capture Zhu Xi's particular understanding of the text, however, it is rendered *Abiding in the Mean and the Constant* in this chapter.

grasp, nothing is better than the *Great Learning*, the *Analects*, the *Zhongyong*, and the *Mengzi*" (*ZZWJ*, chapter 59, in *ZZQS*, vol. 23, p. 2811). Only when they had fully mastered these four texts—referred to commonly since the Yuan period as the Four Books—would Zhu encourage students to turn to the previously authoritative Five Classics (the *Classic of Changes*, the *Odes*, the *Book of Documents*, the *Book of Rites*, and the *Spring and Autumn Annals*).

Of course, it was not simply that the Four Books were briefer and more accessible. For Zhu Xi, they addressed the ultimate concerns of the Confucian school: What is the nature of human beings? What are the sources of human morality? How do human beings tap into these sources? Where and how does evil arise? What is the role of the mind in the self-cultivation process? What is the relationship between humankind and the cosmos?

So full of meaning were these particular texts for Zhu that from 1163 until his death in 1200 he devoted his intellectual energy to preparing, reworking, and refining interlinear commentaries for each of them. His labors on them never ceased. In a letter dating to sometime after 1183, he wrote somewhat plaintively, "I have expended a lifetime of effort on the *Analects*, the *Mengzi*, the *Great Learning*, and *Abiding in the Mean and the Constant*, and have nearly perfected my explanations of them. And yet reading through them recently I found that one or two large sections [of my commentaries on them] still contained errors. I have since been altering them continuously. Sometimes immediately after making an emendation I find still another flaw" (*ZZWJ*, chapter 53, in *ZZQS*, vol. 22, p. 2506). Indeed, his traditional biography tells us that three days before his death on 23 April 1200, he was still revising his commentary on the *Great Learning*, a draft of which he had completed in 1174, a full twenty-six years earlier.[7]

These four texts, which Zhu Xi published together for the first time in 1190, continued to gain in significance. And, in the early fourteenth century, the state formally recognized the Four Books as the basis of the civil service examinations. From this time forward, until the abolition of the examination system in the early decades of the twentieth century, these books remained the core texts in the Chinese tradition. For more than six hundred years, to be literate in China meant to know these essential texts, to be capable of reciting them word for word from front to back. But—and this is critical in appreciating the enormous influence that Zhu Xi exercised in the later imperial tradition—to know these four texts also meant knowing word for word Zhu Xi's interlinear commentary on each. It was his understanding of them

---

7. Wang 1973, 226.

that educated Chinese were expected to master. Zhu Xi's commentary on the Four Books—and his interpretation of the Confucian tradition—thus became as canonical as the texts themselves.

What follows is a translation of chapters one to eleven of *Abiding in the Mean and the Constant*. Zhu ascribes authorship of the text to Zisi, grandson of Confucius, and explains that in the opening chapter "Zisi transmits the ideas handed down by the Confucian school. . . . In the next ten chapters, Zisi cites the words of the Master to complete the meaning of this chapter."[8] Thus, for Zhu, there is an underlying coherence to these chapters.

Translation
Abiding in the Mean and the Constant 中庸[9]

[Zhu Xi comments,] "Zhong 中 *is a term meaning 'neither to one side or the other; nor to overshoot or fall short'. Yong* 庸 *is 'normal or constant'."*

The Masters Cheng[10] said, "To lean neither to one side or the other is what is called *zhong* ('the mean'); unchanging is what is called *yong* ('the constant'). To practice the mean is the true Way of the universe; to keep to the constant is the steadfast pattern-principle of the universe.[11] This work presents the method of the mind-and-heart as passed

---

8. Zhu's ascription of authorship to Zisi is based on limited evidence. So, while it was generally accepted by the later Chinese tradition, textual scholars as early as the Song have cast doubt on it. However sound, the attribution to Zisi has two far-reaching implications: with the assertion that Zengzi, Confucius's disciple, authored the *Great Learning* and that Zisi, Confucius's grandson, authored *Abiding in the Mean and the Constant*, Zhu gives to the Four Books a pedigree of unsurpassed distinction. Second, by including Zengzi and Zisi among the authors of the Four Books, Zhu constructs a direct and unbroken line of transmission of the Way: from Confucius to Zengzi, one of his two greatest disciples; from Zengzi to Zisi, grandson of the Master himself; and finally, from Zisi, or one of Zisi's disciples, to Mencius. The Four Books' embodiment of the direct line of transmission of the Way no doubt makes their centrality in the later Confucian tradition all the more compelling.

9. The translation here is based on the text of the *Zhongyong zhangju* 中庸章句 as reprinted in Zhu Xi 1973.

10. The brothers Cheng Hao (1032–1085) and Cheng Yi (1033–1107), Zhu Xi's spiritual masters, though he never studied directly under them.

11. *Zhong* 中, the first character in the title, means "the mean" and brings to mind passages in the *Analects* (e.g., 6.29, which is cited almost word for word below in *Zhongyong* chapter three, passage 1) and the *Mencius* (7A26). The second character in the title is more problematic. Zhu Xi tells disciples: "*Yong* most definitely refers to 'steadfast pattern-principle,' but if we were to gloss it straightforwardly as 'steadfast pattern-principle,' people wouldn't understand its sense of 'normal or constant.' Now, when we speak of 'normal or constant,' 'steadfast pattern-principle'

down from generation to generation by the Confucian school. Fearing that over time mistakes would arise, Zisi wrote it down in the text we have here, passing it on to Mencius.[12] The text starts by speaking of the one pattern-principle; in the middle, it fans out from this into a discussion of the myriad things; in the end, it returns and treats them collectively as the one pattern-principle. Unfurl it and it fills every corner of the universe; roll it back up and it hides itself in secrecy. Its flavor is inexhaustible. The whole of it is practical learning. The skilled reader turns it over and over in his mind, and once he gets it, draws on it his whole life, finding that it has no limits."[13]

Chapter One

1. What Heaven mandates is called "the nature"; to follow the nature is called "the Way"; to cultivate the Way is called "instruction."

    [Zhu Xi comments,] "'Mandate' (ming 命) is similar to order (ling 令). 'The nature' (xing 性) is pattern-principle (li 理). Heaven, through transformation of yin and yang and the five activities, engenders the myriad things: qi completes their form and pattern-principle is indeed endowed therein. It is as if it had been ordered. And so it is that at birth each person, receiving his endowed pattern-principle, is constituted of firm [hexagram qian], yielding [hexagram kun], and five constant virtues [i.e., humaneness, rightness, propriety, wisdom, and trustworthiness]. This is what we call 'the nature.' 'Follow' (shuai 率) is accord with or obey (xun 循). 'The Way' (dao 道) is similar to path or road (lu 路). If each person follows what is natural to this nature, he will always take the proper path in his day-to-day affairs. It is this that we call 'the Way.' 'To cultivate' is to regulate it. Though 'the nature' and 'the Way' are everywhere the same, the qi 氣 endowment may differ, and consequently it is impossible that there won't be mistakes of overshooting or falling short. The sage takes the path people ought to take and regulates it, thereby becoming a model for all under heaven—this is called

---

is naturally implied" (*ZZYL*, chapter 62, p. 1482; cf. chapter 63, p. 1481–1484, *inter alia*). Thus, for Zhu, keeping to the constant is to keep to the steadfast pattern-principle of the universe.

12. While some scholars as early as the Han had suggested a connection between Zisi and *Abiding in the Mean and the Constant*, it is only in the Song, with Zhu Xi, that the attribution of authorship to Zisi becomes generally accepted by the tradition. The case for attribution, however, is based on limited textual evidence, and thus has been called into considerable question, especially beginning in the Qing period (1644–1912).

13. Zhu Xi adds this introductory remark to the text immediately after the title and his brief commentary on it. The later tradition treats the remark as part of the classic itself.

instruction. Ritual, music, punishment, tools of government, and such are parts of this instruction. It seems that people know that they themselves possess human nature but do not know that it comes from Heaven; they know that there is a Way to carry out matters but do not know that it follows from human nature; they know the sage embodies instruction but do not know that in regulating himself he accords with what we all originally possess. Therefore, Zisi begins the text here by laying it out. What Master Dong [Zhongshu][14] meant by the Way having its great origins in Heaven is this same idea."[15]

2. The Way: it cannot be abandoned for even a moment. What can be abandoned is not the Way. Consequently, the noble person exercises extreme caution about what is not visible to him and is deeply apprehensive about what is beyond the reach of his hearing.

    [Zhu Xi comments,] [16] *"The Way: it is the pattern-principle of everyday affairs and things as they ought to be; and in all of us, it is the virtue of our original nature, embodied in the mind-and-heart. No thing is without it and at no time has it not been so. Therefore, it is not possible to abandon it even for a moment. If it were possible to abandon it, we could not speak of 'following the nature.' For this reason, the noble person is in constant awe. Though he does not see or hear it, he dare not be negligent. Consequently, he cleaves to the essence of Heavenly pattern-principle and does not allow himself to abandon the Way for even a moment."*

3. Nothing is more manifest than the hidden, nothing more obvious than the subtle. Therefore, the noble person, even in solitude, is watchful over himself.

    [Zhu Xi comments,] *"'The hidden' (yin 隱) refers to the obscured (anchu 暗處). 'The subtle' (wei 微) refers to the minute (xishi 細事). 'Solitude' is that place others are not aware of, but you alone are. This passage says that before even the tiniest matter, hidden in obscurity, has yet to take on a trace of existence, its incipient tendencies are already active. Others may not be aware of them, but if you alone are, no affair under heaven will be more manifest or obvious. For this reason, the noble person, being eternally*

---

14. Dong Zhongshu 董仲舒 (176–104 BCE), an influential Confucian thinker and statesman of the Han dynasty (206 BCE–220 CE).

15. Zhu Xi outlines for his readers in the commentary here the metaphysical context that will enable them to understand not only this passage, but the whole of the classic.

16. Occasionally, Zhu Xi opens his commentary with a gloss on the pronunciation of a character as he does here (*"li* 離 is 4th tone"). I have not translated these glosses.

cautious and apprehensive, is especially watchful;[17] *he thereby stops human desire from germinating, not allowing it to develop and grow secretly, hidden from view, and thereby lead him astray from the Way."*

4. Before pleasure, anger, sorrow, and joy have arisen—this we call the mean. After they have arisen and attained due proportion—this we call harmony. The mean is the great foundation of the universe; harmony is the Way that unfolds throughout the universe.

     [Zhu Xi comments,] "Pleasure, sorrow, anger, and joy are emotions. Before they arise is the condition of human nature. It is without the slightest partiality and for this reason we call it 'the mean.' When they arise and are perfectly regulated, this is the proper condition of emotions. There being not the slightest perversity, it is called 'harmony.' The 'great foundation' is the Heavenly mandated nature. All pattern-principles under heaven issue forth from it; it is the Way itself. The 'Way that unfolds' refers to 'following our human nature.' It is that from which all under heaven, past and present, collectively comes; it is the function of the Way. This passage speaks of the virtue of human nature and the emotions to illuminate the idea that the Way cannot be abandoned."[18]

5. Let the mean and harmony be fully realized and heaven and earth will find their proper places therein; and the ten thousand creatures will be nourished therein.

     [Zhu Xi comments,] "'To be fully realized' (zhi 致*) is to push them to their limits (tui er ji zhi* 推而極之*). 'To find their proper places' (wei* 位*) is to be at ease in their places (an qi suo* 安其所*). 'Will be nourished' (yu* 育*) means to fulfill their lives (sui qi sheng* 遂其生*). To control oneself through 'caution' and 'apprehension' [see Zhongyong chapter one, passage 2] and come to achieve an equilibrium of extreme quiescence—one who can hold on to such equilibrium at all times realizes perfect balance, and heaven and earth thereby find their proper places. To refine oneself through*

---

17. The character *jin* (謹) here is a stand-in for *shen* 慎, which Zhu Xi avoids as it is part of the present Emperor Huizong's (r. 1101–1125) personal name.

18. Zhu's remarks should make clear that neo-Confucians do not find emotions themselves problematic; it is excessive or imbalanced emotions that concern them. Note the commentarial strategy Zhu Xi employs here: to underscore for the reader the coherence of the classical text, Zhu explicitly ties this passage to earlier passages in the text, mentioning the "Heavenly mandated nature" and "following the nature" of passage 1 and "the Way cannot be abandoned" of passage 2. This sort of intratextuality is characteristic of Zhu Xi's commentarial writing on the Confucian canon.

diligence and watchfulness and come to respond to everything in the world faultlessly—one who is appropriately responsive in all encounters realizes perfect harmony, and the ten thousand creatures will be nourished therein. It would seem that heaven, earth, and the ten thousand creatures originally are of one body with us.[19] *If our mind-and-heart is set in the right the mind-and-heart of heaven and earth will also be set in the right. If our qi is congenial, the qi of heaven and earth will also be congenial. [Because we are of one body] the end results are like this. This is the ultimate achievement of learning; and it is the special skill of the sage. From the start, it does not depend on something external—as the instruction that it is the cultivation of the Way [see passage 1] indeed resides within. This is a matter of [the Way] itself and its function [see passage 4]; though they are marked by a difference in rest and activity, it is invariably the case that once [the Way] itself is established, function will begin to operate; and so, in reality, it is not that they are two separate matters. Consequently, here they are spoken of together and linked to the ideas in the passages above."*

In this, the first chapter, Zisi transmits the ideas handed down by the Confucian school; it is this that is the basis of his discussion. First, he makes clear that the source of the Way is to be found in Heaven and is unchangeable; and that [the Way] itself, being complete within us, must not be abandoned. Next, he speaks of the essentials of preserving and cultivating it [the mind-and-heart] and examining within oneself. Last, he speaks of the merits and moral influence of sages and spiritual persons. In these matters, he wants students to turn and inquire within in order to get it for themselves—and so eliminate the selfishness (*si* 私)[20] aroused by external temptations and bring to fulfillment their original goodness. This is what Mr. Yang [Shi] meant when he said, "Herein lies the gist of the entire work. In the next ten chapters, Zisi cites the words of the Master to complete the meaning of this chapter."[21]

---

19. Editor's note: As noted in both the Introduction and chapter 1 of this volume, the metaphysical belief that all things are one body and form an underlying unity served as the foundation for the overriding neo-Confucian imperative to care for the world as oneself.

20. Editor's note: the standard translation for the word translated here and throughout this chapter as "selfish" or "selfishness" is "self-centered" or "self-centeredness."

21. Yang Shi (1053–1135) was a prominent disciple of Cheng Yi and an influential thinker in his own right. Zhu Xi offers this remark at the conclusion of *Zhongyong* chapter one. As with his introduction to the text, this paragraph has been treated as part of the classic itself by the later tradition.

Chapter Two

1. Zhongni (Confucius) said, "The noble person practices the mean and keeps to the constant (*zhongyong*); the petty person turns his back on the mean and the constant.

    [*Zhu Xi comments,*] *"Zhongyong is neither going to one side or the other, nor going too far or falling short; it is the normal or constant pattern-principle. It is what ought to be as a matter of Heaven's mandate, abstruse in the extreme. It is the noble person alone who is able to embody it; the petty person turns his back on it."*

2. "The noble person practices the mean and keeps to the constant because, as a noble person, he accords with circumstances to achieve the mean. The petty person turns his back on the mean and the constant because, as a petty person, he is devoid of fear and restraint."

    [*Zhu Xi comments,*] *"In Wang Su's*[22] *edition, the text has, 'The petty person turns his back on the mean and the constant.' Master Cheng also took this to be the case. I am following them here.*

    "The noble person practices the mean, keeping to the constant, because he possesses the virtue of a noble person and, additionally, is capable of according with circumstances in finding the perfect balance. The petty person turns his back on perfect balance and the constant because he has the mind-and-heart of a petty person and, additionally, is devoid of fear and restraint. The mean has no fixed form; its existence accords with circumstances.[23] *This is normal pattern-principle (pingchang zhi li 平常之理). The noble person is aware that [determining the mean] rests with oneself. Consequently, he is capable of being cautious about what he does not see and apprehensive about what he does not hear—and so always practices the mean. The petty person, unaware of this, is indulgent in his desires and reckless in his behavior—and entirely devoid of fear and restraint."*

    The preceding is the second chapter.

    [*Zhu Xi comments,*] *"The ten chapters that follow all expound on practicing the mean and keeping to the constant to explain the meaning of*

---

22. Wang Su's 王肅 (195–256) commentary on the *Book of Rites*, which is now lost.

23. Most commentators understand the *shi* of *shizhong* 時中 in the classic to mean "at all times," understanding *shizhong* to mean "to practice *zhong* constantly." This is a legitimate reading. But wanting to highlight the "situationality" in the practice of preserving the balance, Zhu pointedly comments here, "The mean has no fixed form; its existence accords with circumstances (*suishi* 隨時)."

the opening chapter. Though not composed as a coherent narrative the ideas in them really do form a continuous thread. About the shift here to the term yong 庸, *'keeps to the constant,' from he* 和 *'harmony' (Zhongyong chapter one, passages 4–5), Mr. Yang was correct in stating, 'In speaking of human nature and emotions, we say "zhonghe," ("practicing the mean and harmony"); in speaking of virtuous conduct, we say "zhongyong," ("practicing and keeping to the constant"). The zhong of zhongyong includes the sense of zhonghe, "practicing the mean and harmony."'"*[24]

Chapter Three

1. The Master said, "Practicing the mean and keeping to the constant: is this not perfection? For a long time now few people have shown the capacity for it."

   [Zhu Xi comments,] "To overshoot is to fail to maintain perfect balance; to fall short is not to have arrived yet. Thus, the virtue of zhongyong ('practicing the mean and keeping to the constant') alone constitutes perfection. Still, since all people all receive this same virtue, being zhongyong was not difficult early on. But over the ages instruction decayed and the people have not been aroused to practice it. Consequently, few have shown the capacity for it; this has been the case for a long time now. The similar passage in the Analects (6.29) does not contain the character neng, 'capacity.'"[25]

   The preceding is the third chapter.

Chapter Four

1. The Master said, "The Way is not being practiced, and I know why: the wise overshoot it and the stupid fall short of it. The Way is not understood, and I know why: the worthy overshoot it and the unworthy fall short of it.

   [Zhu Xi comments,] "The Way is the way things ought to be as a matter of Heavenly pattern-principle, in perfect balance and nothing more. That the wise, the stupid, the worthy, and the unworthy overshoot it or fall short of it is owing to differences in their endowments—and so they fail to practice the mean. The wise overshoot knowledge, considering practice of the Way

---

24. By citing Yang Shi's remarks here, the commentary is again intent on demonstrating the coherence of the text for its readers.

25. In this commentary Zhu echoes 1.1 (i.e., *Zhongyong* chapter one, passage 1) and his commentary on it.

to be inconsequential; the stupid fall short of knowledge and, still more, do not know the ways to practice it. This is why the Way is rarely practiced. The worthy overshoot in their practice, considering knowledge of the Way to be inconsequential. The unworthy fall short in their practice and, still more, do not seek how to know it. This is why the Way is rarely understood."

2. "There is no one who does not drink and eat. Yet few know the flavor of what they consume."

[*Zhu Xi comments,*] "'The Way cannot be abandoned' (Zhongyong 1.2). People do not examine themselves; it is for this reason they err in overshooting or falling short."

The preceding is the fourth chapter.

Chapter Five

1. The Master said, "The Way is not practiced—is this not so!"

[*Zhu Xi comments,*] "It is not practiced because it is not understood [see Zhongyong chapter four, passage 1]."

The preceding is the fifth chapter.

[*Zhu Xi comments,*] "This chapter carries on from the previous chapter, explaining why it [the Way] is not being practiced, and introduces the idea found in the next chapter."

Chapter Six

1. The Master said, "Shun! Great indeed was his knowledge! Shun was fond of questioning others, and fond of examining even their simplest words. He would conceal the bad, and trumpet the good. Grasping the two ends he would apply the mean in dealing with the people. This is what made him Shun."

[*Zhu Xi comments,*] "The reason Shun was a person of such great knowledge is that he did not rely on himself alone 'but took from others that by which he could do good' (Mengzi 2A.8). Simple words (eryan 邇言) are words that are easy and accessible—and yet he always examined them carefully to be sure he had not neglected the good in them. Words that were not good he concealed and did not broadcast; good words he proclaimed and did not keep secret. Such were his generosity and intelligence: who among men wouldn't be delighted to speak to him of the good? 'Two ends' (liangduan 兩端) refers to the different extremes that arose out of the discussions with

others. Everything has two ends, as in small and large, and thick and thin.
Within the good itself, he would also grasp 'the two ends,' weigh them, and
select the mean.[26] *Applying it later [in dealing with the people], he would*
choose judiciously and practice it to perfection. If one's internal standards
be not precise, incisive, and free from error, what part could they play here?
It is owing to them that knowledge does not 'overshoot' or 'fall short' (see
Zhongyong chapter four heading) and that the Way is put into practice."[27]

The preceding is the sixth chapter.

Chapter Seven

1. The Master said, "People all say, 'I know.' And yet drive them into a net, a
trap, or a pit, and none will know how to escape. People all say, 'I know,'
and yet having chosen to practice the mean and keep to the constant,
they are unable to hold to it for even a month."

   [Zhu Xi comments,] " 'Net' (gu 罟) is web (wang 網); 'trap' (huo 獲) is
   snare (jijian 機檻); 'pit' (xianjing 陷阱) is hole (kengkan 坑坎). All are
   means of ensnaring wild animals. To choose to 'practice the mean and keep
   to the constant' is to distinguish among the multitudinous manifestations
   of pattern-principle in pursuit of this so-called zhongyong. It is 'to be fond
   of questioning others' (haowen 好問) and 'to apply the perfect balance'
   (yongzhong 用中), the matters referred to in the previous chapter. 'One
   month' (qiyue 期月) is one whole month (zayiyue 帀一月). This is to say
   that people know calamity and yet do not know how to escape it. Even
   more, while they may be able to choose to maintain perfect balance they
   are unable to hold to it. In both of these cases they do not really 'know.' "

   The preceding is the seventh chapter.

   [Zhu Xi comments,] "This picks up from the 'great knowledge' [of Shun]
   in the previous chapter. In addition, it explains why 'it [the Way] is not being
   understood' (Zhongyong chapter four) and introduces the next chapter."

---

26. Some later commentators say that Zhu's remark here about considering the "two ends"
within the good itself is consistent with his view, expressed for example in his commentary on
Zhongyong chapter two, that there is no one absolute right way to proceed—how best to proceed depends on the particulars of each situation 隨時. It remains for the individual to assess
the right "good" course to take in every situation—which is why one requires keen and refined
"internal standards."

27. Shun is an example here of one who practiced the mean perfectly, never overshooting or
falling short; the last line of commentary is meant by Zhu Xi to tie this passage in the reader's
mind to the ideas in the heading of *Zhongyong* chapter four.

Chapter Eight

1. The Master said, "Here is what Hui (Yan Hui) was like as a person: having chosen to practice the mean, when he seized upon the good, he would clutch it to his breast and never let it go."

[Zhu Xi comments,] "Hui is Confucius's disciple, Yan Yuan. 'To clutch' (quanquan 拳拳*) is the appearance of holding tightly (feng chi zhi mao* 奉持之貌*). Fu* 服 *(lit. 'to wear') [in the phrase 'to clutch it to his breast'] is to display (zhu* 著*). 'Breast' (ying* 膺*) is bosom (xiong* 胸*). Holding it tightly and clutching it to his breast is to say that he was able to hold to it. It was because Master Yan truly 'knew' it that he was capable of 'choosing' it and of 'holding' to it like this. This explains how not to 'overshoot' or 'fall short' in practice and how 'the Way may be understood' (Zhongyong chapter four)."*

The preceding is the eighth chapter.

Chapter Nine

1. The Master said, "It is possible to keep balanced family, state, and even all under heaven; it is possible to renounce official rank and salary; it is possible to trample on swords with naked blades. But practicing the mean and keeping to the constant—this may be beyond our capability."

[Zhu Xi comments,] "'To keep balanced' (jun 均*) is to bring peace and order (pingzhi* 平治*). These three matters correspond to wisdom, humaneness, and courage and are the most difficult things in the world. Yet because each is limited in scope, those with the appropriate disposition who exert themselves to the fullest are capable of them. But when it comes to practicing the mean and keeping to the constant, though it may seem easy, if people's sense of rightness is not refined and their humaneness not fully developed—to the point where they are free of even a speck of selfish human desire—they will be incapable of it. These three matters are thought to be difficult, yet are easy; practicing the mean and keeping to the constant is thought to be easy, yet is difficult—which is why few have been capable of it (cf. Zhongyong chapter three)."*[28]

The preceding is the ninth chapter.

[Zhu Xi comments,] "This too picks up from previous chapters and introduces the next one."

---

28. In arguing here for the centrality of the practice of *zhongyong* in the Confucian tradition, Zhu Xi implicitly is arguing for the importance and centrality of the text of the *Zhongyong* and for its inclusion among the core Four Books.

Chapter Ten

1. Zilu asked about strength.

    [Zhu Xi comments,] "Zilu is Confucius's disciple, Zhong You. Being fond of courage Zilu asked about strength."

2. The Master said, "The strength of the South, the strength of the North, or your own strength?

    [Zhu Xi comments,] "Yi 抑 *is a particle of speech meaning 'or.' Er* 而 *means ru* 汝, *'your.'"*

3. "To be lenient and gentle in the instruction of others, to exact no retribution for unjust treatment—such is the strength of the South. The noble person lives by this.

    [Zhu Xi comments,] "'To be lenient and gentle in the instruction of others' means to be forbearing and mild when teaching those who have fallen short. 'To exact no retribution for unjust treatment' means to endure occasions of unjust treatment without exacting retribution. Southern manner is gentle and, consequently, regards overcoming others with the power of forbearance as strength. It is the Way of the noble person."[29]

4. "To sleep on a bed of metal and leather to meet death without remorse—such is the strength of the North. The strong live by this.

    [Zhu Xi comments,] "'To sleep on a bed' (ren 衽) *is to make a mat used for sleeping (xi* 席). *'Metal' (jin* 金) *refers to spears and other arms; 'leather' (ge* 革) *refers to armor and the like. Northern manner is hardy and, consequently, regards overcoming others with the power of daring as strength. This is what the strong do."*

5. "Consequently, the noble person is agreeable in disposition but does not simply go along with the current. Strong indeed is his resolve! He establishes himself in the mean, never leaning to one side or another. Strong indeed is his resolve! When the Way prevails in the state [and he assumes office], he makes no changes to what he held dear before achieving prominence. Strong indeed is his resolve! When the Way does

---

29. Zhu remarks in conversation with disciples that the term "noble person" here is "slightly reckless" (*ZZYL*, chapter 63, p. 1529). For although the strength of the South is admirable, it, like the strength of the North that follows, is not perfectly balanced. Thus, it could not be the "strength" that the truly noble person lives by. The noble person in this passage is in contrast to the truly noble person described in *Zhongyong* chapter ten, passage 5.

not prevail in the state, he makes no changes to what he holds dear even unto death.[30] Strong indeed is his resolve."

[*Zhu Xi comments,*] *"These four matters are what you [ru 汝, see Zhongyong 9.2] ought to consider strength. 'Resolve' (jiao 矯) is strong bearing (qiangmao 強貌), as when the Odes speaks of 'valiant-looking (jiaojiao 矯矯) tiger leaders [i.e., military officers]' (# 299). 'Leaning to one side or another' (yi 倚) is to incline to one side (pianzhuo 偏著). Se 塞 (lit., 'to be blocked') is to be not yet prominent (weida 未達).[31] When the Way comes to prevail in the state, he makes no changes to what he held dear before becoming prominent. When the Way does not prevail in the state he makes no changes to what he has held dear throughout his life. This is a reference to the passage 'practicing the mean and keeping to the constant—this may be beyond our capability' (Zhongyong chapter nine). Those who cannot subdue their own selfish human desires are incapable of choosing to practice the mean and holding to it [as discussed in Zhongyong chapters seven and eight]. What could be greater than the strength of the noble person! The Master spoke to Zilu in this way to restrain his brute force and promote in him moral courage."*

The preceding is the tenth chapter.

Chapter Eleven

1. The Master said, "Exploring the esoteric and behaving eccentrically in order to win renown among later generations: these I simply would not do.

[*Zhu Xi comments,*] *"The character su 素 (lit., 'plain') should be the character suo 索 ('to explore'), according to the Han shu [Standard History of the Han Dynasty]. It [su] would seem to be the wrong character. 'Exploring the esoteric and behaving eccentrically' refers to probing deeply into abstruse pattern-principles and taking unconventional behavior too far. Doing so may be enough to deceive the world and win one undeserved recognition;*

---

30. When the Way prevails in the state the noble person is eager to assume office. When the Way does not prevail, he does not serve, but rather holds on to his ideals in even the humblest circumstances.

31. Zhu's reading of *se* 塞 to mean "to be not yet prominent" assumes the traditional Confucian attitude that once the Way prevails in a state, the noble person has a moral obligation to serve the government—and thus becomes prominent.

*later generations consequently might praise such a person. This is a 'knowing'
that overshoots the mark and does not choose the good, and a 'practice' that
overshoots the mark and does not practice the mean (see Zhongyong chapter
four). This is being strong where one ought not to be strong. How could the
Sage possibly do such things!"*[32]

2. "The noble person keeps to the Way. To go halfway and give up: I, for
    one, am incapable of stopping.

    *[Zhu Xi comments,] "'To keep to the Way' is to be capable of choosing
    the good. 'To go halfway and give up' is a matter of insufficient strength.
    Here, although the 'knowing' is up to it the 'practice' is not. This is not being
    strong where one ought to be strong. To stop (yi 已) is to halt (zhi 止). In
    this instance, it is not that the Sage makes great effort, not daring to give up;
    it is just that his perfect sincerity (cheng 誠) never ceases—so naturally he is
    incapable of stopping."*[33]

3. "The noble person abides in the mean. But to withdraw from the world,
    live in obscurity, and feel no regrets—only a sage is capable of this."

    *[Zhu Xi comments,] "Neither 'exploring the esoteric or behaving eccen-
    trically,' he simply abides in the mean. Being incapable of 'going halfway
    and giving up,' he 'withdraws from the world, lives in obscurity, and feels
    no regret.' This is the virtue of the mean and the constant fully realized—it
    is wisdom (zhi 知) in its fullness and humaneness (ren 仁) in perfection.
    Courage [i.e., the third virtue mentioned by Zhu Xi in Zhongyong chapter
    nine, passage 1] is not required here and yet all is well. This fits our Master
    exactly. But because he himself did not believe that he had made this his
    dwelling place, he says, 'Only a sage is capable of this.'"*

    The preceding is the eleventh chapter.

    *[Zhu Xi comments,] "With this chapter, Zisi's quoting of the Master's
    words to elucidate the meaning of the first chapter of the text comes to an*

---

32. By tying this passage to *Zhongyong* chapter four, the commentary again plays up the coherence of the text.

33. The commentary echoes *Analects* 6.12: "Ran Qiu said, 'It is not that I do not delight in your
Way, Master, it is simply that my strength is insufficient.' The Master said, 'Someone whose
strength is genuinely insufficient collapses somewhere along the Way. As for you, you deliberately draw the line'" (Slingerland 2003, 56). Zhu introduces the term *cheng*, foreshadowing the
classic's preoccupation with the term, beginning in *Zhongyong* chapter twenty. It has the sense
of being entirely true to the good nature one is born with. By referring to *cheng* here, Zhu again
is suggesting how passages in the text interrelate and making the case that *Abiding in the Mean
and the Constant* contains a coherent message.

end. *The gist of these chapters [i.e., Zhongyong chapters two through eleven] is that wisdom, humaness, and courage—the three grand virtues—are the door by which to enter into the Way. It is for this reason that chapters open with illustrations from the Great Shun, Yan Yuan, and Zilu. Shun represents wisdom; Yan Yuan humaneness; and Zilu courage. To dispense with any one of these three is to be without the means to cultivate the Way and fully realize virtue. More on this can be found in [Zhongyong] chapter twenty."*

Bibliography

Gardner, Daniel K. 1989. "Transmitting the Way: Chu Hsi and His Program of Learning." *Harvard Journal of Asiatic Studies* 49 (1): 141–172.

_____. 1990. *Learning to Be a Sage: Selections from the Conversations of Master Chu, Arranged Topically.* Berkeley: University of California Press.

Slingerland, Edward G., trans. 2003. *Confucius Analects, with Selections from Traditional Commentaries.* Indianapolis: Hackett.

Wang Maohong 王懋竑. 1973. *Zhuzi nianpu* 朱子年譜. Taibei: Shijie shuju.

Zhu Xi 朱熹. 1973. *Si shu ji zhu* 四書集注 (*Collected Commentaries on the Four Books*). *Sibu beiyao* 四部備要. Reprint of 1921–1934. Taipei: Zhonghua shuju.

_____. 1986. *Zhuzi yulei* 朱子語類 (*The Classified Saying of Master Zhu*). Edited by Li Jingde 黎靖德 and Wang Xingxian 王星賢. Beijing: Zhonghua shuju.

_____. 2002. *Zhuzi quanshu* 朱子全書 (*The Complete Works of Master Zhu*). Shanghai: Shanghai guji chubanshe and Hefei: Anhui jiaoyu chubanshe.

Further Readings

Chow, Kai-wing, On-cho Ng, and John B. Henderson, eds. 1999. *Imagining Boundaries: Changing Confucian Doctrines, Texts, and Hermeneutics.* Albany: SUNY Press.

Gardner, Daniel K. 1986. *Chu Hsi and the Ta-hsueh: Neo-Confucian Reflection on the Confucian Canon.* Cambridge, MA.: Harvard University, Council on East Asian Studies.

_____. 1998. "Confucian Commentary and Chinese Intellectual History." *The Journal of Asian Studies* 57 (2): 397–422.

Henderson, John B. 1991. *Scripture, Canon and Commentary A Comparison of Confucian and Western Exegesis.* Princeton, NJ: Princeton University Press.

Makeham, John. 2004. *Transmitters and Creators: Chinese Commentators and Commentaries on the* Analects. Cambridge, MA: Harvard East Asian Monographs (Book 228).

Key Terms of Art

The following list contains the translations standardly used in this volume for various key Chinese terms, followed by common alternative renderings for these terms that appear in other published translations.

Ai 愛—love (care)

Ai 哀—sorrow (grief)

Benran zhi xing 本然之性—original nature

Cheng 誠—sincerity (integrity, authenticity)

Chu ti ce yin 怵惕惻隱—alarm and concern (commiseration)

Ci rang 辭讓—deference and yielding (modesty and complaisance)

Dao 道—Way

Dao li 道理—pattern-principle of the Way (principle of the Way)

Dao xin 道心—heart-mind of the Way (heart of the Way, mind of the Way)

Fa 法—regulation (law, standard)

Ge wu 格物—investigation of things

Gong 公—public oriented (public, common, just)

Gongfu 功夫—purposeful practice (spiritual practice, work)

Jing 敬—reverential attention (reverence, respect)

Ju 懼—fear

Junzi 君子—noble person (gentleman, cultivated individual)

Li 理—pattern-principle [plural: pattern-principles] (principle, pattern, reason)

Ming 命—mandate (decree)

Nu 怒—anger

Qi 氣—[Romanized only: no translation given] (psycho-physical matter, vital energy, vital matter)

Qi 器—concrete things (implements)

Qing 情—feelings (emotions)

Qizhi zhi xing 氣質之性—*qi*-material nature (physical nature, material nature)

Ren 仁—humaneness (benevolence, complete goodness)

Ren xin 人心—human heart-mind (human heart, human mind)

Shi 士—literati (literatus, scholar)

Shi fei 是非—approbation and disapproval (right and wrong, approving and disapproving)

Shu 恕—sympathetic concern (empathy, sympathy, altruism)

Si 私—self-centered (selfish)

Si duan 四端—four beginnings (four sprouts, four germs)

Tai ji 太極—supreme ultimate (great ultimate, supreme polarity, supreme pole)

Ti 體—the thing itself or thingness itself (substance)

Tian 天—Heaven ["heaven" when clearly referring to the sky] (nature)

Tian li 天理—Heavenly pattern-principle (natural principles)

Wu 惡—hate (dislike)

Xi 喜—happiness (joy)

Xin 心—heart-mind (heart, mind)

Xing 性—nature

Xing er shang 形而上—above form (above physical form)

Xing er xia 形而下—within form (below form, below physical form)

Xiu wu 羞惡—shame and disdain (shame and dislike)

Xu ling 虛靈—capacious luminousness (spirit, intelligence)

Yang 陽—[Romanized only: no translation given]

Yi 意—intention [used in the technical sense as the initial manifestations of the heart-mind, which can then develop into a commitment (*zhi* 志) or desire (*yu* 欲)] (thought, idea)

Yi 義—rightness (righteousness)

Yin 陰—[Romanized only: no translation given]

Yong 用—function (operation)

Yu 欲—desire

Zhi 志—commitment (will, intention, volition)

Zhi zhi 致知—extension of knowledge

Zhong 忠—devotedness (loyalty)

Zhuzai 主宰—master-governor (master, governor, ruler)

Index